aurora metro

Founded in 1989 to publish and prc
press has specialised in new drama and fiction, winning
recognition and awards from the industry.

new drama
Best of the Fest. new plays celebrating 10 years of
London New Play Festival ed. Phil Setren
ISBN 0-9515877-8-1 £12.99

Six plays by Black and Asian women. ed. Kadija George
ISBN 0-9515877-2-2 £7.50

Seven plays by women, female voices, fighting lives.
ed. Cheryl Robson **ISBN 0-9515877-1-4 £5.95**

Young Blood, five plays for young performers. ed. Sally
Goldsworthy **ISBN 0-9515877-6-5 £9.95**

European drama
A touch of the Dutch: plays by women. ed. Cheryl Robson
ISBN 0-9515877-7-3 £9.95

Mediterranean plays by women. ed. Marion Baraitser
ISBN 0-9515877-3-0 £9.95

other
How Maxine learned to love her legs and other tales of
growing up. ed. Sarah Le Fanu **ISBN 0-9515877-4-9 £8.95**

The Women Writers Handbook eds. Robson, Georgeson,
Beck. **ISBN 0-9515877-0-6 £4.95**

Sian Evans

Born and brought up in Bridgend, South Wales. Plays include: *Insect Life* (BBC Wales 1993), *Underdog* (WTW, Oval Theatre 1994), *Dancing on the Turf* (Radio 4 1994), *Little Sister* (Made in Wales Stage Co. 1996), *Asleep under the Dark Earth* (National Theatre 1997), *Mary Kelly* (Theatre Clwyd 1998).

Translations/adaptations include: *Britannicus* (Sheffield Crucible 1990), *At Fifty She Discovered the Sea* (Liverpool Playhouse 1992), *Badenheim 1939* (Second Stride Theatre Co, Riverside Studios 1995) and *Tiderace* (BBC Wales 1996).

Television drama: Episodes of *Peak Practice* (Carlton 1997/8), *Touching Evil* (United 1998/9).

Awards - Arts Council Translation Award 1992 and Gulbenkian Award to develop work in film 1993.

Cheryl Robson

Born in Sydney, Australia she has lived in the UK since 1969. Worked for the BBC in film and production, before founding Women's Theatre Workshop and Aurora Metro Press. She has developed, produced and published the work of many UK and international writers.

MA in Playwriting Studies at Birmingham University (1991). Her plays include: *O Architect!* (New End Theatre 1989), *The Taking Of Liberty* (Steam Industry 1992), *Simply Hostile* (WTW Man in the Moon 1994), *Versus* (Arts Catalyst /Young Vic 1996).

Awards include: Winner of Croydon Warehouse Theatre's Playwriting Festival in 1990. Arts Council Writer's Bursary and Option Awards, Pandora and Raymond Williams Publishing Prizes.

eastern promise

seven plays from central and eastern europe
editors: Sian Evans and Cheryl Robson

Jenufa, her step-daughter

The Umbilical Cord

Tulip Doctor

The Tender Mercies

Nascendo

The Chosen Ones

Belgrade Trilogy

AURORA METRO PRESS

Anglo-Romanian Bank Limited

Funded by
THE
ARTS
COUNCIL
OF ENGLAND

We gratefully acknowledge financial assistance from The Arts Council of England and the Anglo-Romanian Bank.

With thanks to: Alison Spiby, Graham Starkey, Janet Gordon, Susan Croft, Malgorzata Semil, Marian Popescu, Sladjana Vujovic, Gillian King.

Contents

Foreword
by Gerald Lidstone

In 1985 I was the designer for a tour of *Top Girls* by Caryl Churchill that toured through Eastern Europe. The play provoked considerable response, particularly amongst the women in the audience. It was explained to us that it was rare to see a play not only dealing with issues relating to the lives of contemporary women but that it had a particular irony for them in Eastern Europe, dealing as it does with sexual politics and the employment of women. Politically, many of the changes in legislation which occurred in Britain in the 1970's, specifically affecting women (The Abortion Act, The Divorce Reform Act, The Equal Pay Act, The Sex Discrimination Act) had already been written into the new post-war constitutions of East European Countries. However, they seemed to have had no social effect whatsoever. The choice for women was not between a career or staying at home and raising a family, it was how to do both at the same time. Work was a necessity for most. The play itself made it clear that while there may have been individual women who had succeeded, the condition of the majority of working women had not changed in anything but superficial ways. The production provoked fascinating post – show discussions inevitably turned to the subject of women playwrights – the answer we were given was much the same as that told to the editors of this volume: they don't exist.

They were of course there; it was just that the overwhelmingly male theatre establishment was unaware of them. With very few exceptions, artistic directors and senior dramaturgs were men who were primarily interested in the reinterpretation of 'classical' work, as this was the main mode of cultural/political opposition to censorship. The infrastructure for the development of new writing did not exist, as even the studios of the state theatres were considered too large to take a risk with an unknown writer. Both the Ministries of Culture and many established theatre practitioners actively discouraged small fringe venues and companies. The usual reasoning was that the quality of work produced outside of the state system could not be guaranteed and as the state had a responsibility for culture, it would not endorse it. Even in those countries which did have an alternative 'fringe' movement such as Czechoslovakia the gender bias was still very evident.

There is evidence that things are just starting to change. In Romania two of the independent theatre companies in Bucharest are led by women. Merle Karusoo has recently been appointed as director of The Estonian Drama Theatre and in Slovakia Darina Karova, director of the Nitra Festival, now holds a senior post within the Ministry of Culture. Izabella Cywinska who was briefly the Minister for Culture in Poland is now head of the independent funding body Fundacja Kultury and there must be more that I'm unaware of.

In Britain, over the last 15 years there has been a steady increase in the number of women playwrights performed and acknowledgement that they have been at the forefront in challenging both the content of plays and in particular the linear narrative form.

However in 1991, the Director Annie Casteldine in her introduction to *Plays by Women* (Vol. 9) commented that out of 228 productions in 40 regional repertory theatres in Britain only 10 were by women and in the West End only 3 plays out of 61 were by women. Although women were represented on stage as performers and in the audience (where they formed the majority), they were still not well represented as directors or writers. The subject matter, the location of the action and crucially the agenda of the majority of work continued to be from a male perspective.

The advances in presenting the work of women writers since this time have been primarily due to the support of particular theatres and crucially to the publication of plays by women.

That they are available to be studied in schools, universities and to be produced has been instrumental in bringing the diversity of women's writing to the forefront of contemporary theatre. That is why this volume, **Eastern Promise** is so important. I hope it is the first of many. In one direction the publication of *Jenufa, Her Step-daughter* asks the question: how many other works by women are there to be 'discovered' from this period? In another, the quality, relevance and insight of *The Tender Mercies* heralds the arrival of a major new talent in European writing. Each of the plays in this carefully chosen collection contributes to a view on the recent history of Eastern Europe that is seldom expressed. Their translation and publication in this volume and subsequent staging, will I hope, mean that they will reach a wider audience and the recognition in their own countries which they deserve.

Introduction
by Sian Evans and Cheryl Robson

This is the third in a series of plays by women from different regions within Europe. **Mediterranean Plays by women** covered countries that were geographically close but politically divided. It brought together a wide spectrum of female voices, tackling personal and political issues such as partition, fundamentalism and cultural identity. **A Touch of the Dutch** focused on a small country at the heart of Europe - the Netherlands, where the influences of French, German and English theatre could be keenly felt. The subjects explored reflected the modern concerns of a western nation – eating disorders, AIDS and sexual abuse. This was matched by the innovation of the playwrights in terms of form and content, demonstrating their sophisticated understanding of contemporary theatre.

In this collection: **Eastern Promise** we bring together seven women writers who have all experienced living at a time when their countries were part of a larger political entity. For Gabriela Preissova, it was the Austro-Hungarian Empire, for the others, the soviet bloc. Some of the moral and political dilemmas their characters face range from the killing of a child, to the betrayal of a comrade, to reinventing oneself as a way of living in exile.

When we began to research this collection in 1993, we were told repeatedly by dramaturgs, directors and cultural advisors that women playwrights did not exist in the former soviet bloc countries – why not look at plays by men? In countries with emerging democracies, the roles women carry out are an important indicator of the degree of equality and the openness of a society to new ideas. We wanted a different perspective on central and eastern Europe to the one commonly presented by the media – refugees, food queues and starving orphans. Women's lives in these countries remained a mystery, overshadowed by the images of tanks, land mines and rebel forces. After a good deal of research we began to unearth some names – Daniela Fisherova (Czech), Aspazija (Latvia), Ludmilla Razumovskya, (Russia). By travelling to European theatre conferences we were able to speak to theatre practitioners themselves and we discovered many women[1] playwrights struggling to make their voices heard, encountering hostility and prejudice but still managing, against the odds, to have their plays staged. By publishing these plays and bringing them to a wider audience, our understanding of these events and people can be enlarged. While we enjoy the passion and intelligence displayed within the range of work included, we hope the playwrights will benefit from further productions of their work in other countries across the English-speaking world.

The plays have been arranged in such a way that the perspective changes from the stability of a village community united by values of church and state, typical of life at the end of the last century, through worlds in which notions of morality, humanity and community are severely tested or abandoned altogether. In this way, the collection reflects the enormous changes which have occurred across Europe during the last century and the repercussions of war, revolution and the repeated shifting of boundaries.

Where these contemporary plays differ from those written in the West over the same period, is the continuing use of absurdity, of events turning full circle, of an intense atmosphere of living on the edge, of madness prevailing, of language being both a weapon and a gift, of allegiances shifting, of identity crumbling. While playwrights in the West have tended to move away from tackling wider social and political issues in the '90s, for playwrights in central and eastern Europe, the personal and the political remain irrevocably intertwined.

The Plays –
Jenufa, Her Stepdaughter

Produced for the first time on November 9th, 1890, at the National Theatre in Prague, the play fuelled a fierce controversy between the advocates of realism and their opponents. It was slated by the critics, who wrote: 'Everything in it is covered by the frost of baseness, vulgarity, foolishness and contemptibility...' but it was defended by the director of the theatre, who wrote to the newspaper: '...it would be a fatal error, if the National Theatre were to close its doors to new movements...' which ensured the debate went on and paved the way for the style of realism in Czech drama to become established.

---

[1] see Appendix.

Unfortunately, the controversy led Gabriela Preissova, the 28-year-old author to give up playwriting altogether.

Based on two real but separate crimes, Preissova set out to portray 'a barren woman haunted by the longing for a child'. The Kostelnicka character provides a fascinating female role, a woman full of pride in her achievements as a widowed working parent, who has devotedly brought up her step-daughter. She is also a highly respected member of the church, who is entrusted to lead processions, cure the sick and oversee burials. Jenufa, her step-daughter who has an illegitimate child and is abandoned by the father, Steva, tests the Kostelnicka's strict moral principles in the play. The Kostelnicka's efforts to avoid the ensuing scandal lead her into deceit, humiliation and ultimately, murder.

Janacek saw the play as a tragic love story and was attracted to the Slovak setting and folkloric elements. His adaptation of the play into an opera libretto, involved editing out details of characterisation and plot. Preissova's play offers us a more psychologically complex Kostelnicka as the central character in a community whose moral attitudes are implicitly questioned.

The Umbilical Cord

With echoes of Witkiewicz' play *The Mother* (written in 1924), Krystyna Kofta creates the stifling scenario of a sick and bedridden mother requiring those around her to repeatedly enact her memories of hunger and imprisonment. An intense three-way relationship between the mother, her son and the nurse is skilfully developed in which co-dependency precludes the possibility of any of them breaking out of the cycle of ritually re-playing the past. This is a play, which asks the question: how can we break free from the past? It examines how an individual's sense of guilt and experience of suffering can paralyse those around her.

'It is written almost with tenderness. It is an epitaph of …an entire generation, the members of which suffered 'moral defeat' when they had to steal a bicycle to save life… and in their torment dreamt to 'live long and safe like animals' though they knew that 'their life amounted to just a moment of relief before massacre'.

(Tomasz Kubikowski, Dialog.)

Tulip Doctor

Set within a revolving kaleidoscope comprising several rooms, this experimental play demonstrates the extraordinary imagination of the young Vera Filo. She attempts to deconstruct and parody the form and content of the modern play, with a cast involving several Salvador Dalis, a dragon and an angel. A bizarre murder mystery unravels, in which the dead discuss their own deaths and reflect on their past lives. There are many reflections – scenes repeated with dialogue modified; the opening three scenes are repeated in reverse order at the end. We are asked to make our own connections and our own meanings as the absurd and the surreal collide in a sequence of fragmented scenes. There is a war going on outside but none of the characters in the play shows any interest in this or in the cyber soldiers in their sequinned uniforms who frequently pass by. It would require a talented design and production team to realise the diverse technical and visual elements of the play.

The Tender Mercies

War is very much at the heart of Sladjana Vujovic's powerful and award-winning drama in which a female captor undertakes the brutal re-education of two prisoners. In the first part language is used by one prisoner as a weapon to dehumanise and humiliate another. In the next part we see psychological abuse in action and in the final part, the female captor takes on the role of passive-aggressive, encouraging one of the prisoners to beat and finally kill his former friend on the promise of release. A critic in *The Scotsman* wrote:

'The roles of tormentor and victim are thus infinitely interchangeable, as are their tribal ideologies of national superiority...
...her dazzling play upon the savagery of war approaches a universal statement.'

The play has been compared to Pinter's *One for the Road* in its economic use of language to convey a world of brutality. It transferred from Edinburgh in 1993, where it won a Fringe First, to be produced elsewhere in the UK and Europe.

Nascendo

Alina Nelega's play deploys the world of the maternity hospital as a metaphor for a nation in the act of rebirth. Set on the eve of the revolution, we are in a world of women, where class and ethnic divisions create conflict and anxiety about the future runs deep.

When the outside world enters in the form of a wounded young man, both the women and the hospital staff are suspicious of the intruder, leaving him to die, rather than nursing him back to health.

The play offers the opportunity for ensemble playing, a range of roles for women and implicit social criticism of a society divided against itself.

The Chosen Ones

Elena Popova won the first European Play competition with this atmospheric end-of-century piece about three generations of a family – father, daughter, grand-daughter and their respective relationships. Set within the confines of a decaying grand apartment, allocated to the father for services to the previous regime, the various occupants squabble over the apartment and its contents in a humorous reminder of the wider territorial conflicts. The laid-back central character, Irina provides us with insight into a woman coming to terms with her loss of status and money, thrown out of her job, unable to commit to a relationship, uncertain about the future. Both sad and funny, with subtle characterisation, the Bonner Biennale programme described the play as: 'a poignant portrayal of post-communist society.'

Belgrade Trilogy

Sharp and darkly humorous, Biljana Srbljanovic's exploration of life in exile provides a thoroughly contemporary work of modern angst. Contrasting various groups of Yugoslavians in Prague, Los Angeles, Sydney and Belgrade over the course of one New Year's Eve, she deftly raises questions about the meaning and value of freedom when it comes with a loss of cultural identity. The difficulties for each of the characters in coming to terms with their new situation provide the tension and dramatic conflict within each of the worlds we see. Although there is a buried sense of longing to return home, the final scene in Belgrade in which a pregnant woman sits alone in the dark as people off-stage count down to the New Year, leaves us with a feeling of dread as to exactly what the new year might promise.

Theatre in central and eastern Europe

During the communist period, theatres acted as a focus of dissent and defiance in much of central and eastern Europe. Although play texts were censored, it was impossible to control the way an actor spoke his or her lines. The use of irony, a subtle gesture or expression could convey one meaning while the words conveyed another. With Party members on the boards of theatres, controlling programming, employment and budgets, performers and directors found ingenious methods of subverting the mainly classical repertoire.

Alongside these large, state-subsidised theatres, sometimes known as stone theatres, smaller spaces with flexible companies grew up, particularly in Prague where the development of 'small form theatre' soon attracted audiences. In contrast to the worthy and well-paid ensembles of actors and directors in the mainstream theatres, those who worked in the smaller theatres set about deconstructing texts, playing with genre, merging sketches, songs and cabaret in an attempt to keep the theatrical event both alive and capable of expressing the complex reality of life under communist rule. Following purges against playwrights, performers developed verbally minimal pieces using mime, dance and physicality. In this way, the smaller theatres helped to raise the political consciousness of the people in Czechoslovakia and contributed to the events, which led to the collapse of the political system in 1989.

After 1989, many of the mainstream theatres throughout central and eastern Europe seemed to lose their way. Now there were no restrictions on their programming, what were they to do? They were no longer needed to act as communal meeting places to express anti-communist sentiments and many theatres consequently experienced a loss of audience. They also suffered from cuts to their state subsidies – a financial crisis, which led some theatres to programme populist musicals and comedy, raising ticket prices to increase box office revenue. Others rented out their spaces for conferences or to independent touring companies. The reciprocal arrangement between theatres, for companies to tour within the communist bloc, no longer applies so that touring productions are generally limited to visiting national festivals. The situation for smaller independent groups, lacking any subsidy, is more difficult with the scrabble for funding desperate. The number of freelance artists is growing while ageing and underemployed actors in the mainstream theatres do little but wait for retirement.

Within the mainstream theatres there are too many large spaces and very few studio spaces where small companies can try out new work. This encourages the programming of classics and literary adaptations and discourages the innovative and risky, as the need to increase box office revenue to make up for lost subsidy prevails. So far, very few of the larger theatres have closed but their dominance is threatened by the growth of smaller venues, especially in countries like Russia where dozens of studio spaces are opening up and the competition is fierce.

At a recent conference in Prague, hosted by the Open Society Institute, theatre practitioners were asked: 'Who is the key agent of change in the performing arts?'

'...Some felt that the individual artist's vision must have primacy and carry enough clout to provoke change. Others believed that the new entrepreneurs' managerial talent can create sufficient conditions for artists to develop and implement their vision. Others put more faith in sophisticated politicians, especially on the local level, who may be eager to enhance their city's image by supporting the development of the arts. The dictates of a mass audience, the whim of sponsors looking for popular and safe products and the corroding influence of the market were seen as potentially endangering factors, pushing the dynamics of change in a negative direction, away from commitment to quality and unique artistic identity.'

(Reform or Transition: the future of Repertory Theatre in Central and Eastern Europe.' ed. Dragan Klaic)

New writing in the theatre

Many of the playwrights working in central and eastern Europe find themselves at a disadvantage. Whereas playwrights in the UK have access to theatres such as the Royal Court and the Bush Theatre and companies such as Paines Plough and Soho Theatre Company which are focused on developing and premiering new work, the situation in the former soviet bloc countries is hardly encouraging of new writing. There are few dramaturgs or Literary Managers employed to work with new writers in the theatres and very few literary agents who can promote and market the work either nationally or internationally. In addition, if a new play is written in a minority language there is the added cost of translation. Playwrights often see their local repertory theatre as their only option for having their work staged and these large theatres often see new writing in terms of fashionable imports from the West such as Yasmina Reza's play *Art*. In Moscow, groups of theatre students get together to stage new work in smaller studio spaces or within the framework of a theatre festival. This is at least offering playwrights the chance to see their work produced and to develop skills, although the life of such spaces is generally limited.

In Romania, there are two important new initiatives:

'New writing in Romania has been mostly dealt with (since 1990) by means of a national play contest called *Best Play of the Year*. The winning plays have been published by Unitext, a small Romanian theatre publisher. The other new initiative by Alina Nelega, author and editor, is Dramafest, an annual festival in Targa Mures dedicated to new plays.

Major difficulties arise whenever a new play is presented to subsidised theatres because managers, directors and critics don't have enough appreciation of them to include them in the repertoires. For many years directors have turned to classic works as the stimulus for 'freshening up' the reps. It's only since 1989 that many new ideas have forged ahead in Romanian theatre which is still dominated by the former system.

The dramaturg is not yet present in the theatre community and there are no university courses to open up minds to this valuable function in the theatre. It's only occasionally that directors such as Victor Ioan Frunza and Mihai Maniutiu have worked with dramaturgs. Usually, plays are treated in the same way as literary texts, which have been adapted for the stage, which are not really 'plays' but prose.

For women playwrights, it's not a question of facing more difficulties than a man. It's just that there's not yet a culture nurturing the new plays. What's different is the situation for women directors. Many of the graduates of Universities or Faculties of Theatre in Romania are women.

In 1997/98, for instance, the number of productions created by women in professional theatres (not the puppet theatres) is some 20% of the total. Usually, they face almost the same difficulties as their male colleagues of the same age, but there are also some more due to their being women. A current opinion I've often heard is that: 'Theatre directing is not for women'. It's something which comes from a deeper sense of an archaic male structured way of living. The question has been dealt with by the communist regime too, when the Party would claim by way of a percentage quota the level up to which women could be 'visible' from a socio-professional point of view. The same with youth etc.

Among the few women playwrights in Romania, Alina Mungiu-Pippidi is now a well-known author. Her winning play *The Evangelists* (1992) led to a furious reaction in the religious milieu and was subject to many polemics. No theatre has so far dared to put it on. Alina Nelega began to make a name for herself with *Nascendo* and the production succeeded in demonstrating the quality of the subject she chose. Already published or in rehearsals are plays by Nina Tântar and Ioana Craciun. When I edited the first collection of new Romanian plays in 1991, I included one of Ioana Craciun's plays, titled *Fair River*. Nina Tântar 's *Ubu and Milena* was shortlisted for the 1997 *Best Play of the Year* competition.'

(Marian Popescu: Theatre critic, Lecturer at The University of Theatre and Film Bucharest and The University in Sibiu, Director of Unitext.)

A new generation of playwrights in central and eastern Europe is coming to prominence, tackling new subjects in new ways. What they need is a theatre community willing and able to stage their work, valuing the new voices within their own borders who can truly represent the lives and experiences of their own people at a time of rapid change. One of the selected playwrights, the Belorussian Elena Popova found that post- *perestroika,* after years of struggling against the censors, there was a new and receptive audience for her work:

'For me, political theatre, the theatre as an ideological platform, is a thing of the past. Demonstration and Revolution were powerless to change the human soul in any way. The salvation of the world lies in the individual's striving after perfection...

The path of logic and reason do not always lead to the Truth. But what can be more precious than the living Word or the Breath of Life, or the quivering of existence?'

(Elena Popova, Minsk.)

Appendix: Short-listed writers: Helena Albertova (Czech), Keva Apostolova (Bulgaria) Marketa Blahova (Czech), Anna Bojarska (Poland), Lada Kastelan (Croatia), Blaga Dimitrova (Bulgaria), Olga Dioszegi (Hungary), Slavenka Drakulic (Yugoslavia), Madeja Dragova (Bulgaria), Ksenia Dragunskaya (Russia), Daniela Fischerova (Czech), Eva Lachnit (Poland), Teresa Lubkiewicz (Poland), Olga Mukhina (Russia) Vida Ognjenovic (Montenegro), Ludmilla Razumovskaya (Russia) Nina Sadur (Russia) Tsveta Sofronieva (Bulgaria) Lelde Stumbre (Latvia)

The Plays

Jenufa, (Her Step-daughter)

Her Step-daughter is one of a group of late 19th century plays which are performed regularly and with popular success in Czech theatres, and yet are virtually unknown in the English speaking world. They are the work of writers living in a society which has emerged from the 'National Revival' of the first half of the 19th century, and is confident about its Czech identity; a society in the process of building such landmarks of today's Prague as the National Theatre, the National Museum and the Rudolfinum concert hall.

These plays, known as the 'village drama', are set in specific regions of Bohemia and Moravia, identifiable by the dialect in which the dialogue is written and, in their original productions, by the accuracy of detail in staging and costuming. Whereas the upper and middle classes in the cities of Prague and Brno were still largely German speaking and looked to Vienna as their model, the country-side was seen as the cradle of the true Czech character. The themes and situations were also realistic, in that they dealt with the genuine conflicts of individuals in a society rooted in the beliefs and traditions of the past, but faced with adaptation to new ways of life. The role of women is a recurrent theme, as in *Maryša* by the brothers Mrštík, in which a young woman is forced to marry an older man to accommodate her father's business interests, and eventually poisons him. Preissová's only other play – *The Farmer's Woman* (1889), adapted from her own novel, was the story of a woman's doomed attempts to live an unconventional life with the man she loves. The shocked reaction of the public to the theme of *Her Step-daughter* persuaded her to abandon writing for the stage.

Her Step-daughter is at least known to the world in its version as Leoš Janáček's opera *Jenůfa,* in which he adapted the theme, to put the emphasis on Jenůfa herself, and the development of her character. Preissová was more interested in Jenůfa's step-mother, the 'Kostelnička' or sacristan – normally a position for a man. The Kostelnička has taken on a man's role not only as sacristan and spiritual authority, but also as breadwinner for the daughter of the first wife of her late (and profligate) husband. At the same time she clings so desperately to traditional values of honour and respectability that she is driven to murder. It is this state of the modern soul that Preissová is most interested in unravelling.

Barbara Day.

Jenufa, (Her Step-daughter)

by Gabriela Preissová
translated by Barbara Day

The play was first performed in 1890 at the National Theatre in Prague, Czechoslovakia.

CHARACTERS

Kostelnička Buryjovka Granny Buryjovka's daughter-in-law
Jenůfa Kostelnička's step-daughter
Granny Buryjovka a farmer's widow and housekeeper at the mill
Števa Buryja Buryjovka's grandson
Laca Klemeň half-brother to Števa
The Foreman of the Mill
The Mayor
The Mayor's wife
Karolka their daughter
Kolušina a farmer's wife
Barena a servant at the mill
Jano a cowherd
Two old women
Three young girls
Musicians, Villagers

There is an interval of one year between Acts I and II, and two months between Acts II and III.

ACT ONE

Early evening. A water mill in a peaceful place in the hills. Stage right, in front of the farm house, a porch with wooden pillars. A hillside, bushes, some trees and, at the back, the millstream. Buryjovka is sitting on the porch, choosing seed potatoes from a pile in a basket, cutting out the eyes and throwing them into a pannier.

*Laca, a dark-haired young man, is sitting on the trunk of a tree stage
left, carving a whip-handle with a knife. Jenůfa stands on the bank of
the millrace, a pot of rosemary in one hand, the other shielding her
eyes as she gazes into the distance.*

JENUFA (*to herself*) It's getting dark, and Števa hasn't come! All
night I was afraid, I could barely wait 'till morning – but then
again, the morning... oh, it was a bad sign... (*in desperation*) Oh
sweet Virgin, answer my prayer – if they take Števa away... if
they stop us getting married... I'll kill myself – or I'll be damned
forever for the shame of it!

BURYJOVKA Jenůfa, dear, something's keeping you from your
work, what is it? Do I have to get all the potatoes ready with these
old hands? Not one of you lifts a finger to help. You used to be
such a sensible, hard-working girl, and now you've changed
altogether. Laca tells me it's not his work, as a journeyman... the
Foreman's gone off to look after something or other at the mill
and young Jano and Baruna have to see to the animals. Everyone's got some excuse or other – and now you as well, you're
leaving it all to me. The potatoes have to be planted tomorrow,
and there's only half a basket ready! And these old eyes of mine
can't see as well as they used to.

LACA (*spitefully*) There's a lot more that those old eyes of yours
haven't seen! You keep on asking me to help you, but you're just
trying to keep me in my place, a hireling to look after the estate. I
know perfectly well I'm not... not your *real* grandchild. I used to
feel it whenever I came here, a poor little lad trying to creep close
to you while you were hugging Števa and stroking his hair and
whispering 'golden as the sun!' You used to push me away –
even though I was an orphan too, barely four years older than
Števa. If you'd just cough up my father's share of the mill...
twelve hundred guilders... then I could go off wherever I wanted,
couldn't I?

JENŮFA (*on her knees by the millrace, turns*) Laca, you're always
being so rude to Gran, then you expect her to help you out.

BURYJOVKA I'm just an old witch to him – not even a
housekeeper, let alone family!

LACA (*to Buryjovka*) And you're making Jenůfa work today... *today*, when she's waiting to find out if Števa's been enlisted? If it weren't Friday, when Aunt Kostelnička comes for the butter, she'd be over there with Števa.

JENŮFA (*to herself*) How much does he know? He can see straight through people with those piercing eyes of his. I won't give anything away – the spiteful man... (*to Buryjovka*) Gran, don't be cross with me, I'll make up for it. I remembered my rosemary was starting to die so I just went to dip it in the stream. (*with a sigh*) And if it dies – you know what they say, all the happiness in the world goes with it.

JANO (*runs to Jenůfa*) Jenůfa! Jenůfa! I can read, I can read! Do me some more!

JENŮFA Wait, until I've been to town, Jano. I'll bring you a reading book and you can read that. And then I'll teach you to write, and you'll be glad of it. But you'd better get off to work now, or we'll have Gran scolding you as well.

JANO (*runs off*) I can read, I can read – Jenůfa taught me to read!

BURYJOVKA Well, my girl, you should be pleased with yourself. You taught Barena how to embroider and how to read too. You should have been a teacher, you reason like a man – you take after your step-mother.

JENŮFA (*with a sigh*) Oh, Gran... my reason... my reason was long ago washed away in the stream!

SCENE 2

The Mill Foreman enters, in his town attire, dusty with flour, and stops by Laca.

FOREMAN What are you working on, young man? That could be a fine handle for a whip!

LACA This knife's blunt, it'll take me two hours at this rate. Could you sharpen it for me?

FOREMAN Of course I will.

(*He pulls out a small whetstone from his pocket and begins to sharpen the knife. Meanwhile Laca tries to pull the scarf from Jenůfa's head with the whip-handle.*)

JENŮFA (*without looking at him*) Laca – Laca, you've always been a bit crazy.

LACA   You wouldn't mind if it was Števa, would you?

JENŮFA   Števa wouldn't behave like that.

LACA   Because you never let him out of your sight.

JENŮFA   You can't leave someone alone, can you? It's more than anyone can put up with! What has it got to do with you? You just take care yourself!
(*She crosses the porch to the living room. After a while she comes back and sits by the basket, working diligently on the potatoes.*)

LACA (*to the Foreman, watching her as she leaves*) She'll make a charming sister-in-law, don't you think? That's what I've got to look forward to!

FOREMAN   Well, she's got plenty of charm, it could turn a man's head… carries herself as proud as a peacock, and she could draw the soul from your body with those grey eyes. The other day the miller over the hill told me he'd come Easter carolling and courting the girls. 'Mind,' I said, 'we've only got the two young women, Jenůfa and the cowgirl.' And he said, 'That Jenůfa's worth a hundred other girls!' I don't know why I'm telling you; those eyes of hers have already got to you – haven't they?

LACA   Me? (*derisively*) If you'd been here just now you'd have seen how much I love her. She was crying over her rosemary. She's got no idea I put two worms in the roots, so it would wither away like this marriage she's planning with Števa.

FOREMAN   You know, Laca – I find it strange, the cruel things you do because – you're not as hard as you make out, are you? And it seems to me you always get flushed whenever Jenůfa's around.

LACA   Rubbish – you keep out of it.

FOREMAN   Look, I'm on your side, you know. I'm not an orphan, my parents are still alive, but they've always left me out of things, like you. As I'm the youngest, there was nothing left for me to inherit. If it weren't for you here, holding everything together, what would be left of the mill and the farm? Števa may be the miller in name, but he doesn't know anything about it and since the mill's been rented out, all he's done is have a good time with the money. They call him the manager, but all he manages is getting down to the inn, and that's it. On Sunday, at the village dance, he bought drinks for all the young recruits.

LACA Try telling Gran or Jenůfa that.

FOREMAN It's in his blood... the recklessness. Takes after his father. Your poor widowed mother, fifteen years older than him, so much in love she made the mill over to him, then he started throwing money around. It was lucky he died so soon after she did. And then there's his brother, your Aunt Kostelnička's husband, hard to find another rogue like that one – he'd have sold his best shirt for a drink.

LACA Jenůfa never says a word against him.

FOREMAN A father's a father. He behaved himself well enough with his first wife, Jenůfa's mother. They'd only been together a year before she died – but his second wife, Kostelnička, he put her through hell. Well, one shouldn't speak ill of the dead, but I'm sure I'll live to see the day when Števa goes bankrupt and the mill will be yours, as it should have been.

LACA Jenůfa isn't like them.

FOREMAN Indeed she is not. Perhaps she takes after her mother. And then she was brought up by Kostelnička.

LACA Jenůfa keeps Števa in order. It's just as well she's so thrifty and sensible.

FOREMAN To what end! Even Kostelnička couldn't hold her man down. Neither could your mother.

LACA My mother's mistake was falling madly in love with my stepfather.

FOREMAN Isn't it the same with Jenůfa? Blind love?

LACA But – he hasn't got her yet. If he's enlisted today, there'll be no wedding.

FOREMAN They didn't take him! I met the messenger down by the stream – only chose nine out of the lot, and Števa wasn't one of them.

LACA (*jumps up*) No! What kind of justice is that! He's built like an ox – I wasn't half as strong as him at that age, and I had to suffer three years in the army.

FOREMAN Always had the devil's own luck – born under a lucky star. If his parents were still alive, they'd put a stop to his marrying an impoverished cousin. As for that old grandmother of yours, she's gone weak in the head. Jenůfa's her grand-daughter too, and because Kostelnička brought her up, she thinks she'll pass on all that wisdom. Such an exceptional woman. The priest's put her in charge of the chapel, and leaves the sick and dying to her.

LACA   Of course, all Števa can see is a pretty face. You know she's already his third girlfriend, he just dropped the other two! I'd bet anything, if Jenůfa caught the smallpox and her face was scarred with pockmarks, Števa would drop her like that and start looking for another.

FOREMAN   Well, there's your knife. I don't think it can be sharpened. Ah, here comes Kostelnička now, and the Mayor's wife's with her. *(he greets them and exits.)*

SCENE 3
Laca doffs his cap without saying anything and gets on with carving the whip-handle.

JENŮFA *(breaks off her work and kisses her stepmother's hand)* Welcome, Mother! *(to the Mayor's wife)* And you too, Madam! God be with you! *(runs back to her work.)*

MAYOR'S WIFE And with you, my child! I know you're surprised to see me. I've been up to the brow of the hill, where somebody cut and stole our winter crop, and on the way back I ran into Kostelnička. So I was glad of her company, it makes the walk pass more pleasantly. *(to Laca)* And what are you doing Laca, all alone? My girls would like you to come and visit.

LACA   That's kind of you, madam. But if I did come, the gossips would start saying how you wanted to marry me off to one of your daughters.

BURYJOVKA *(rising)* Why, there you are, my dear. Come and join us.

MAYOR'S WIFE I'm afraid Kostelnička's in a hurry. She's like a whirlwind – always on the move.

KOSTELNIČKA *(her speech and bearing are more dignified than that of an ordinary village woman)* I don't like standing around, it only leads to gossiping. And I have to earn my living. Only yesterday an old man came to my house for a bite of food, and was curious to know how much my husband made as verger. I told him, 'I don't have a husband – they call me Kostelnička because I'm the one who looks after the chapel and I'm the one who leads the girls at funerals and festivities. But honour is my only reward. It's true, this hand is kissed with gratitude and respect (*she gestures with her hands*) more than if I were some great lady.' He was wondering how I manage to make a living for myself.

MAYOR'S WIFE Surely people pay you in kind for your good advice so you don't need to peddle your cloth from door to door?

KOSTELNIČKA It's easy for you to say so. (*to Jenůfa*) My child, I bought something for you today from the German woman – a length of cotton, it hangs like silk. I saw the same thing on my rounds, on rich people in the town. I can't give you money, but you'll have a trousseau fit for the daughter of a lord. Your real mother couldn't have done more.

JENŮFA God will reward you, mother.

BURYJOVKA Kostelnička adores you as if you were her own daughter. She always takes such pride in you.

MAYOR'S WIFE (*tartly*) Kostelnička's step-daughter or the draper's step-daughter – *my* daughters are never the equal of Jenůfa. And people take it for granted she'll be the miller's wife here. I'm sure you'll manage that – they don't call you the wise woman for nothing.

KOSTELNIČKA I take no notice of idle talk; let them look after their own daughters – my step-daughter's as good as any of them. You don't need to make a point of our poverty. I'm from a decent home. I brought money to my husband's farm, and six cartloads of goods – and if the poor soul hadn't squandered it all... I've never complained... I kept it all to myself, and then I started to make a living selling cloth – even though it was hard for me at first, going from house to house like a common peddler. My Jenůfa won't have to suffer like that and she's more right to the mill than any outsider!

MAYOR'S WIFE I was only speaking the plain truth. You packed her off to the mill quick enough before Christmas, as soon as my husband – Števa's guardian – kindly persuaded the authorities to declare Števa of age, so he could take over the mill… and with Laca just back from his military service too… well, it's hardly proper to parade a girl in front of two such eligible young men.

KOSTELNIČKA Proper! They're family! Jenůfa is Buryjovka's grand-daughter and Števa's cousin… they were brought up together. There's only three years between Števa and Jenůfa, they went to school together, and Laca – he used to carry Jenůfa on his back across the stream. As a little boy he promised to marry her. It was always: 'I'll build a fine house, Jenůfa, just for you and me, and we can live there together!' He spent more time with us in our quiet cottage than in his own home, even though it was out by the lake, and we got it cheap from the quack because children thought it was haunted… That boy gave his heart to her, long before he went off to the army.

LACA (*jumping up distressed, waving his hand at her*) Kostelnička!

KOSTELNIČKA It's nothing to be ashamed of, Laca – once I caught him at night, setting up a fine May tree outside her window… he must have walked five hours through the woods to find it. But the Lord God decided otherwise. I don't think Števa will be any great catch for Jenůfa, so don't you (*she laughs proudly*) try and tell me what's proper. Jenůfa promised herself to him of her own free will – out of love. And her wealth – to grow up decent and unspoiled like the lily in the field – not even the Count would have reason to be ashamed of such a bride.
(*Jenufa is fearful, she hides her face.*)

BURYJOVKA I agree with every word, my daughter… And what made you so late today?

KOSTELNIČKA I had to get the girls together, to organise the funeral procession for the blacksmith's daughter from Vobora. She died of diphtheria… I was with her till the end.

BURYJOVKA God be praised, you've a strong spirit. So many ill and dying you've cared for.

KOSTELNIČKA I'm not afraid of the dead – it wouldn't bother me to spend a night in the churchyard. She had a difficult death, the blacksmith's daughter – fighting to breathe. Her mother couldn't bear to watch. It's fortunate for her she's got more daughters.

BURYJOVKA That's no help to a mother; she'll grieve just as much for this daughter.

KOSTELNIČKA If you're born to live in poverty and degradation – surely it's a thousand times better to be out of this world?

MAYOR'S WIFE But one's own flesh and blood... You wouldn't understand, Kostelnička. The good Lord never gave you a child – but I've buried two.

KOSTELNIČKA No, he didn't. But I've watched our cat, our little scrawny cat, every time some wild animal's eaten her kittens, she's prowled around the house and mourned for them. I've always thought to myself, 'there you are, she's a mother too!' What would she have done, if her kittens were still alive? She would have brought them up, taught them their craft and set them up on their own.

LACA So what are you saying? That women are like cats?

KOSTELNIČKA No, I'm saying that human beings are on a higher level than the animals because they have souls, and good will, and reason. (*points to Jenůfa and raises her voice*) Look at Jenůfa, who I raised! She's not my blood, not a part of my body – but I stayed awake all night with her, I gave her the best food, I prayed for her, punished her, blessed her and brought her up to be honest. And the priest said to me, when I sold my Marian thaller, given to me at my christening – my Marian thaller which I'd hung on to through all the hardship – when I sold it to buy food rather than leave my poor sick Jenůfa and take some work, the priest said to me, 'Buryjovka, I take my hat off to such a mother.' (*more quietly*) And that priest is still alive; you can ask him yourself.

MAYOR'S WIFE No-one's trying to reproach you; I meant no harm.

KOSTELNIČKA I'm wasting my time here... wasting time... They're waiting for me at the gamekeeper's as if I were some messenger from heaven. The gamekeeper's wife has a swelling on her leg and I have an ointment for it. How much butter do you have for me to sell?

BURYJOVKA Five pounds of butter and three pounds of cheese. Barena, bring it up from the cellar. And there's a piece of cheesecake in the oven, that Jenůfa baked today for Števa.

KOSTELNIČKA Thank you, no. I'm not hungry and there are
people needing my help, so I won't stop for food. I'll just collect
the butter. *(she goes inside.)*

SCENE 4

BURYJOVKA Whatever's the matter, Jenůfa, why don't you go in
and help your mother? Are you still upset about that telling off
she gave you last Friday, when you forgot to help the other girls
prepare the Virgin's little garden on the chapel altar?

JENŮFA   Oh no – I deserved it. But please, Gran, don't make
me go with her!

BURYJOVKA Child, you worry me. Ah well, they say every girl
loses her senses nine times before she becomes a bride.
(In the distance the sound of music and singing can be heard)

'They don't want to be soldiers
'cause soon they'll have to marry
I'm glad to be a soldier
For marriage, I'll not tarry.

If you've got pots of money
then pay and don't get taken
but I don't have a penny
so beggar, I'm forsaken.'

*The Mill Foreman enters; Števa is not far behind, accompanied by
the Magistrate and the musicians.*

SCENE 5

FOREMAN   Here's Števa, with all his friends round him – he's
over the moon now he hasn't been picked for the army! You can
see it on him a mile off!

JENŮFA *(jumps up)* Not picked! Dear God, you heard my prayer!
Gran dear, *(she kisses Buryjovka)* Števa wasn't chosen!

Števa enters stage left with four fiddlers – he has had quite a lot to drink, but is merry, rather than unpleasantly drunk. Jenůfa runs to greet him.

JENŮFA   My own Števa!

ŠTEVA (*his auburn hair in a lock over his forehead; he holds himself unsteadily upright, and with his left hand raises a hat decorated with flowers high over his head, with his right, he beats time to the music*) And I must be a soldier, farewell to love! Huzza!

(Kostelnička appears on the threshold. The Mayor is in a merry mood, not drunk, waving his hat in time to the tune and laughing.)

MAYOR'S WIFE (*to the Mayor*) Old man, what are you doing with them! Do you think they need you, you old goat?

MAYOR   I'm here to support our young recruit. It was thanks to me he didn't get picked. I simply stood there by his side, and those gentlemen know very well who I am. (*grinning*) We showed them what our village is worth, we gave them a small barrel, well half a hogshead, of old wine to drink our health! I'm the Mayor in Oborany, I'm the authority here. Let them all see we're not misers here in Oborany!

MAYOR'S WIFE   You old fool, what are you doing throwing your money around like that? Just wait till we get home! You want to be best friends with a young spendthrift like Števa, do you? Well, you just wait!

MAYOR   Oh, stop your blithering, woman! (*grinning*) It wasn't me who paid, it was him – it didn't cost me a penny – just four kreutzers for tobacco, and then I had a few drinks with them. So there you are, you stupid woman, you silly old biddy... you think you can teach the Mayor how to do his job, do you?

MAYOR'S WIFE   It's high time you got home with you! This is no place for you... you shouldn't be mixing with these young people. It's not right. And I'm in a hurry. We're not waiting for Kostelnička, as she always thinks she's a cut above the rest of us. (*takes her husband by the arm*) Have a good time! And good night to you all! (*to her husband*) Get a move on!

MAYOR (*leaving with her*) Stop nagging, can't you!

They exit.

SCENE 6

JENŮFA (*reproachfully*) Števa, dear soul, you've been drinking
again!

ŠTEVA   You saying I'm drunk? Jenůfa, you say that to me?
Don't you know, I am Štefan Buryja? I own the mill, and all the
land around it. Anyone round here would lend me as much as I
asked for. What does he say, (*turning to the musicians*) the
innkeeper Rotbegr, what does he say? And the gentlemen there,
from the army, they know I can pay for it – that's why they let me
go, and that's why all the girls are so nice to me. This little lot,
(*he shows the flowers in his hat*) one of the village girls gave
them to me, as we rode through Oborany. (*he turns to the
musicians*) What've you stopped playing for? Play Jenůfa's song:
(*they play*)

> 'They have built a tower
>   on the yonder plains
>   it's not built of marble
> but of handsome swains.
>
> The dome of that tower
>   glistening and tall
>   is my only darling
>   fairest of them all.
>
> But the dome has fallen
>   from the tower steep
>   now my dearest darling
>   holds it for her keep.'

ŠTEVA   She likes it, the little angel likes it. You shall be paid
for that! There you are, my hungry hares!
(*he takes handfuls of coins with both hands from his pockets and
throws them to the musicians. They go down on their knees to
collect them, then start playing again, with everyone singing
along. Števa turns to Jenůfa*)

Come on, Jenůfa, come! (*he takes her round the waist*) That's
how we'll go to our wedding, with music… they'll have to
accompany us the whole way!

KOSTELNIČKA (*claps her hands and stops the musicians from
playing*) And that's how you'll go through life is it? And you,
Jenůfa – you'd go down on your knees too to pick up the pennies,
would you? Just like my late lamented husband, with that big
farm of his! It's in the family. He was another golden-boy, a fine
figure of a man – he wormed his way into my heart so that I
longed for him even before he married his first wife and then
again when he was widowed. My mother warned me – even then
his eyes were wandering – but I wouldn't listen! Still, I never
went whingeing to her afterwards. Not when he got drunk week
after week, until he was always drunk, and not when he started
running up debts and throwing his money around…
(*Števa is startled – Jenůfa is crying*)
I tried to reason with him but he started beating me, so I spent
many a night hiding out in the fields. So you see, I've known it
for some time now that the Oborany miller is not worthy of my
step-daughter.

JENŮFA (*interrupts her in desperation*) Calm down, please mother!

KOSTELNIČKA I've kept quiet long enough, because I knew you
loved him – you're young and you follow your heart, while I have
to act as your head… and I want everyone to know that you're not
chasing after his money. First thing tomorrow you'll come home
to me. I'd take you this minute, but I'd rather you and Števa said
goodbye on good terms – as is proper for a future bride – and he
needs to be sober for that. I want you to tell Števa that I shall
allow you to get married when he has gone a whole year without
drinking. Both of you are still young – you have to be patient.
And Jenůfa, if you don't listen to me, if you put Števa's wishes
before mine, then God will be the one to punish you – believe me.
(*Števa is shocked; he leans back against one of the pillars*)

LACA (*gratefully*) Kostelnička, you've dropped your shawl – and let
me kiss your hand.

Kostelnicka leaves.

SCENE 7

BURYJOVKA Kostelnička, please – oh, what a hard woman she is! He's not such a bad boy, our Števa – nor was that husband of hers – my son. There are a lot worse than he was. Whatever came over her? What if he did have a drop too much once in a while? Go and lie down, Števa, go on with you. You overdid it a bit, that's all. You're young, it's only natural, those friends of yours were leading you on. You there... musicians, get off home with you, you're the ones causing all the trouble.

The musicians leave.

Jenůfa, my dear, don't cry... everything will be all right, you'll see. Every couple has its ups and downs.

LACA (*to himself*) Stroke him nicely, the brave boy, just stroke him nicely!

JENŮFA (*quietly to Števa*) Števa, I know you were only behaving like that because of high spirits – but there have been other times... Števa, please Števa, try and behave. Please don't make my mother so angry. You see how wretched I am! I'm scared to death they'll all know my guilt. I'm so afraid of being punished for it. Night after night, I can't sleep. Remember, dear soul, that the Lord God has helped us already. You don't have to go into the army, so we can get married now. I'm so worried... As it is, mother will have enough to reproach us with once she knows. You know how much she thinks of me – you've heard her. I don't know what she'd do if we don't get married straight away. I don't know what *I* would do! Oh, Jesus Christ!

ŠTEVA Stop making such a face. You know Aunt Kostel-nička's always got on my nerves, because she thinks so highly of you, and so poorly of me. Well, I wish you could both see how all the other girls treat me!

JENŮFA (*angry*) But you shouldn't take any notice of them any more – I'm the only one who has any right to you – I'd have to kill myself! (*she grabs him by the shoulders and shakes him*) How can you be like this to me – my God – so weak, so pitiful!

ŠTEVA (*trying to calm her down*) I'm not saying I'd leave you like that... Jenůfa...

Laca enters, at a distance.

You were always the prettiest of them all, with your cheeks like rosy apples...

BURYJOVKA Alright. Enough talking. Leave it all till the morning, when his head is clear again. Get off to bed, my boy – go on, off with you!

Števa and Buryjovka both go inside. Jenůfa goes to sit down by the basket of potatoes, and head down, continues to cut them up.

SCENE 8

LACA (*comes downstage with whip handle and knife in hand*) So for all his fine boasting, Števa's been taught a lesson by Kostelnička!

JENŮFA He's still a hundred times better than you'll ever be!

LACA (*choked with emotion*) Is he? (*bends down to pick up the bunch of flowers dropped by Števa*) Look, Jenůfa – he's left the flowers he was given by one of those girls he says is nice to him. Let me pin them on you...

The maid Barena appears on the doorstep

JENŮFA (*stands, proudly*) Yes, let me have them! I can wear such flowers with pride – they're part of the honour my Števa receives.

LACA (*to himself*) Yes, go on, be proud of him but all he sees in you are your cheeks, fresh as apples... and yet he's a hundred times better than me, of course. (*he looks at the knife in his hand, feverishly*) This knife could ruin those lovely cheeks forever. What does he care about your soul – your sweet soul that you promised to me so long ago! (*to Jenůfa*) My dear girl, my little lamb... Take these flowers of yours – here. (*even more excited, he approaches Jenůfa, the flowers and the knife in his right hand*)

LACA   ... but I can't let you have them for nothing. (*tries to embrace her.*)

JENŮFA   Don't you dare, Laca – I'll hit you!

LACA (*leans over her, and as she resists him, draws the knife across her face*) Why do you hate me?

JENŮFA (*screams*) My God! You've cut my face! (*presses her shawl to her cheek.*)

LACA (*falls on one knee beside her, holding her in his arms*) What have I done! Jenůfa – Jenůfa – my darling, my dearest! I loved you... I've always loved you! Water – get some water!

Barena wrings her hands, Jenůfa runs inside. The Foreman and Buryjovka enter.

FOREMAN   What's going on?
(*Laca jumps up, holding his head in his hands.*)

BARENA   Something dreadful! Laca was teasing Jenůfa for a kiss, but he was holding a knife and it cut her face... he didn't mean it to happen. Thank God he didn't cut her eye!
(*The Foreman runs inside to find Jenůfa.*)

BURYJOVKA Oh boys, boys! Why do you cause me such grief! Don't you know it's madness to play about with a knife in your hand? Where is she?

FOREMAN (*re-entering*) Grandmother, come and look after Jenůfa, she's near fainting. And send for Kostelnička, the wound needs her care.

BURYJOVKA My God, is it as bad as that?

FOREMAN   She won't die from it – but she'll carry the scar for the rest of her life.

Buryjovka hurries inside; Laca, overwhelmed, comes to and runs off.

Laca, don't run away, I know you did it on purpose – but I promise not to say anything!

Lights fade.

ACT TWO

A room in a Slovak cottage. The walls are covered with religious pictures and carvings; there is a stoop of holy water by the door. A stove, a bed, a linen chest, a clothes-rack, a shelf with some plates, a few chairs. A picture of the Holy Virgin by the window. There are two doors, one to the outside and one to Jenůfa's room.
Jenůfa is dressed in ordinary clothes. On her pale face a dark scar can be seen, not deep but noticeable. She sits on a chair by the table, sewing, her head bowed over her work. Kostelnička is with her. She approaches the side door of the room and opens it.

KOSTELNIČKA I'll leave this door open, to let a little warmth into your room. Why do you keep going to the window to pray, like a lost soul? It's not good for you, you should try to get some sleep.

JENŮFA I can't help it, I can't seem to find any peace.

KOSTELNIČKA (*with a sigh*) Yes, I know – neither can I. Your distress has upset me so much, from the day I brought you home to heal that wound on your face. And when Števa stayed away from us, and when I told you off for wanting to die, and when you confessed everything to me – then, then I thought I would die as well. But you've been such a big part of my life, I knew I had to help you. I've been so worried about hiding you here, fretting over your shame... I told everyone you'd gone into service in Vienna – until the day Števa's son came into the world. And even in his dreams his father cares nothing! (*she takes a cup from the stove*) I've brewed some poppy-seed for you, to help you sleep. All these sleepless nights have left you a shadow of yourself. You need to take care of yourself – try to keep healthy – you have someone to live for, the child's going to need you. You're the only one he can depend on. He'll never know his father – that shameless man. (*more kindly*) Come on, I don't even want to think of that swine!

JENŮFA (*drinks a little and quickly returns the cup to Kostelnička; hurries to the door of the room, looks inside*) I thought for a moment little Štefka was awake! But he's sound asleep...

KOSTELNIČKA You're always spoiling that child. You'd do better praying to the Lord to relieve you of it.

JENŮFA (*returns to the table and takes up her sewing*) But he's so sweet and good… eight days old, and he's not cried once.

KOSTELNIČKA He'll make himself heard all right... he'll torment you... it sucks the blood and reason out of me – it will come out that I'm hiding you and your shame, and that I've lied to everyone about it.

JENŮFA   Why didn't you let me go somewhere a long way away? Then I wouldn't have been here to see or cause you any pain.

KOSTELNIČKA Let you end up in despair? Let you be guided by your sins... into the arms of Števa perhaps? People would still have found out.

JENŮFA   You said yourself, when we were at the mill, that sometimes it's better to be dead.

KOSTELNIČKA You think by disappearing off, the shame wouldn't find its way back here? People, newspapers, officials, they find out everything and make it known here, there and everywhere.

JENŮFA   Mother, I've admitted my sins a thousand times, and I can't tell you how much I've suffered but, since it's already happened, I should put an end to it once and for all rather than putting you through all this.

KOSTELNIČKA Put an end to it! How can I put an end to being part of you? I brought you up, I put all my hopes and pride into you, and for it all to be brought down to this – this – I had such hopes for you. (*sighs deeply*) Oh, dear God!

JENŮFA   If Števa could see his little boy, he would help us!

KOSTELNIČKA This is what I see happening... complete humiliation... If I go and beg him to marry you – he'll be even less likely to marry you. Ohhh!... if only that child did not exist!

JENŮFA   The poor little mite has done nothing wrong.

KOSTELNIČKA A mite, yes, that's what it is, a mite that has eaten my heart. And when I look into its eyes, I see your fine bedfellow.

JENŮFA   If Števa could just see the sweet babe, he'd take pity.

KOSTELNIČKA Don't deceive yourself. Not once has he come to find out what you were doing in Vienna. Laca was the only one who made his way here to ask after you. Did Števa show a scrap of conscience, when he learnt what happened to you?

JENŮFA   Maybe he was afraid of you, mother.

KOSTELNIČKA And which of us two should get down and beg first? Him, that loose fellow, or me, whose hand people kiss in gratitude?

JENŮFA (*puts her sewing down and stands up*) Mother, I don't feel well. I'm going to lie down.

KOSTELNIČKA (*gives her the cup again*) Drink this up first, so you'll have a peaceful night's sleep. The bed's made up and I've lit the lamp.

JENŮFA (*drinks up*) Good night, mother! (*She exits.*)

SCENE 2

KOSTELNIČKA (*closing the door behind Jenůfa*) Oh, my poor girl... that window of yours has been blocked up these last twenty weeks – that fine young man of yours hasn't managed to find his way to it. Wait, just wait... I didn't tell you that today I've asked him to come here so we can sort everything out... and the child, pale like Števa, I hate the sight of them both. (*in despair*) Oh, how I prayed, how I fasted, that it would never set eyes on this world! All in vain. A week old now, and no sign of dying. What else can I do but let Jenůfa go to Števa?... so he can abuse her... and even for that I'll have to grovel before him. (*there is a rattling at the door*) There he is! (*she locks the door to Jenůfa's room and opens the front door*) Is that you, Kolušina?

SCENE 3

KOLUŠINA (*enters*) Good evening and God be with you. What's this, Kostelnička – keeping the door locked? You've always kept the door on the latch, even though you live so far from anywhere. No-one would dare steal a thing from you. They know you'd see right through them.

KOSTELNIČKA They steal from the priest's house, so why wouldn't they dare to steal from me? The contents of this chest alone would be worth their while. Look at this! (*she opens the chest which is filled to the brim*) All of it ready for Jenůfa – nothing but the best. Look at these blouses. She has more than a dozen, some of them worth ten guilders at least.

KOLUŠINA   My goodness, all that just for a step-daughter! When I think of the times the women used to run you down... but that was years ago, when your poor husband was still alive, before you were so well-known... they used to laugh at you for going on pilgrimages to pray for a child. They'd say, 'Well, the Lord God must have his reasons for not granting her a child.' They would have been only too glad to find fault with Jenůfa, but they couldn't find any, although they did go on about you sending her to help out at the mill with all those men there. Still, a step-mother like you – you're one in a thousand!

KOSTELNIČKA   What have you come for, Kolušina? And how is your servant, is her cough better? Was that syrup I brought any use to her?

KOLUŠINA   Oh, yes... she was pleased. It did her a lot of good, and she's blessing you all the time.

KOSTELNIČKA   I need no thanks. As long as I have the chance to do some good... that's what pleases me most.

KOLUŠINA   Today, my dear Kostelnička, I've come to you for some advice... it's hard to say exactly... I'm almost ashamed to speak of it... Well, what do you say to this? My husband, the poor old thing – why, his hair's already white, well, he can't stop saying how pretty and clever the new innkeeper's wife is, and he can't take his eyes off her... Do you think that's right? It makes me ashamed...

KOSTELNIČKA   Does he spend a lot of money at the inn?

KOLUŠINA   I never leave him more than sixpence in his pocket. I don't let him waste money! But as I say, he's always sneaking in there to stare at her, as though she were a holy picture.

KOSTELNIČKA   Let him stare at her, and when he does simply say to yourself, 'the poor old fool, he's going dotty...' Those wise words will help you get rid of your envy, so no-one can laugh at you any more. Oh Kolušina, there's nothing more important than stopping people from seeing your shame and misery – none of them will help you, they'll just spread the gossip.

KOLUŠINA That does make me feel a little easier. God reward you, Kostelnička. I'll send you a chicken. Now you don't seem yourself either – are you sad about something?

KOSTELNIČKA I'm getting on. At my age one year feels like ten. And I'm worried about Jenůfa.

KOLUŠINA Where is she... in service?

KOSTELNIČKA She's in Vienna. She writes to me that she's poorly all the time, she's got a fever. I wrote to her to come back – but she's not going to look very well.

KOLUŠINA I know you'll be able to help her... so she's in Vienna, is she? The neighbours were saying she'd gone to Brno.

KOSTELNIČKA No. Vienna. It's a big city, a person can get lost there like a drop in the ocean. But she's in service with a respectable family and they think highly of her.

KOLUŠINA I should think they do! A gifted, clever girl like her! That Števa up at the mill has a blot on his conscience, abandoning her for that scar on her face.

KOSTELNIČKA Abandoning her! That's nothing but stupid gossip. Just wait a while – maybe even today he'll come to plead with me. Tell everyone it was my doing. I did it! Everyone knows he was about to have the banns called – people should remember when it was – before the accident, when he came back from the recruitment – and I said he'd have to wait a year without once getting drunk... But he didn't listen – so be it. My Jenůfa can do quite well without him... so I sent her to Vienna, to help her forget about him.

KOLUŠINA Now Števa's courting the Mayor's youngest daughter. People say they're engaged.

KOSTELNIČKA Is that so? Never mind... in any case, his half-brother Laca is a more respectable young man by far. And he's been coming here every day to ask after Jenůfa. He's still upset he caused that injury to her face... and he'd be very happy to marry her! But listen – Števa will certainly be here soon. So make sure, please, make sure you tell everyone, that he's coming here to plead with me.

KOLUŠINA I'll certainly do that. Good night to you. (*she leaves.*)

KOSTELNIČKA (*opens the door into the bedchamber and looks at the bed*) She's asleep – sound asleep. I was right to give her the poppy-seed tea... at least she won't witness my humiliation.

Števa enters.

SCENE 4

ŠTEVA (*uneasily*) Aunt – you sent a note to say I should come – that if I didn't come, something terrible would happen. What is it, you want to tell me?

KOSTELNIČKA (*shows him the door of the inner room*) Come... (*Števa hesitates*) Well, why are you waiting?

ŠTEVA   I'm afraid... Has something happened – to Jenůfa?

KOSTELNIČKA Jenůfa is well, and so is the child.

ŠTEVA   It's arrived?

KOSTELNIČKA   A week ago. (*reproachfully*) Not once did you come to ask after her!

ŠTEVA   I thought about it, all the time... it made me quite wretched. Then after you'd attacked me, Aunt – after you'd pers-ecuted me the way you did – and then when Jenůfa's beauty had been spoiled... well, it wasn't my fault.

KOSTELNIČKA Then go in.

ŠTEVA   I'm afraid. Is she really there? Is she back from Vienna?

KOSTELNIČKA She's asleep. (*she opens the door to the room*) No-one's been in here these five months... Jenůfa wasn't in Vienna – she was hiding here. Go and take a look at your child, your boy – we called him Števa after you. I christened him myself.

ŠTEVA   Poor little thing...

KOSTELNIČKA Yes, but it's Jenůfa who's worse off by far. I was so sure the child would die... after all her suffering, it would be born weak and sickly – that I'd be able to lay it to rest in sacred ground and that no-one would know about it. But he's healthy and strong. He wants to live – that's the only reason I called you.

ŠTEVA   I'll pay for its keep, just as Jan Kapica did with his woman. Please, dear Aunt, don't go telling anyone it's mine.

KOSTELNIČKA (*catches him convulsively by the hand and pulls him towards the door*) Come and see her – see Jenůfa. Poor lost soul... What did she do to you? What harm did she do so that you brought her to this, and now you won't help her? You never came near us... she's given up all hope thinking you were angry because of my severity... she even wanted to poison herself by crumbling match-heads into her milk. But like her guardian angel I found out about it – I found out what she was planning to do, and that evening, that terrible evening, she told me... on her knees, she told me... Števa, at that moment the cruelty of fate cut down my life. I'd gladly leave this world – if it would help Jenůfa. It's on my conscience that I sent her to your mill!

ŠTEVA   But my dear Aunt – there are thousands of women in her position... and with some help, she'll still be able to get married...

KOSTELNIČKA Married? To whom? – Only to you! The poor thing... the number of times she wanted to send for you or to go and find you, but I wouldn't let her. I thought the child would die and she wouldn't need to ask you for anything. I was afraid of being humiliated, if I'd let you have Jenůfa in spite of my prohibition... because I knew she'd never be happy with you, you'll never make her a good, reliable husband.

ŠTEVA   How you still persecute me. They don't have any of your fears at the Mayor's. They're willing to give me the prettiest of their daughters. And the Mayor's wife tells me that once I've sown my wild oats, I'll make a good husband.

KOSTELNIČKA There's nothing else for it... you're forcing me to beg you – even though people will point at me and say, '...there goes that proud Kostelnička, oh, wasn't she pleased that Števa agreed to marry his disgraced girlfriend!... How she boasted about having brought up her step-daughter and kept watch over her – it's a good job the Lord God didn't entrust her with children of her own! And then she sent the girl off into the charge of that senile old woman at the mill – right into Števa's hands!'

ŠTEVA   But my dear aunt, it's not such a great disaster... people don't have to find out about it. It would have been worse if

Jenůfa had died – that's what I was afraid of. The best thing would be if you both moved away from here.

KOSTELNIČKA Alone – without you, Števa? What about the little boy – he is the image of you? Come and see him, Števa! (*she falls on her knees*) I implore you on my knees, I, who the priest himself tells people to take their hats off to... Števa, take them both as the law of God commands! (*Števa hides his face in his hands*) Don't forsake my step-daughter – the joy of my life – however unhappy she'll be as your wife – don't leave her lost and disgraced... think of her name and my name... Are you crying? (*she rises and takes his hand*) Come and see them, Števa. Take your son in your arms and make Jenůfa happy!

ŠTEVA (*pulls his hand from hers*) Dear aunt, this would make even a stone weep, and I am not a hard man. Ask me to give her half of all I own – I'd mortgage the mill... ask me whatever you want... ask me to take my own life – I'd do it – but I can't marry her. It would be a disaster for us both.

KOSTELNIČKA Why should it be a disaster for you?

ŠTEVA Because... because I can't do it... because I'm afraid of her. She was always so sweet and merry and then, suddenly – even at the mill – she started to change before my eyes – she started to be like you... forceful, unhappy. Her eyes became sad, which I couldn't stand, and when I saw her that morning after the recruiting, with her face cut – and with those sorrowful eyes – I lost all the love I once had for her. It's not my fault, as God is my witness. And you, Aunt... don't be angry with me for being honest... I'm afraid of you as well – you're so strange, so terrible – like a witch who would haunt me. And then, I'm already engaged to Karolka – so there's an end to it.

KOSTELNIČKA (*cries in terror*) Števa!

JENŮFA (*from her room, in her sleep*) Mother! A stone is falling on me!

Števa gives a start and runs out of the door in fright.

KOSTELNIČKA Are you awake? No, she sat up in bed in her sleep and he saw her... She sleeps again. (*she locks the door to the room*) He ran away, the wretch! Without even going near the child – his own flesh and blood! (*greatly agitated*) Oh, I have it in

me to destroy the mite and throw it at his feet and say, 'Take that
on your conscience!' (*collects herself*) And then what? Who
would save Jenůfa? Oh, I saw it all coming!

The door opens. Laca enters.

SCENE 5

LACA   It's me, Aunt. I was passing... you know how I like
coming to see you and talking to you. But then I saw some woman coming in, and as soon as she left, a young man. It was Števa –
I recognised him when he rushed out. What did he want? Is
Jenůfa back?

KOSTELNIČKA She's back.

LACA   Will they get married?

KOSTELNIČKA No... She didn't even speak to him.

LACA   Then let me have her, dear Aunt... just like you used
to say I could! You said yourself he'd never give up his wild
ways – he was drunk again at the inn last night, playing cards till
midnight. And you said yourself, another reason you couldn't let
her marry him – he's her first cousin, so they'd have to get permission from Rome, which would never lead to a happy union.
She'll be happy with me. I'll treasure her. Even with that scar on
her face, I'll be a happy man.

KOSTELNIČKA   I would give her to you, Laca, and if I knew
she was settled with you, I would die happy. But when I tell you
everything, you won't care for her any longer...

LACA   Nothing would make me leave her... nothing in the
world! Even if she were old and ugly and twisted, or married to
someone else – my heart would never belong to anyone else. I've
been so close to her, since we were children, I don't know why – I
don't know how to express it.

KOSTELNIČKA   Laca, you have to know everything first –
then you can test your love. You're the first person I'm telling this
to. No-one else must know. I'd rather die. Jenůfa... poor lost
girl... she was never in Vienna... I've been hiding her here the

whole time, in that small room. A week ago she gave birth to a boy – Števa's child.

LACA   Aunt – it's not true? You're only testing me!

KOSTELNIČKA As God is my witness, I'm telling the truth, and with a heavy heart, because I know you mean well.

LACA (*darkly*) Oh… this is more than I can stand… it's as though a stone's crushed my head… and I'd have to take that, that – Števa's child?

KOSTELNIČKA (*paces the room in distress, clutching her head in her hands.*) Laca… the way it is – the child… no longer lives. The boy died…

LACA   Does Števa know?

KOSTELNIČKA Yes.

LACA   That was why he came here again… He wants to get Jenůfa back, and leave Karola.

KOSTELNIČKA   Maybe… I don't want to know him any more. I'd only want to get revenge – revenge to his life's end!

LACA   Where is Jenůfa? I want to see her… As long as I don't have to look at that child… she should know I'll do what I've promised. Even her guilt won't put me off.

KOSTELNIČKA   Wait – first I have to explain everything to her – she's still so upset, still grieving. It was only yesterday the boy died, I buried him myself.

LACA   Where?

KOSTELNIČKA In the graveyard, before dawn. I sprinkled the earth with holy water and hid the child there in a little coffin. At least he won't have to suffer any shame. And I christened him myself – it's allowed, in time of need.

LACA   You did well… and no-one knows about it, I'm glad… Poor Jenůfa.

KOSTELNIČKA Števa won't tell a soul, and I didn't even tell him what happened to the child.

LACA   If I could speak to Jenůfa… don't worry I'll talk to her gently… tell her first – not to be afraid of me – and that I've really loved her since we were children…

KOSTELNIČKA Not yet… *(she thinks)* Go and find out when Števa's going to marry Karolka.

LACA   But I've only spoken to him when I had to, for over
a year now.

KOSTELNIČKA I didn't mean you have to ask him yourself. Go
and find out from someone in the Mayor's household. (*with
mounting tension*) Go! Go and find out when the wedding will be!
I have to know! Go!

LACA   Bless you – I'll be back shortly. (*he leaves.*)

SCENE 6

KOSTELNIČKA (*alone*) Shortly... while I have to live through a
complete eternity, perhaps a complete salvation... if I were to put
the child out to be fostered? No, Jenůfa would never agree... in
any case, she doesn't know how to lie. Nothing except the child is
in the way... that shame... for life... I could redeem her life...
God knows best how things really are, and what awaits such a
poor mite in the world. (*she takes a shawl and wraps herself in it*)
I'll take the boy to the good Lord now... the pain will be shorter
and lighter than for a child destroyed by convulsions or diphtheria
... He can go to the Lord now, while no-one knows anything. In
spring, when the ice melts, there'll be no trace left... and I'll have
saved one adult life – Jenůfa's good name, and my own... (*going
out of her mind*) People are like wasps... how they'd attack us –
Jenůfa - and me too... 'Do you see them? (*pointing*) Look at her,
look at Kostelnička!' (*she slips into the inner room, returns with
the child, wrapping it in a shawl*) 'Fathered by sin, like Števa's
wretched soul!'

She runs out, locking the door behind her. Jenůfa enters.

SCENE 7

JENŮFA   Mother, my head is heavy, heavy as a stone... Help
me! Where are you, mother? (*slowly looks round*) This is her
room... I... (*rubs her forehead*) stay inside... in the inner room...
I have to hide there, (*alarmed*) so no-one notices me. Mother's
always telling me off – it cuts me to the quick... It's evening – I'm
allowed to open the shutters. Dark everywhere... only the moon

shining on miserable people, and a sky full of stars... Števa still
hasn't come – maybe he never will! If only he'd seen his little
boy... how he opens his blue eyes... and where is my little Števa?
He isn't crying – it's as though I could hear him... Where did you
take him? *(she runs into the inner room and back)* Where's my
little boy, my joy? *(she turns over the eiderdown)* He's crying,
moaning, so faintly, yet I can still hear him. Don't hurt him, good
people – it was me who was guilty – me and Števa. Where have
you put him? He'll fall down... down! The frost will devour him,
the cruel frost! Don't leave him! I'll come and rescue him. *(cries
out)* Wait! *(falls on the floor. After a moment drags herself to the
door and gropes at it with her fingers. Quietly)* Where am I? This
is mother's room... the door's locked. *(happily)* I know...
Mother's taken him to the mill! To show them Števa's son!
(anxious) But I must pray for him – here at the Virgin's shrine.
(she takes the statue down from the wall and kneels to it) Hail,
holy queen, mother of mercy, our sweetness and our hope! To
you, do we cry, poor banished children of Eve. To you do we
send up our sighs, our mourning and weeping in this vale of tears.
Gracious advocate, turn your merciful eyes towards us and after
our long exile, show us the blessed fruit of your womb... Jesus...
Oh tender, loving, oh sweet Virgin Mary! And save Števa for me,
please... don't let him go, oh holy Mary, mother of God!

*(Towards the end of the prayer we hear a rattling at the door.
Then a banging at the window.)*

SCENE 8

JENŮFA *(jumps up)* Who is it?

KOSTELNIČKA Jenůfa – is that you? Are you up? Open the
 window – open it. *(she speaks apprehensively, breathing heavily
 and shivering.)*

JENŮFA *(opens the window a little)* What do you want mother?
 Have you got little Števa with you?

KOSTELNIČKA *(by the window, startled)* Did you see me?

JENŮFA No, I didn't, but I thought you must have him, when
 he wasn't here.

KOSTELNIČKA   Here's the key, open the door... I can't do it, my hands are shaking... from the cold... I went to chop a piece of ice for tomorrow – for the washing.

JENŮFA (*closes the window a little but not completely; goes to the door and unlocks it*) Where is little Števa? Did you leave him at the mill? (*happily*) Perhaps Števa will bring him back and sit down with us? Do you think he will, mother... for the sake of the dear little child?

KOSTELNIČKA Jenůfa, you're out of your mind... May the Lord rest you, but you don't know yet what terrible thing has happened. You've been in a fever these last few days... your little boy has died and today... peacefully, I buried him.

JENŮFA (*falls to her knees by Kostelnička, leaning her head in her lap*) My joy, my little boy... dead? (*chokes*) Mother, my heart's aching so much... you always said it would be better for him... that I couldn't do for him what the Lord in heaven can do. Now he's dead, he's a little angel... but I'm lost without him, my heart is so heavy – it's breaking...

KOSTELNIČKA Thanks to the Lord God, give thanks! He has delivered you. You're free again and you still have hope.

JENŮFA   Did you put the holy pictures in his little coffin and did you make the sign of the cross for me instead of my weak hand?... And what about Števa, mother? You promised me you'd send for him. He must know too... he will grieve with me.

KOSTELNIČKA Don't even spare him a thought – curse him instead. How well I knew him! He came here when you were fast asleep and saw the child... I went down on my knees to beg him, but all he wanted to do was to pay for it all, just to pay.

JENŮFA   God forgive him!

KOSTELNIČKA He said he was afraid of you now because you're scarred, and afraid of me too because I'm a witch. And he's promised himself to the Mayor's daughter. Don't give a second thought to that drunkard... instead... think about Laca. He knows everything... I told him it all and he's forgiven you. That's the kind of love that's true and dependable... (*pause*)
Here he comes now...

Laca enters.

SCENE 9

LACA (*to Kostelnička*) Aunt, there was no-one home at the Mayor's. (*sees Jenůfa*) Jenůfa! (*approaches her, holds out his hand*) God bless you, Jenůfa – how poorly you look. Won't you let me help you?

JENŮFA (*gives him her hand*) Thank you, Laca, for all your concern during the past months, when you couldn't see me. I've listened to you and mother talking, many times from the attic. You see... I'm so wretched.

LACA   But you'll be well again. You'll get over the loss of the child, and Števa – he would never have respected you. You're better off without him.

JENŮFA   You know, I've always thought of life on this earth quite differently than it really is... now I feel as though I've come to the end.

LACA (*sadly*) And you wouldn't consider marrying me, Jenůfa?

KOSTELNIČKA (*feverishly*) Of course she'll marry you, Laca. She will... now she's come to her senses again and she can still be happy. I will bless you. Ahh, she doesn't realise how hard it's been for me to bring this about. *(sinks in the chair.)*

JENŮFA   Mother speaks like a child... how could you marry me, Laca? You know I don't love you, and I'm so pitiful, so repulsive.

LACA (*gently*) Jenůfa, it wasn't just your pretty face I loved. It was as though, long ago the Lord God joined your soul with mine... I used to dream about it when I was in the army... at night, when I closed my eyes, while the others were still carousing, I was close to tears, because they'd dragged me so far away from you... I used to go over in my head everything I was going to tell you once I came home... but when I came home – you only had eyes for Števa. I was so jealous, I was so angry, my darling... I felt so lost – believe me.

JENŮFA   Laca, you are strange, you know... They always said you were wild and even cruel... but maybe, you do have a good heart.

LACA   No I don't, Jenůfa, I don't – but then, maybe I could have, if we were together.

JENŮFA   When you talk about wanting me – I almost believe you do love me and mother wants it so much – she's been through hell because I've been such a fool... I could marry you and be a good and grateful wife but think it over carefully! I'm not rich or respectable, I'm not even pretty any more... and I've lost the thing that counts for most in this world – love. Do you still want me as I am?

LACA   Yes, Jenůfa I do – if only we could be together! *(takes her in his arms and kisses her on the cheek)* This scar, it's my doing and in spite of it you are still loved, my dearest!

JENŮFA *(moved)* Then I'll gladly take you for better or for worse... But, Laca, promise me you'll let me be on my own from time to time... let me be by myself sometimes... believe me, occasionally I need to be alone...

LACA   I understand that, Jenůfa. I'll leave you alone, for as long as you want me to.

JENŮFA   Now mother will be at peace – once she can give us her blessing.

KOSTELNIČKA *(with an effort she pulls herself together and goes to her)* You see – I've done well after all! And now I bless you from my heavy heart... May the Lord God keep you from harm, and may He bless you with health, wealth and happiness... but the person who was the cause of all this trouble... I curse him. The woman who marries him would do better to lose her mind than cross his threshold! *(sinks into a chair)* Woe to him and me! *(a short silence during which the breeze opens the window and the wind whistles)* Do you hear that howling – that whining? *(cries out)* Hold me! Stand by me!

LACA *(puts his arm round her compassionately)* What's the matter, dear aunt?

JENŮFA   Aren't you well? *(to Laca)* She stayed up with me, so many nights and by day she wears herself out... it's too much for her, poor woman.

KOSTELNIČKA Stand by me! Laca, stay! *(looks round in terror)* Close that window!

JENŮFA *(goes to close the window)* Laca, wrap her in a shawl, and I'll make up the fire. I think she's caught cold, poor soul. What a storm outside, and a frost – but the sky's alight with sparks. Oh, you're better off out there, my little boy, than with us in this sad world...

KOSTELNIČKA (*supporting herself, rises*) You see – you see – he is better off out there – there he is fine! (*again she shudders in fear*) Jenůfa, Laca – hold me – it's as though death himself were peeping in on us here.

Lights fade.

ACT THREE

Kostelnička's room. A white tablecloth on the table and a flower pot with rosemary; a few sprigs tied with a ribbon on a plate. A bottle of wine, a few glasses and a plate of pastries.
Jenůfa is sitting on a chair, dressed for her wedding, a prayer book and a scarf in her hand. From behind, Kolušina ties a scarf round her head. Laca is standing next to Jenůfa. Granny Buryovka is sitting by the table. Kostelnička crosses the room, in feverish disquiet and suppressed suffering; she looks very tired and ill. Jenůfa appears more refreshed than in the Second Act, but very serious.

KOLUŠINA   Aren't you feeling sad, Jenůfa?

JENŮFA   No.

LACA   Why should she feel sad? I'm not ever going to let harm come to her.

KOLUŠINA   It's usual for girls to be sorry to lose their freedom. Goodness, when I remember how silly I was – I cried my eyes out – even though I was marrying a good, upright man. There's nothing to fear from marrying a good man.

KOSTELNIČKA (*startled*) What's that rattling at the door? Who's there?

KOLUŠINA (*opens the door*) Welcome! Don't be so frightened, Kostelnička. It's the Mayor and his wife. *(they enter.)*

SCENE 2

KOSTELNIČKA   So you're here? Welcome!

MAYOR (*holding out his hand*) God be thanked... Did we startle you?

KOLUŠINA It's because she's not well. She's frightened of everything.

MAYOR We were all invited. Karolka too – only she's waiting for Števa – they'll come together.

JENŮFA (*standing*) Welcome!

LACA Greetings!

KOLUŠINA (*by the table*) I don't know what's better first – pin on the rosemary or offer a drink. I'm here to help today. Kostelnička has been so frail since her illness.
(She offers the drink and then the rosemary.)

MAYOR One can see that – she's fading! Always such a strong woman you were, fit as a fiddle. (*drinks a toast*) Well – here's an end to your worries, and everything will be right again.

KOSTELNIČKA I'm making everything ready for Jenůfa's wedding to a good man, so I've no need to worry. But I do feel – that I'm fading. Do you think it will be over soon?
(She points to her breast.)

MAYOR'S WIFE Is it your chest?

KOSTELNIČKA That too. But it's my head that's worse. (*clasps her head*) Oh – what a torment it is! Sleep doesn't help – I have to get up – I have to – to just get through it all.

JENŮFA Mother, God will make you better!

KOSTELNIČKA I don't want to be better... no... Long life would be terrible... and there... (*comes to her senses*) Today's your wedding day, Jenůfa – and I'm pleased about that.

JENŮFA We brought it forward for your sake, because that's what you wanted.

MAYOR'S WIFE (*to her husband*) Even if people do look sick, it's not right for you to tell them so to their face. (*to Kostelnička*) Anyway, you don't look so bad... and how dressed-up you are! A new blouse of the best silk – you're more dressed-up than the bride! What on earth has got into Jenůfa's head, going to her wedding dressed like some gloomy widow?

KOSTELNIČKA She... she... Why, the greatest ladies go to the altar dressed as plainly as she. I saw the burgomaster's daughter from Belovec at church for her wedding. She was wearing an ash-coloured dress and a black hat without flowers. So why can't Jenůfa just go dressed in her ordinary clothes?

MAYOR'S WIFE The gentry can wear whatever's in fashion – but it's different in a village. Well, I wouldn't go to the altar without a wreath and a ribbon. Even if someone paid me a thousand guilders – I wouldn't go!

KOLUŠINA All the same, she'll always be a proper and clever woman.

KOSTELNIČKA Come and look at her trousseau! I laid it out in the inner room, for it to air. I got it all together myself and you don't see a trousseau like that every day.

They go into the inner room, leaving Jenůfa with Laca.

SCENE 3

JENŮFA There, Laca, I knew people would remark on how I'm dressed for the wedding.

LACA (*takes a flower from the pocket of his jacket*) Jenůfa, I did bring you this flower... it's from the gardener in Belovec. Won't you take it?

JENŮFA Thank you, Laca! (*fastens the flower to her bodice*) Oh, Laca – you deserve better than a bride like me!

LACA Silly, don't talk about it. When Aunt Kostelnička first told me, it was a blow – but I forgave you at once. And I've sinned against you... and I'll make up for it all my life. I know you loved Števa, more than anything else, but now you don't think about him any more. And I'll be so proud of you – of you, just as you are.

JENŮFA My heart's beating so fast today... but I don't feel like crying. I'm so sorry for you – you, who stood by me in my misfortune – you, not Števa. But Laca, we should move away from here as soon as possible! Far away, to another place... mother is longing to move away as well – and perhaps another place will help her get well again.

LACA   You know I'll throw away all my stupid plans for you. There was nothing good in me before. I had nothing but envy in my heart for Števa – I would have cheated him out of everything. But you made me make it up with him – and I overcame all that hatred in myself – overcame it all, because I have you with me. I've invited Števa to the wedding, just as I should and he promised as a brother to come and bring Karolka with him. And look – there they are now.

Števa and Karolka enter.

SCENE 4

KAROLKA   Good day to you all. Števa was such a long time dressing, I thought his legs were rooted to the ground. I was afraid we were going to get here too late. Jenůfa and Laca – may God bless you and make you happy. I'll be watching you sadly today, Jenůfa, as I'll soon be following you to the altar. But then, I hope I'll be dancing a lot too, because everyone has to dance with the bride. What a pity you're not having any musicians, just like a staid old couple! That's not a proper wedding!

JENŮFA   Dear Karolka, our vows aren't based on merry-making. We thank you for your good wishes...

KAROLKA   And now you, Števa, you must congratulate them!

ŠTEVA (*embarrassed*) I'm not like Karolka, I'm no good with words...

JENŮFA   It doesn't matter, Števa – shake hands with your brother. You each have your own gifts. You, Števa, you're a fine figure of a man – and you, Laca, you're one of God's good souls.

KAROLKA   All you have to do is tell Števa he's good-looking, and he doesn't know what to do with himself.

JENŮFA   Is he still so silly? To put such trust in a fine face, which could spoil, wrinkle or decay, in no time? It would be just as foolish and ridiculous if, say, a year ago, I'd looked down from the mill to the village, through the roof of the chapel, and imagined I saw a happy couple standing there in fine clothes.

LACA   When will your wedding be?

ŠTEVA   If the banns are read these two Sundays, in two weeks' time.

KAROLKA (*jokingly*) Oho, that's only if I agree! Perhaps I'll say no! People tell me all sorts of things about you!

ŠTEVA   If you did say no – I'd have to end it all! All these weeks I've been behaving myself just for your sake!

JENŮFA   There you are, Števa, that's true love! God grant you never suffer for it!

The Mayor, Kostelnička and the others return.

SCENE 5

MAYOR'S WIFE You've set her up well. It's a credit to you, considering you're only her step-mother after all.

KOSTELNIČKA Well, no-one can say I gave up my Jenůfa to some good-for-nothing layabout.

MAYOR'S WIFE (*to herself*) That reminds me... I said the same of Števa once. She may be sick, but she's as conceited as ever.

MAYOR   That was certainly some inspection tour in that room back there! If I hadn't had a cigar to light up, all that grubbing around would have got on my nerves.

KOSTELNIČKA Števa is here – Števa! He's come to bring us more bad luck! (*to Laca*) You begged me to invite him along with the Mayor, but I can't bear to look at him.

LACA   Jenůfa insisted I make my peace with him. After all, he is my half-brother. In any case, we'll soon part when we move.

KOSTELNIČKA Yes, Laca, far from here – I can hardly wait.

SCENE 6

Barena enters with three young girls carrying a posy of rosemary and muskrose tied with coloured ribbons.

BARENA   Good day to you all! I know we're not invited, and we won't trouble you for long – but even though you don't want to make this a big occasion, we had to come to congratulate Jenůfa and to do some singing for her. You see, she was our first singer –

our teacher – and we all loved her. So, Jenůfa and Laca, all of us want to wish you lots and lots of good fortune, as much good luck as there are raindrops in a downpour, and to sing you a happy song. Sing, Anesa!

ANESA   'Oh, my mother, my dear mother!
              Let them make me a nice dress
                 For my wedding,
                   Mother mine!'

CHORUS   'Oh my daughter, my dear daughter!
              You are young, much too young,
                 To be married,
                   Daughter mine!'

ANESA   'Oh, my mother, my dear mother!
              You were also very young,
                 When you married,
                   Mother mine!'

(They repeat the chorus.)

BARENA *(gives Jenůfa her posy)* This is from us, Jenůfa!

JENŮFA   Thank you, my dears, with all my heart. I'm touched by your kindness!

MAYOR   Well, it was a nice enough song, but it's time now – it's nearly nine o'clock.

LACA   The priest told us to be at the church at nine.

MAYOR   Then hurry with the blessing – we must get on.

(Laca and Jenůfa kneel in front of Buryovka.)

LACA   I humbly ask for your blessing in the name of my family.

BURYOVKA   I bless you in the name of the Father, the Son and the Holy Ghost. Laca, don't think any ill of me!
(The couple kiss Buryovka's hands.)

MAYOR   And now you, Kostelnička. You know what to say just as well as the priest.
(The couple kneel before Kostelnička; she raises her hand. A noise outside, Kostelnička recoils in fear. Two voices can be heard from outside.)

FIRST VOICE The poor thing! How could some beast do this to a child!

SECOND VOICE What god-forsaken creature could have done this?

KOSTELNIČKA Child?… What child do they cry of?

MAYOR   What – what is it?

Jano enters.

SCENE 7

JANO   Mayor – they're looking for you.

MAYOR   What? What is it?

ŠTEVA   What's happening?

JANO   Don't you know yet? The brewery workers found a frozen child under the ice. *(everyone exclaims in horror)* They're bringing it here on a board. The poor thing looks almost life-like, wrapped in swaddling bands with a red bonnet on its head. It's terrible, everyone's upset and crying – come on!
(He runs off. The Mayor and his wife, the girls, Kolušina, Laca, Jenůfa and Karolka follow him. Only Števa stands frozen to the spot, with Kostelnička and Buryovka by the bed..)

SCENE 8

KOSTELNIČKA Jenůfa – don't go there!… Hold me! Protect me! They're after me! *(she sinks down by the bedstead, and grips it convulsively, watching the action in terror.)*

BURYOVKA But daughter, daughter, you're going mad – it's your illness! You've had a fright.
(Števa runs off. Karolka grabs him at the door.)

SCENE 9

KAROLKA *(grasps Števa by the hand)* Števa, it's terrible… The wedding ruined like this... If I were the bride, I'd be in tears.

ŠTEVA　　　I couldn't move… as though that cry had cut my legs from under me… and I'm still afraid.

JENŮFA *(from outside)* Oh my God – my God – it's my little boy!

LACA *(pulls her inside)* Jenůfa, Jenůfa – come to your senses! What's come over you? People can hear you! Calm down and think!

JENŮFA *(pulls herself out of his grasp)* Let me go – it's little Števa – my little boy – mine!

The Mayor enters, with swaddling bands and a red bonnet in his hands. The others follow. The door remains open. People peer inside and push in.

SCENE 10

JENŮFA　　　Don't you see? – His swaddling bands – his cap. I dressed him in them myself! My little Števa – the joy of my life! Oh, you people, what a way to bring him to me – without a coffin – without a wreath!

ALL　　　Oh God!

JENŮFA　　　Can't you leave him in peace! They've gone off with him somewhere in the ice and snow! Števa, run after them – hurry up! He's your son!

LACA　　　Jenůfa, come to your senses, that can't be your child!

JENŮFA　　　Oh mother – how did you bury him?

MAYOR'S WIFE *(to her husband)* Do you hear that? They know all about it… Kostelnička and all the rest!

MAYOR　　　I can see that for myself … but I have to act official-ly, as well… *(he wipes the sweat from his brow)* I don't want to be involved in this. It's all such a terrible mess!

FIRST VILLAGE WOMAN That's how she did away with the child!

SECOND VILLAGE WOMAN She brought the child back from Vienna. Stone her!

LACA *(threateningly)* Don't you dare lay a finger on her! You'll die first! I know how to use my fists, you know!

MAYOR   It all has to follow the course of justice – the
authorities will want to know the truth.

LACA   It wasn't Jenůfa who did it – I know that! Yes, she
did have a child with my brother Števa, but it died. Kostelnička
buried it. I tell you, I'll stake my life on it. You'll have to take me
away first, before it's proved.

MAYOR   Maybe she'll go of her own accord. You see she's
not denying it.

KOSTELNIČKA (*gets up with difficulty*) Don't forget about me!
You don't know a thing about it! I did it! It's my crime and my
punishment. Don't punish Jenůfa. This is God calling me to
judgement.

ALL   Kostelnička!

KOSTELNIČKA   I destroyed the child born of Jenůfa and
Števa – I alone. I wanted to save Jenůfa's life, her happiness and
my own. The horror, the shame... weighed me down, of having
led my step-daughter into disgrace. (*falls on her knees*) God alone
knows how unbearable it was, thinking that two lives had to be
lost for the sake of the child... (*pause*) Jenůfa was never in Vienna
... I hid her in her room and one night when she was fast asleep
because I'd given her a sleeping draught... I took her child, took
it to the river. There was a hole in the ice near the bank and I
pushed the child into it.

KOLUŠINA   My God – can this be Kostelnička?

KOSTELNIČKA It was dark. He didn't struggle... didn't even cry
... I only seemed to burn my hand... and my head was on fire... I
must have been beside myself... and when it was all over I realised that... I was a murderer... and that was when it started tormenting me. I told Jenůfa the child died while she was asleep. Have
pity on her – don't blame her – don't punish her – she's innocent.
Take me – judge me – stone me – wretched woman that I am!

JENŮFA   Oh, mother – under the ice – No! (*in a frenzy*) Leave
me!

LACA   Dear God... a curse has fallen on Kostelnička.
Jenůfa, I started all this, when I deliberately scarred you so Števa
would leave you... all this misery has come from that. Oh –
you'll be free of me, Jenůfa – the curse has worked – before you

crossed my threshold! And I loved you more than life itself... I would have been a good man! *(chokes.)*

KAROLKA *(to Števa, who has been standing by the window)* Is this on your conscience, Števa? *(throwing her arms round her mother's neck)* Oh, mother, I can't stand it. Take me away – I won't marry Števa. I'd rather jump in the river. Take me home! Take me home!

MAYOR'S WIFE Karolka, my Karolka!

Karolka forces her way out, followed by her mother.

KOLUŠINA That's his punishment! No girl will want him now, not even an honest gypsy!

Števa, his face buried in his hands, forces his way out. Kolušina leads out the devastated Granny Buryovka.

SCENE 11

JENŮFA *(with control, turns to Kostelnička)* Get up, dear step-mother... There are plenty more trials and tribulations ahead of you. I don't blame you, but you've saved my life only to make it impossible for me to go on. *(helps Kostelnička to get up.)*

KOSTELNIČKA Why are you making me get up? Don't you know they'll take me away? *(in terror)* Oh! *(runs to the door of the inner chamber)* No! I mustn't do it! They'd blame you, Jenůfa!

JENŮFA Let them blame me – my dear. There's no pain could hurt me as much a second time – none.

LACA Jenůfa – you're usually so reasonable – are you out of your mind?

JENŮFA Don't be afraid, Laca. God doesn't listen to weak people – and such people never know what they can stand, what they can go through. I won't do anything against the will of God – I'll go far away... and drag myself through life. Only, God willing, better than I did before. I'll prove to you I can rise above my past... and my dear stepmother... now I realise, she doesn't deserve to be rejected. Don't condemn her... give her time to repent! God may even forgive her!

KOSTELNIČKA Jenůfa – my poor, dear, daughter... it's all for your sake! It would be easy for me to go in there... (*pointing to the inner room*) I've often thought about it... when the time came... I'd finish it all. But I have to go before the court and they'll summon you as well! Because they suspect you... This is the greatest sacrifice I can make for you, my dear. You're the one who can forgive me – for now I see I've always loved myself more than you. I denied myself everything for you, everything except my pride. A real mother would have suffered shame and humiliation for your sake. Don't call me: 'Dear mother!' any more. You didn't inherit my nature or my blood... now I take my strength from you and from the hope you give me! God may even forgive me! (*turning to the Mayor*) Take me away!

JENŮFA   May God comfort you, mother!

The Mayor takes Kostelnička by the arm and they leave. The crowd surges and rushes after them, leaving Laca and Jenůfa in the room.

SCENE 12

JENŮFA   They've gone... Laca, go too. You see how imposs-ible it is for your life and mine to be one. God be with you – and remember, you're the best man I've ever known in this world. Yes, you hurt me once on purpose – but I forgave you long ago. You did wrong for love, and I did the same.

LACA   You're really going away, for a better life? Take me with you, Jenůfa.

JENŮFA   Don't you know I'll have to go to court, and they'll all rebuke me?

LACA   Jenůfa, I can go through all that, if I have you. What will they mean to us, when we have each other?

JENŮFA   I'll always have that martyred child of mine inside me... you know. (*sombrely*) Think about it, Laca – what a sad life we'd have together...

LACA   You'll get through it – and I'll get through it with you!

JENŮFA   Laca – my dear – (*overwhelmed*) Come! Love makes me warm to you – not the kind of love which drew me to Števa – but the kind that lasts a lifetime and pleases God himself. Once we've come through all this... I'll be your wife... and when I leave and have to go before the court, your hand must guide me... and it will give me strength to know I'm not alone – with the man who loves me by my side!

Lights down.
The end.

Gabriela Preissová

Born in 1862, in Kutná Hora near Prague. From childhood almost to the end of the century she lived in the Slovácko region of Moravia, where she was fascinated by the local traditions and dialect. Her first published writings were *Tales from Slovácko*, one of which, the *Beginning of a Romance* was used by Leoš Janáèek as the basis for his first opera. Both her plays were also set in Slovácko, *The Farmer's Woman* (National Theatre, Prague 1889) and *Her Step-daughter* (National Theatre, Prague 1890). Both were also turned into operas; *The Farmer's Woman* as *Eva,* by J.B. Foerster and *Her Step-daughter* as *Jenufa* by Leoš Janáèek. Preissová, who died in 1946, never again achieved the success of her earlier works.

The Umbilical Cord

The subject of a sick relationship between mother and child, and then adult is present throughout my creative work.

In my novels, they are the knots impossible to untangle between mother and daughter. Even though I have several novels and a collection of short stories to my name, this problem remains unsolved. The mutual emotional blackmail and the impossibility of independent life seemed to me important, especially in our culture, in which young people do not move away from home and as adults, find themselves under the control of their parents, especially mothers, so that growing up stretches out interminably, giving us in effect old children.

The Umbilical Cord was from the beginning a dialogue. At first, I heard it in my head, then I placed it in the closed, stuffy space of an apartment. I wrote it with the small stage of television theatre in mind, where you can show in close-up, the games a mother plays out with her son.

I was surprised when two well-known Polish theatres staged it and in 1999 the Australian premiere is to take place. I did not consider it to be theatrical in the traditional meaning of the word. The television production of it seemed to me the most interesting. The response was good, so I busied myself with writing my next play, *Professor Mephisto's Salon*, in which my other obsession revealed itself: time and the unwinnable battle against it. Mephisto is a woman, a plastic surgeon, Faust is Faustina, who wants to keep her youth at all cost. This play has not yet been staged, although there are several directors interested in it. This time I have encountered difficulties, since it has been judged to be a feminist play, and feminism in Poland is considered to be the ideology of witches. Maybe that is why I wrote the novel: *In Praise of Witches.*

Krystyna Kofta

The Umbilical Cord

by Krystyna Kofta
translated by Joanna Mludzinska

First performed at the Ateneum Theatre in Warsaw in 1990.
Directed by Szczepan Szczykno.

CHARACTERS
Mother
Rose, her nurse
Leo, her son
David, her husband, father of Leo
the Doll, little Leo

The mother should be played by an actress much younger than
indicated by the age of the play's heroine. Leo and David should be
played by the same actor.

ACT 1

A large room in a villa. French windows open onto a patio. In an
enormous bed sits the fat, massive Mother. She is strong, full of life
and loud. Her huge breasts push out a low-cut nightdress decorated
with frothy lace. Mother is still a very coquettish woman. On the bed
is a special table on which she sets out the cards. She turns the cards
smoking a cigarette. She burns her fingers. The ashtray is full of
cigarette ends. Mother is a little deaf, which is why she talks very
loudly. Sometimes, when excited, she shouts.

MOTHER   A journey and an important meeting! Must be with
   St Peter. *(laughs, shouts)* Rose! Do you hear? A journey!!!
   (with an energetic gesture she throws the cards off the table onto
   the floor, puts out the cigarette.)
Rose enters from the patio; she has a nightgown over her shoulder,
also pink, the same as the one Mother is wearing.

Rose is a young woman: about 30 years old, peasant looks, a pretty face with no make-up and a good figure hidden beneath a snowy white nurse's uniform. Fair hair drawn up under a cap. She collects the cards off the floor, puts them onto the table, removes the ashtray, takes the table and leans it against the bed. Rose speaks emphatically, with a peasant accent.

ROSE   You're going nowhere, that we do know. But we have to change the nightgown anyway. It's as filthy as muck.

MOTHER   No, no! Rose, please, it's still clean. Fresh linen is so cold! I always get the shivers from it. Dirt keeps you warm. *(Mother defends herself against Rose, who, in spite of her protests, changes the nightgown, hiding Mother from the audience with her body.)*

ROSE   That's true, dirt keeps you warm. And it stinks! Phew!

MOTHER *(giggling)* You know I'm ticklish!
(Rose takes the dirty nightgown in two fingers and carries it with disgust like a stinking fish by the tail. She takes it out through the door and comes back. She sits on a chair by the bed, takes an orange from the pile arranged on a silver platter and begins to peel it. Mother devours the scene with starving eyes, swallowing hard. Rose's fingers are practised. She divides the orange into segments and puts them in Mother's mouth. Outside the window we hear a bicycle bell. It is a sharp sound, coming from nearby. Mother is chewing)
Someone's ringing.

ROSE   It's no-one, just kids on bikes.

MOTHER   Must they ride around right outside my window?

ROSE   Obviously they must. Shall I turn the television on? You ought to occupy your mind with something.

MOTHER   I can't look at them any more.

ROSE *(putting the next segment of orange in Mother's mouth)* Look at whom?

MOTHER   At any of them.

ROSE   All old people watch.

MOTHER   One or the other, either I'm not old or I'm not a
person.

ROSE   Maybe there's a film on.

MOTHER   In my head there's a film from half a century ago
running all the time. Don't try to distract me, Rose, you know
what you're supposed to be doing.

ROSE   Again?

MOTHER   There's no escape from this. You have to keep trying
until you succeed.

*(Rose goes up to the built-in cupboard, which couldn't be seen
before and opens it. The cupboard is full of shoes arranged on
shelves. From the floor right up to the ceiling.)*

ROSE   Which ones?

MOTHER   Get the sporty walking shoes ready. They're the
most comfortable for everyday running around.

*(Rose reaches up on her toes and gets down a pair of black
walking shoes. Mother is watching every move carefully)*

No, not those, I can see that you want to send me on my final
journey.

ROSE *(speaks rudely, impatiently)* So which ones, then?

MOTHER   The grey ones, of course. Where you come from, in
the country, they only wear black ones, eh? You've been with me
so long, and you haven't learned a thing! You're so thick, Rose.

ROSE   The servant is like the mistress.

(She bows low with irony.)

MOTHER   The only thing you don't lack is cheek.

*(Rose puts the black shoes back with a bang, takes down the grey
ones, throws them by Mother's bed, puts the table on the bed, lays
a rug on it, and the shoes on the rug. Now she takes down from a
shelf a box with shoe polish and brushes. All these actions she
carries out angrily. Mother begins to clean the shoes. First she
puts polish on them, spits on them slightly and polishes them with
a soft cloth, then with a brush. She is actually caressing the shoes.
Mother begins cleaning)*

The most important thing on a journey is to have comfortable
shoes. *(she spits on the shoes)* These shoes know more about my
life than you do, Rose. You'd never believe it but I used to be like
a spinning top. I rushed around everywhere.

ROSE *(peeling another orange, preparing a stock of segments)* Oh yeah! A likely story!

MOTHER   Don't you believe me?

ROSE *(brutally forcing a segment of orange into Mother's mouth)* I'll never believe anything you say ever again. *(she turns her back to Mother and eats a piece of orange.)*

MOTHER *(chewing)* There are those for whom immobility is a blessing. They spend all their lives lying down. I know people like that. But me? Just think, Rose, I, the most mobile of all women, a born wanderer, in bed for the last ten years because of a stupid paralysis of the legs. That's what you call blind fate. It strikes you and that's it. But never mind. The only thing that matters to me is Leo. I live for him. Put my shoes on, Rose. *(Rose uncovers Mother's legs and puts the shoes on her inert feet)* I can't feel a thing, still nothing, but it must pass sometime, what do you think, Rose?

ROSE   You always say that I don't think. *(moves Mother's feet about energetically, as if Mother was marching on parade, counting as she does it)* One, two, one, two, three, one, two, one, two, three… Anything?

MOTHER   Nothing, nothing again.

ROSE   It's all finished: crawling around the rubbish dumps, collecting mouldy bread, pretending you're a beggar, when you're sitting on millions. How ashamed Master Leo must have been, it's hard to imagine it! *(All the time she is moving Mother's feet as if marching.)*

MOTHER   It's better to be ashamed than to die of hunger. When you've been through hell, you're plagued by the fear of hunger. *(she falls silent breathing heavily as if exhausted by walking)* Enough. This march to nowhere has made me tired. Take them off and put them away.

ROSE *(takes the shoes off and puts them away on the shelf. She also puts away the cleaning stuff. After a while)* I wonder what fear has to do with pretending?

MOTHER   At first, you had to put them off the scent, and then later it became like an addiction. Yes. Fear gets into your blood, draws you in, and the world which disgusts you, that draws you in as well… *(she spits out the membranes from the orange, gets them* *all over her)* Oranges are deceptive. Membranes and water and nothing else. They make money on membranes and water.

ROSE   I'm supposed to be the country bumpkin but you're the one who eats like a pig.
(takes a huge handkerchief out from under Mother's pillow and wipes her mouth. Then she picks up the remains of fruit with the handkerchief and throws it in the bin. She puts the handkerchief back under Mother's pillow and reaching deeper, takes out a plastic bag full of crusts of old bread. Mother throws herself on her treasure, like a lioness, wrenches the bag away from Rose and clutches it to herself)
I wonder what else we'll find there.
(she digs under the pillow on the other side, takes out two silver knives)
Oh yes, I might have guessed. Knives again! You'll hurt yourself one day, and then what?

MOTHER   Then I'll die injured. These knives are blunt. You can hardly cut with them. *(she puts a large lump of dry bread into her mouth and eats it with relish)* Meat. Meat! My kingdom for a piece of meat! This fruit diet is killing me. You can't assuage your hunger with water. But what could you know about hunger, Rose? *(the next piece of bread disappears into her mouth.)*

ROSE   Not so greedily, you'll choke and I'll have a lot of unpleasantness that I didn't look after you properly. You talk about putting people off the scent. What's the point, when no-one's looking anyway?

MOTHER   They are looking. They're always looking. And even when they're not looking, they find something. Rose, dear, I've got a little favour to ask you. You know how fond of you I am, give me a glass of cherry brandy, I'm so agitated today…

ROSE   First please give back the bread.
(Mother quickly puts the next bit in her mouth, takes another one and hides it under her pillow, thinking she does it without being seen, then slowly gives the bag to Rose.)

MOTHER   But you will give me a glass?
(Rose goes over to the dresser with the bag, puts it down, and takes out a bottle of cherry brandy.)

ROSE *(leaning on the dresser)* You have to rely on me don't you?
Because of the stupid play-acting, you've forgotten who you
really are. I know all these lies now. On Mondays: not a drop of
foreign blood – God and country, on Tuesdays, what is it you
say? Oh yes, I know, a fabulous mixture *(she mimics the old
woman)*, on state holidays, an atheist, and on Sundays, Lord bless
us! *(she folds her hands and bows deeply)* And I'll tell you
another thing, it's one big con, why do you pretend in front of me
after all these years?

MOTHER   I've had better friends than you, Rose and yet
they've given me away. Better to know nothing – when it comes
down to it, it's better to have confusion. Pretending is not a con,
it's a human privilege. It's an act. Animals don't act. Have you
ever seen a pig acting a giraffe? Everyone acts. Even you Rose, a
simple country girl, always have to act. So, Rose, have a drink
with me. To pretence!

ROSE *(pours out and passes the glass to Mother)* I don't drink.

MOTHER   Cherry brandy is the best fruit, full of vitamins.
*(They both laugh. Rose eats an orange. Mother has a hearty
laugh; Rose's is a bit shrill.)*

ROSE   You say I act. How can I not act, when you've even
changed my name?

MOTHER   We had a servant called Rose before the war, so I
got used to the name.

ROSE   Forty-five years is enough time to get unused to it.
*(Mother drains the last bit of cherry brandy, wants to say
something, chokes. Rose bangs her on the back as hard as she
can. Mother gasps for air. She calms down. Rose takes the glass
from her hand. Mother looks at her beseechingly, puts out her
hand in a begging gesture)*
There we are, pretending to be a beggar, you can do that
perfectly. *(she pours out the next glass and gives it to Mother,
then sits on the chair with her hands on her knees and listens
calmly.)*

MOTHER   Pretending to be poor! Do you think it's nice going
around in tatters and breathing in the mouldy stink of rubbish
heaps? *(she slurps her drink)* Or maybe you think it's a pleasure
digging around with a metal pole and hitting the rotting body of a

rat? Oh, at least the rat was dead. And the people around me? Those were the rats from the whole town. What could I do, I had to protect Leo. I didn't fancy rotting in prison, and Leo certainly wouldn't have survived that. He is delicate, like every true artist... *(she closes her eyes. Suddenly she is silent. She drops off to sleep and snores a little. Rose gets up and begins to pace up and down the room, as if she were counting the steps. She goes up to the French windows, back to the chair, then goes in the opposite direction, round the room. She circles like a caged animal. She opens her eyes as suddenly as she closed them, shouts)* Stop walking, Rose. Don't you understand how much every unnecessary step of yours hurts me?

ROSE *(sits heavily on the chair)* I thought you'd fallen asleep for good at last.

MOTHER What do you mean 'for good'? Fallen asleep? I don't know what sleep is. For ages all I've known is naps. I've taught myself not to sleep. Sleep blunts vigilance and brings death. I couldn't sleep, protecting little Leo. Birds and their vigilance have nothing on me... If you only knew, Rose, how tortured I am, how tortured... But I don't want to die, isn't that strange.

ROSE What's strange about it? If something's running away from you, you chase it, don't you? A sick person's life is running away, so he tries to catch it. Simple.

MOTHER For you everything is simple. I think that the animal inside each person wants to live at all cost. You'll do anything for life, humiliate yourself, degrade yourself, perform any foul deed. And that's right, life is worth just that. There, then... It wasn't the human being inside me, it wasn't the human being that scratched the roots out of the frozen ground with claws, it was the animal, which is superior to the human. If you don't let it dominate, you die... Oh, God when I think about it I feel hungry again. Meat! Give me meat! *(Rose gives Mother a piece of orange)* Pass me the little trunk, Rose, it's the only thing that comforts me.

ROSE Strange, that what comforts you is the worst.

MOTHER Everything seems strange to me, and nothing is strange in all this strangeness.

ROSE All muddled in the head. You should run to the end of the world from these memories. I'll put a film on.

(she puts a film on the video. We can hear machine gun fire, people screaming, more machine-gun fire. Mother puts her hands over her ears, hides under the duvet. Rose turns the sound off, leaves the picture.)

MOTHER *(peeps out from under the duvet, begins to speak to Rose, who is following the action on screen)* I've already been to the end of the world, seen what it's like, smelt the bitter smell. I won't run anywhere. You're right, it was the worst period of my life. But it was life, you understand? Life!!! Do you hear? Stop staring at those stupid pictures.

ROSE Hard not to hear, the whole neighbourhood can hear. *(Stares at the screen again.)*

MOTHER Let them hear. Let them know. What do I care about that scum? Then I was really living, now, even if I was cured by that miracle worker who touches you with his healing hand, I wouldn't get up, even though I want nothing more than to walk a few steps, but I've put down roots in this bed and for various reasons it's better this way… Give me the little trunk then.

ROSE Of course it's better. Indolence is always better than work for a lazy person. *(Rose pulls out from under the bed a little trunk; a dirty little cardboard trunk, which is falling apart. She wipes it over with a cloth, puts it on the bedside table. All Rose's actions are obviously part of a ritual. We can see that during the years spent with Mother she must have carried them out hundreds of times. As she does them, Rose glances over at the TV screen. Mother hugs the little trunk to her chest as if it was a baby, who didn't want to go to sleep. After a while, she opens the trunk and pulls out a greying, child's shirt, which must have once been white. She presses it first to her chest and then to her lips.)*

MOTHER Oh, this is the little shirt Leo was baptised in. My God, if you had only seen! In the dark of the night, a priest disguised as a commissar, or the other way round, but to you that's immaterial, you prefer to watch the machine-gun massacre… If anyone had given us away then… No, no. It's better not to think about that.

ROSE *(laughs quietly, watching the screen)* Of course it's better.

MOTHER   That's just what you say, when you think about something too much. If it got out death or exile to the interior.

ROSE   Look, look. Now they're going to execute him.

MOTHER *(looks at the shirt carefully against the light, finds a hole in it, passes it to Rose)* Rose, mend it, do you hear? Mend it, you'll go quite daft.

ROSE   Oh, he's down already. That's it for him. *(takes the shirt from Mother, reaches for the sewing things and begins calmly darning, glancing every now and again at the screen.)*

MOTHER   There's no return from there. From where I've been.

ROSE   So how come you came back? You've supposedly been there.

MOTHER   Yes, I've been there. And not supposedly but with absolute cruel certainty. There's no return from there, but you'll always find someone who comes back from a place from where there's no return. *(she takes a little cap out of the trunk, speaks softly, almost lovingly)* Look at this sweet little cap, I knitted it myself on needles carved from wood by a Ukrainian, I remember only too well where I got the wool from: I unravelled some woollen socks of David's when he didn't come back… I've told you about this…

ROSE *(looking at the screen)* A million times.

MOTHER   What a fool David was, in spite of his exceptional intelligence. Look at his portrait.
(Rose lifts her head and looks at the huge portrait hanging above the bed. It is a photograph enlarged to life size, framed in an oval shaped gold frame. In the photograph, a man in spectacles, a peaked cap and plus fours stands leaning on a bicycle, as if he was about to go on a picnic. He stands slightly sideways, so we can see a small rucksack on his back.)

ROSE   In my opinion Mr David looks very clever in those spectacles. Master Leo looks very much like him. *(starts to laugh again.)*

MOTHER   What's so funny about a son looking like his father?

ROSE   It's a pity you're not watching, honestly, he's just done a flying eagle!

MOTHER   What language! The eagle is sacred to us. A flying
eagle indeed. I don't even know what that means. Won't you ever
learn to speak in a civilised manner, Rose?

ROSE   Now, look what's going to happen... Go on I'm
listening.

MOTHER *(thoughtfully)* Yes, Leo has his face but my hair, his
voice but my temperament. Sometimes, when Leo speaks, it's as
if I heard David, maybe that's why he's always here. Yes, as if I
had them both. Oh that David! Seventh generation intelligentsia!
He always boasted of that. *(she begins to mimic David)*
'I've got nothing better to do, so I'll go and visit the tomb of
Tamburlaine. You musn't let any opportunity go past to learn
something new.' *(she goes back to speaking normally)* And how
could a man like that survive?
*(Rose darns the next hole, looks at the screen, but seems to be
engrossed in her own thoughts)*
Are you listening to me? Turn that box off. You're supposed to
listen to me. That's what you're here for, I pay you for that as
well.
*(Rose gets up, turns off the TV, comes back, sits down, looks at
Mother with hatred)*
Could David survive? I ask you? Could he survive? He was
condemned to death, like that whole family of his. Just think,
wearing plus fours and a peaked cap, there in their country! But
that's not important. The most important thing is that Leo had
warm ears. It was very good wool, soft, mixed with angora and
sheep's wool, that's why little Leo never had an ear infection, and
you know what his ears mean to Leo!
*(passes the cap to Rose. Rose smells it, grimaces and gives it back
to Mother together with the folded, darned shirt. Mother puts
both away in the trunk.)*

ROSE   These rags should be washed for once, they're
bound to have hundred year old moths and lice in them.

MOTHER   Mind what you say. They're not rags; they're my
little Leo's clothes. You can't wash them or they'll fall apart.

ROSE   About time. After half a century all clothes are rags.
It's a disgrace. You treat them as if they're the relics of a dead
child, but Master Leo's alive and well. It's time to forget about
that and burn these rags. Master Leo will be fifty soon.

MOTHER   Yes, Leo will be fifty soon, but little Leo is still four years old and travelling with me through those awful lands. What can you know about motherhood, Rose – about a miraculously saved child? You the loner with a heart of stone.

ROSE *(hides her face in her hands, weeps quietly and desperately. Her back trembles. She speaks through her tears)* A real bulls-eye there. Straight from your soft heart. Soft as a scrap of fat dead meat. *(she pulls herself together at last. She calms down, wipes her eyes with her apron. She gets up and begins to tidy the room. She shakes the table-cloth out on the patio, gets the feather duster and sniffing occasionally begins to clear away spider webs.)*

MOTHER   Happy the one who can weep, who still has tears. How many deaths have you seen? A few. Maybe a dozen. In hospital, in bed, a luxury, or maybe one chance murder on the street, and that's all. And me? Valleys full of dead bodies, mountains of remains, forests of frozen stiffs, can you imagine? And in this landscape, little four year old Leo, with his eyes wide open… And you weep, because I've hurt you with a word, think, Rose, what are you crying about? You're safe, I pay you well. You're as snug as a bug in a rug.

ROSE *(stands on a stool and speaks as she stops clearing the spider webs)* That's all fine, you've just forgotten one thing. No-one else would last longer than half an hour here. *(vindictively)* Maybe you've forgotten what happened the last time I left? And the time before? *(she jumps down from the stool with the duster in her hand and brandishes it threateningly over Mother's head)* What did you get up to, to get me back? Master Leo couldn't get anyone else to take the job.

MOTHER   You are made for me and I am made for you as the left side is made for the right side. I've grown fond of you, Rose. Wouldn't it be marvellous if we could all die at the same time: me, Leo and you? That would be real paradise. *(she pulls out a piece of dry bread from under the pillow and begins to crunch away at it.)*

ROSE *(sits on the edge of the bed)* Personally I can do with out that great favour. What's paradise for one person can be hell for another. Anyway, even in paradise, you would be thinking about that other hell.

MOTHER *(she is tired and slips down on the pillows, speaking softly and quietly)* That village near Samarkand, that's me and Leo, if you take my memory I'll give you my immortality.

ROSE   Thanks. I've got my own. What do I need two for?

MOTHER   The more the better. That's the rule.

ROSE   That's greedy talk.

MOTHER   Rose... Rose...

ROSE   You want something again. I can feel it.

MOTHER   You know what, Rose, please.

ROSE   You do go on about those feet!

MOTHER.   Try them again. Just one more time. The last time today, maybe I'll feel something.
(Rose gets up, uncovers Mother's feet. She goes to the dresser, takes out a long, sharp pin, comes back to the bed and jabs Mother hard, first in one foot and then the other)
Nothing, nothing. Nothing, still nothing. When they come I won't be able to run away.

ROSE   How many times do I have to say it? No-one's going to come? The war's over. *(she moves Mother's feet around, humming a march.)*

MOTHER   Don't let them trick you. It will never be safe here. This cursed piece of land is a bloody scrap with huge dogs tearing at it. You were born during a short break, Rose... they're asleep, but they'll wake up again. They always do, so they can bring death...

ROSE *(arranging Mother's legs under the covers)* The world is wiser, no-one wants to die.

MOTHER   The world is wiser, but people are stupid. The worst thing is to drop your guard. I don't believe in the wisdom of the world. I have to practise escaping. I can't let my guard down.
(Mother leans out of the bed, resting on her hands. She moves her palms, moves her body, drags behind her the heavy, powerless legs. They fall with a thud to the floor. Mother attempts to drag herself across the floor. She does so with a great effort. She falls. She lies unmoving, her face on the floor. Panting heavily, she lifts herself up on her hands and crawls, or rather moves her hands dragging the rest of her body after her. Rose, sitting on the edge

of the bed, observes her efforts)
I am strong… strong… I am strong… *(she falls)* But I'm very
strong, aren't I Rose? *(she lies on her stomach with her hands
stretched out in front of her.)*

ROSE Yes, yes. You're very strong.

MOTHER (lifts her head) I was always strong. We crawled for
hours. I would put little Leo on my back and off we'd go. Once I
lost him in the snow. You always have to try… Always, right to
the end. *(she crawls on again)* Yes. To the end.

ROSE You're eighty years old now!

MOTHER *(stops and speaks angrily)* Do you mind, not eighty.

ROSE You'll be eighty in a year's time. Big deal.

MOTHER A year to you and a year to me are not the same
thing. Anyway it's not a question of age. I've seen them smash
the skulls of babies and strangle old people. It didn't take more
than a few seconds. *(She starts crawling again. She is getting
better at it.)*

ROSE So they'll do what they like with us in any case.
(She follows Mother around like a referee at a boxing match.)

MOTHER You don't understand. That's what they want.
Surrender and immobility. But I'm still alive and so is Leo. So
survival is possible.

ROSE Only by chance.

MOTHER Oh, no. It's not chance. Look at me. An old wreck.
Useless legs, but I crawl along and I'll never give in. My
worthless life counts too.
(She crawls with stubborn determination.)

ROSE I would let them kill me.

MOTHER That's just words, just words… *(she is panting
heavily, deathly exhausted)* Stupid words.

ROSE All that pain! That awful memory! I can't take any
more. You can end it all in a second… There, see! I always leave
the bottle of pills full, so you have it to hand. *(she goes up to the
bedside table, takes the bottle of pills, pretends to empty its contents onto her hand, leans her head back pretending to swallow)*
And that's an end to it.

MOTHER   Give up your life with a walkover? You don't know
what you're saying, child, or who you're saying it to. I have to
live for Leo, I feel like life's heroine, I'll never give up and don't
ever suggest that wicked thought to me again… there are heroes
on the garbage heap too. *(she speaks lying down – she has turned
over onto her back, put her hands under her head as if she was
resting in a meadow, and looks up at the ceiling)* If sin exists in
the world then that is it. *(she speaks calmly)* Your generation
doesn't know how to live. A bottle of pills to hand and that's the
end of it. I lie looking at the ceiling and I see the sky… it's
beautiful… And in the sky…

ROSE *(with irony)* I know. Clouds and birds.

MOTHER   Yes, clouds and birds. Irony, nastiness. Everything
of ours you put in inverted commas, and you have nothing of your
own. Nothing.

ROSE   We can't have anything of our own, because we're
slaves to those who should have passed on a long time ago…

MOTHER   Rose! You shouldn't have said that! You've never
said that before.

ROSE   So fire me. By all means. Tell me: 'Go, Rose,' and
I'll go… Why don't you say that to me? I know why. Because I
might go and a parasite can't thrive without its host, cut off from
it – it dies. Parasites! Not only did they survive while others were
dying but they claim to be better than us – they demand respect,
care, love. There's no credit in surviving! Remember that no-one
has a right to anything! Anything. You old folk talk as if you'd
chosen to be taken away and killed. But it happened to you just as
it could happen to us. No credit. It's fate. No-one's fault. Judge
those who killed, sentence them – don't poison your own people's
lives. That's the truth. *(she goes up to Mother, picks her up under
the arms and tries to drag her to the bed.)*

MOTHER *(grabs her round the knees)* You can't go, Rose, you
have to stay with me. Leo can't look after me. He's a great artist,
you know that.

ROSE   Yes, he's a great artist. He's very rich. He can afford
to put you into very good care in a nursing home. Even in Switzerland.

(Mother begins to cry. Rose is also sobbing; she sits down beside

*Mother on the floor. Mother strokes Rose, cuddles her to her
chest.)*
What do I care if Master Leo is a great artist? He doesn't notice
me at all. It's all the same to him, whether he sees an empty chair
or me sitting on it. You don't respect me either.

MOTHER   Be patient, Rose. It's not long now. I don't know
whether it's a sin that I'm still alive... I promise you, Rose, I'll
die soon. You won't leave me? Rose, say you won't leave me?

SCENE 2
*Mother is lying still on the bed, stiff. She looks dead. Rose walks up
and down the room, preparing things, little bottles, bowls, gauze,
cotton wool. She arranges it all on the table near the bed. She sits on
the edge and looks at Mother. She leans over her. She touches her
face in various places. She takes a powder compact and powders her
whole face with pale powder and the cheeks with rouge. She paints
the lips with a bright lipstick. She puts mascara on the eyelashes. At
this moment we hear a bicycle bell outside the window. Very close.*

MOTHER *(sits up terrified, looking like a dead body suddenly
coming to life)* Oh sweet Jesus! They're coming for us!

ROSE   Oh great. Everything's smudged. Lashes no good at
all.

MOTHER   I heard a bell.

ROSE   Its kids on bicycles. I tell you that a hundred times a
day.

MOTHER *(holds her hand to her heart, breathes heavily. After a
while, calmer)* Just do the eye shadow.
*(Rose takes a piece of cotton wool and wipes off the smudged
mascara. She carries out Mother's request, then reaches for a
bottle of nail varnish)*
Not that one. That colour looks like blood. Use the cyclamen pink
one.

ROSE *(takes the cyclamen pink varnish and paints Mother's nails,
glancing at the television as she does it)* Look at that samurai.
That's the chief. He can cut off ten heads at once.

MOTHER *(laughing)* As long as the victims are the same height. *(she stops laughing)* I'm worried about Leo. The Japanese are a cruel nation.

ROSE   We'll do the eyelashes again. Look up. And don't close your eyes! Don't close them!

MOTHER   I'll tell you something, Rose. I believe in every cruelty. Goodness has its limits but cruelty knows no bounds.

ROSE   Just sit still a moment longer. Right. Good. *(she goes away from the bed and looks at Mother from a distance.)*

MOTHER   Pass me the mirror.

ROSE *(passes her a small mirror in a silver frame)* Mirror, mirror on the wall, who's the fairest of them all?

MOTHER *(looks at herself in the mirror, from the side and full face)* A bit more rouge on the cheeks. Leo likes me to have a high colour. *(Rose spreads rouge over Mother's cheeks)* How do I look?

ROSE   Like a goddess. From the Quaquito tribe! *(They both laugh.)*

MOTHER   He should be here.

ROSE   It's almost an hour's journey from the airport. *(she takes a bottle of perfume and anoints Mother behind the ears.)*

MOTHER   I'm beginning to get anxious. I feel hot, like when… And here in the cleavage…

ROSE *(pours half a bottle of perfume onto Mother's hand)* Careful, or we'll have to do the injection. *(she pulls a syringe and needles out of her pocket, reaches for an ampoule. She fills the syringe and approaches Mother with the needle aimed at the old woman.)*

MOTHER *(covers herself up, squeals, giggles)* No, Rose, please, not that, I'll be good. Or maybe in the leg, try the leg.

ROSE   Not in the leg. An injection has to hurt. We'll do it in the bum today. *(she tries to uncover the place she has selected for the injection. Mother defends herself. Her arms are strong. A fight begins on the bed. Half joking, half serious.)*
Oh my God, Master Leo's back! *(she quickly restores Mother to order.)*

At this moment the door to the room opens and Leo bursts in. He is about fifty years old, with an imposing head of greying black curly hair. He is wearing evening dress, all a bit crumpled. When Leo enters Rose stands by the patio door.

LEO   I see everything is as per normal. Home at last! *(Leo has the face of the man in the portrait, only without the spectacles. In his hand he holds a huge bunch of roses. In the other hand a travelling bag. In spite of his tiredness, he is very dynamic. He gestures a lot, puts the bag down, runs up to Mother's bed with the roses, kneels, kisses her hand, she kisses his hair. Leo appears not to notice Rose)* You look younger and younger. Every time I come back I find a younger mother. Soon you'll look like my sister. See how I've rushed to get here. I haven't even changed. *(He throws the bunch of roses onto the bed covers.)*

MOTHER Dear little Leo, let me see how you look. Nothing bad has happened to you? *(During their greeting Rose stands leaning on the frame of the patio doors and observes the scene. Her face is inscrutable.)*

LEO *(runs up to the black travelling bag and raises it in the air)* There's a present for you in here but you won't get it until tomorrow! *(puts the bag down and returns to Mother.)*

MOTHER I was just telling Rose that the Japanese are a cruel race...

LEO *(only now notices Rose)* Ah, Rose, how are things with you? Everything alright? How has she been behaving?

ROSE   How's she supposed to behave? The same as usual. *(She shrugs her shoulders, takes the flowers off the bed and puts them in a vase. She goes out taking the vase with her.)*

MOTHER Tell me all about it. What did you play?

LEO   What could I play? Chopin as usual. *(Rose returns with the vase, into which she has put water. She arranges the roses, playing with the arrangement.)*

MOTHER And for the encore?

LEO   Chopin as well.

MOTHER I like Chopin too, but you never play him at home.

LEO   I can get changed at last. At home I play for pleasure. *(takes off his shoes, leaves them in the middle of the room. Then pulls off his jacket and throws it to Rose. Rose catches the jacket and hangs it on the back of the chair.)*

MOTHER   Scriabin, nothing but Scriabin. *(Leo takes off his trousers, throws them to Rose. She does as above.)*

LEO   I've got Chopin in my fingers, but Scriabin in my heart. *(he takes off his socks, rolls them up in a ball and throws them under a chair.)*

MOTHER   Oh my little Leo, my dear little Leo!
(Rose collects up all Leo's clothes and carries them out of the room. She comes back in a moment with an old track-suit. She gives it to Leo who has lain down on the bed beside Mother.)

LEO *(stretching)* Thanks, Rose. You can go to your room now.

ROSE   Thank you sir.
(Leo puts on the track-suit. He flings himself off the bed, does a few knee-bends, then carries out a few violent Kung-Fu movements.)

MOTHER *(rocking with laughter)* What barbaric exercises. Quite unacceptable. Leo, enough of this! *(she speaks sharply, as to a disobedient child)* Please sit down next to me. This will only end in tears.
(Leo obediently sits on the bed beside Mother. He crosses his legs in such a way as to be able to reach his foot easily. He begins to fiddle with his toes.)

MOTHER   Was the ovation very long?

LEO   Of course it was long.

MOTHER   A standing one?

LEO   What do you think?

MOTHER   I think they thought you were wonderful.

LEO *(begins to bite his fingernails)* That's what they said.

MOTHER *(slaps his hand)* What's wonderful in Japanese?

LEO *(bites the nails on his other hand)* I haven't a clue. The Japanese speak English.

MOTHER   Really? All of them? *(again slaps Leo's hand lightly)* Stop biting them. A pianist with bitten finger nails!

LEO   All of them. It's getting dark. I ought to go to bed.
I'm very tired.

MOTHER   Carry on then but stay with me a bit longer son, I
feel so lonely... The darkness is coming again.

*(They sit for a while in the quiet darkness, listening to the
cricket's song. They are lit only by the light of the moon. You can
hear the howling of a dog. After a while, asthmatic coughing,
which stops suddenly. A huddled figure slips past the window.)*

MOTHER   What was that? Who is it? I'm frightened for you all
the time.

LEO   It's nothing. Just the full moon.

(The sound of the dogs howling gets nearer.)

MOTHER   It's howling for death. *(she grabs Leo's hand.)*

LEO   It's only the full moon. It makes the night bright.
The sound of the dogs howling seems menacing. But it's nothing.
Nothing. *(they begin to talk in whispers, with intimacy.)*

MOTHER   It's the night for travelling, and I can't run away.

LEO   You won't escape even if you run. Running away is
the same as immobility. *(he pulls her hand out of his and begins
to stroke her head.)*

MOTHER   On bright nights like this, on such nights of travelling, I ran away, carrying you and protecting you. I protected
myself, protecting you. Danger was flight. Fast steps and slow
ones, crawling, dragging oneself along under the lightening sky,
Oh God, when I found a field of beetroot... that taste, do you
remember?

LEO *(holds her hand again)* It was so long ago...

MOTHER   Long ago? What are you saying – it's as if it was
yesterday! I dug my teeth into that hard red beetroot. You didn't
even have the strength to cry from hunger – hard and red like
them. *(she laughs with a low, croaky laugh)* I dug my teeth in and
ate, ate one after the other, my mouth's watering at the very
thought of it, I have to cheat my hunger. *(she reaches for a
cigarette, Leo helpfully lights it for her)* I ate so long, 'til my jaws
ached. We lay for a long time after that in the beetroot field, and I
felt the milk swelling up in my breasts. And you drank the red
milk... you were four years old then, with teeth sharp as nails,
you bit me and it hurt... oh, I tell you, believe me, the pain of

feeding you was sweet to me... *(Leo has gone to sleep, as if his mother's words were like a lullaby. She speaks as if she was singing, rhythmically)* And then the road again. The road means steps. *(The howling of the dogs. Again a hunched figure moves past the window, clanging metal. The figure with the bicycle slips past again.)*
Death must be somewhere near here, Leo, I can feel it... oh Leo, why didn't we die of hunger then? Together? We should have died then... death would have been beautiful – so unjust. The death of a child is always beautiful and pathetic, together like that, the two of us, united... Now I'm afraid, Leo, I won't survive my death. Swear to me, you won't leave me alone when I'm dying. I saved you, you can't save me, but don't leave me alone... Swear to me! *(she pulls Leo by the hair, wakes him up.)*

LEO   What, have they come for us?

MOTHER   Swear to me that you won't leave me alone when I'm dying. On your knees!

LEO *(gets up, stretching, and kneels down)* I swear. Why don't you believe me? I've sworn so many times.

MOTHER   You've sworn each time you wanted to run away.

LEO *(gets up violently, stands over Mother)* Because it's sick! Sick! You destroy everyone around you. You keep holding me back with your dying. As long as I can remember, you've always been dying, either from fear or from life... you were always dying...

MOTHER   I can't die until you're safe.

LEO   So you'll live forever.

(The howling of the dogs gets louder again.)

MOTHER   A bad omen, bad omen. Those dogs there, do you remember? Eternally hungry skeletons covered in skin...

LEO   I remember people like that.

MOTHER   How quietly, desperately, they howled!

LEO   It carried across those great expanses... There were millions of everything there.

MOTHER   Millions and us two among them, running away, only us, *(with irony)* because your father preferred to visit the tomb of Tamburlaine.

(More coughing outside the window, and the metallic clanking of chains)
See what's going on outside the window. Such an uneasy night. Full moon.

LEO *(goes up to the window and chases away invisible figures)* Oy, ghosts, demons and spooks, clear out, leave my mother alone! Be off with you! Go on! Go on! *(he carries out a few quick kung-fu moves.)*

MOTHER *(laughing)* You can always make me laugh. Put the light on your father.

LEO   Now this point in the repertoire! Leave him in peace in the other world. You're not only tormenting the living but also the dead. He never had a moment's peace. Let him live the spirit life – listen to the silence. Even the crickets have gone to sleep.

MOTHER   Put the light on him, please. I won't be able to sleep without that. It could be the last time.

LEO   You're always doing that – blackmailing me with your death. *(he lights the lamp and directs the light towards the portrait.)*

MOTHER   Close the curtains, they can see us.

LEO   Who?

(Leo and Mother look at the portrait in silence.)

MOTHER   I'd like to know myself, who's watching us now.

LEO   The moon. Does he work for them too, according to you?

MOTHER   Don't mock. He's only lighting their way. Your father! Yes, your father, oh, that David! Intelligentsia for seven generations was a fat lot of good. Intelligentsia doesn't help when you're lying under a soldier's boot. And that boot always tramples brains first. With all his wisdom, your father was a fool, do you understand? He went off to see the tomb of Tamburlaine! Foreign, hot Samarkand, he doesn't know the language, puts on… Do you know what? Do you remember?

LEO   Yes, I remember. I was already four years old.

MOTHER   Do you see him? Like he is on this photograph. In his plus fours, his peaked cap, there, in their country. In all that dirt and poverty, like a lord on a picnic. My God how I laughed,

how I cried, when he went off on his journey with his little
rucksack on his back, me standing in the doorway saying goodbye
to him, you with me, holding on to my leg, laughing when I
laughed, crying when I cried. We waved goodbye to him. Do you
remember? *(she begins to wave goodbye. She plays out that scene
looking at the portrait. She wipes the tears which do not flow.)*

LEO *(also waving like a child)* I remember. Enough.
*(He lowers the lampshade. The circle of light encompasses only
Mother in her bed.)*

MOTHER   I warned him. He wanted to go, so he went. Let's
have a drink and then let's separate for the whole long night. You
have no idea how tiring that David can be. *(she lights a cigarette,
inhaling deeply)* As bad as he was in life, maybe even more so. I
didn't have to listen to him going on then, but now I have to,
because he talks inside me. Oh that foreign spy! Who goes around
in plus-fours? A spy. The stupidity of this intelligent person calls
for divine retribution. It was pointless saving him. He could have
stayed here and gone up in smoke with the rest of his family. He
never forgave me for saving him.

LEO *(goes up to the patio doors, pulls them back a bit and looks out
into the dark)* He must have died there, where they killed everything that was different. Don't speak of it any more.

MOTHER *(angrily)* I must speak. I must and I will. This is my
everlasting death. The eternity of death. Eternity is exactly that –
everlasting death. You take your own death with you. That's why
I don't want to die, although my life isn't worth a hill of beans.
Your father's life was worth at least as much as my diamond as
big as an eye.

LEO *(going up to Mother's bed)* It's lucky someone turned up who
was willing to take that dead stone in exchange for a worthless
life. *(he stands by Mother, but would like to go. Mother grabs his
hand, pulls him to sit down. Leo sits leaning a little.)*

MOTHER   You know very well who it was. The bastard went a
long way. God be with him.

LEO   Or the devil. That's the rule. All regimes put the
same people up on a pedestal and kill the same people. It's an
absolute rule. From the death camp to the concentration camp
from the concentration camp to the tenth pavilion. You have to be

born with a silver spoon in your mouth to get through a net like that. *(he strokes Mother's hair tenderly.)*

MOTHER   David certainly wasn't. He was born unlucky. He didn't believe in human cruelty. He was constantly surprised. *(she mimics his voice)* 'It's unbelievable, it's just impossible.' *(back to normal)* I always say: 'Only goodness has limits, cruelty knows no bounds.' I kept telling him, that... but he never, ever...

LEO *(stops stroking Mother's hair)* Stop now. Stop! *(shouting)* That was half a century ago! I'm sure Father was very grateful...

MOTHER   Gratitude kills love. Because he was grateful to me, he preferred to have himself killed. I snatched him from death, so it was me who took him from his family. I saved him, and they died. Do you understand? Only the sacrificial smoke remained. Gratitude kills love.

LEO   And you always demand gratitude. You demand it of me as well.

MOTHER *(softly, lovingly)* Remember, Leo, those dry crusts, which I saved for you?

LEO *(springs up, paces round the room like a caged animal)* I don't want to remember. I don't remember anything. I was four years old! *(when Leo finds himself by the bed, Mother passes him a piece of dry bread taken from under her pillow, he takes it as if in a trance and begins to crunch it. He calms down, walks calmly now, as if going for a walk.)*

MOTHER   We always have to be ready. They might come in at any moment and we'll have to run. I am afraid for you, Leo. All it takes is a bright night, the howling of a dog... Actually I'm afraid of dark nights as well, I'm afraid of the days, of the sun, of the rain... everything's against me.

LEO   It's against me just as much as against you. For half a century you've kept me by your side, I can't have a normal life. It's grotesque... a grown man at his mother's side.

MOTHER   It won't last much longer. Time is on your side.

LEO   You've been talking like this for ten years, every day. Go on, take a tablet, maybe you'll go to sleep... *(He pours water from a jug into a glass, passes it to Mother with the sleeping pill.)*

MOTHER *(swallows the pill, doesn't drink the water. She puts the hand with the glass out towards Leo)* You forgot something. You promised. *(she speaks in a little girl voice)* Did you think I would forget?

LEO *(pours a glass of the cherry brandy and passes it to her)* You drink a lot.

MOTHER   Before I stand in front of my God I'll be sober. It really won't be long now, but don't begrudge me these last hours. Now, when each day is the success of defeat, and every night is the defeat of success of the day survived... You have your music, and I have only you, Leo, only my little Leo... My real illness isn't the paralysis of my legs, but the paralysis of time – being stuck in the past. Every second distances me from them – every minute brings me closer to the unknown. The other was terrible, but past, and the past is known. I remember it, because I survived. And you, Leo, say: 'Half a century has passed.' What's half a century to remember so many unknowns? I have to look back and see every danger, that could have happened, I have to think about what we avoided... *(she yawns, talks more and more slowly, the sleeping pill begins to work)* ... wandering through those endless open spaces... paralysis of the legs is a sentence forcing me to think... oh Leo, I'm so exhausted by all this, so unfulfilled... *(Closes her eyes, opens them with a great effort, checking, whether Leo has gone away.)*

LEO *(quietly, in a whisper, soothingly)* You can sleep safely. I'm beside you, don't be frightened. Shh, it's perfectly safe, your eyelids are tired, they are so heavy...

MOTHER *(opening her eyes for a moment she speaks clearly)* They're not heavy at all. They're as light as paper.

LEO *(laughing with Mother)* You are impossible. You always have to spoil everything. Here's your present. When you wake up in the morning, you'll see what it is. Now, sleep well. I'm going to bed. I can hardly stand.

He kisses Mother on the forehead and on both cheeks, tucks the bedclothes round her and goes out, quietly shutting the door behind him.

ACT TWO

A large room which looks like a marital bedroom. White furniture, a double bed, a dressing-table with a mirror in a gilt frame. On the dressing-table there are lots of cosmetics and perfumes. Open wardrobes. In the middle of the floor stand suitcases ready packed. A woman in a fur coat is struggling to close one of them. She has her back to the audience. When Leo enters the room, the woman lifts her head and looks at him. It is Rose, who now looks quite different. Her face, delicately made up, is beautiful, but racked with pain.

LEO   What's happening, Rose?

ROSE *(straightening up)* My name is Eve again.

LEO   Yes, I thought so. It was hanging in the air today.
(He goes up close to Rose.)

ROSE   I'm going away, moving away, leaving. Whatever you prefer.

LEO   Again?

ROSE   This time for real. After all, you said, 'Thank you Rose, you can go.'

LEO   We've been playing this game for ten years – why do you want to go today? *(he tries to put his arms around her.)*

ROSE *(pulling away)* Why? Because I didn't do it yesterday. And because I can't be bothered to carry on acting out this feeble play. I didn't think I'd be acting in a theatre for one actor and two spectators for ten years. Burlesque plays always enjoy the longest runs, don't they? Well, you cast me in this burlesque tragedy of errors. It's a completely new, unknown genre. Today's the tenth anniversary of the day I took on the part of nurse to your mother. The action of this play never moves forward, it goes backwards fifty years with your mother's constant talking. I can't live in your past any longer.
(she bends down and pulls a long white dress out of the suitcase. She shows it to Leo, puts it up against herself, then speaks to Leo in a voice that is very quiet and broken)
Can you even remember who I was? You stopped remembering out of fear that your mother might notice something. Would you give up your art for me?

LEO   Why should I give it up? What are you getting at? I do very well out of it. *(he takes the dress out of Rose's hands, breathes in its scent, behaves like Mother does with little Leo's clothes)* Of course I remember this dress. You had it on then. Ten years ago, when I came to your dressing-room. It smells!

ROSE   Of mothballs. Yes, my name was Eve then. This is Eve's dress. Eve was playing Juliet. These are Eve's clothes and those are little Leo's clothes. *(she speaks mechanically. Suddenly she snatches the white dress from Leo, throws it on the floor and stamps on it viciously.)*

LEO   Oh my God, I can't stand this. *(he covers his face with his hands)* Anything, but this. Thank goodness I took you away from the theatre! Really, Rose! These overblown gestures! It's an awful scene, stop it.

ROSE   Real despair is theatre to you. Your emotional development is arrested at age four. You're frozen like petrified rock, because that's how your mother wanted it. Bloody four year old Leo with his bloody shirts and caps.

LEO *(imprisons Rose's hands in his; speaks looking into her eyes)* Really, Rose? Really? You sleep with a four year old child? You paedophile! Go on, kiss little Leo, kiss him! *(he is playing around, trying to kiss Rose. She turns her head away, begins to laugh herself. But it is laughter mixed with tears.)*

ROSE *(she speaks standing very stiff in his arms)* I hate that child in you. That child in you is enough for you, but I want a real child, do you understand? Can you grasp that, that a woman wants to have a real child? You're afraid of your mother! She wouldn't survive that! Her time has come. She may not survive. Do you know, sometimes I trip over an umbilical cord, which joins you, a cord as thick as a python.

LEO *(letting Rose out of his embrace)* Why do you talk such rubbish? You know very well you'll never leave. I remember everything, Rose. I came to your dressing-room after the performance. You were sitting with your eyes closed, tired as a dog, in that tiny dressing-room... it stank of the sweat of Romeo, that old fool...

ROSE   I remember it too! You came in like the lord of the universe. The finest performer of Chopin of all time – a man who can't stand Chopin. Get stuffed and stop going on about love!

Sentimental idiot. You love only your mother and yourself! I remember when you said: 'My mother has lost the feeling in her legs, Eve. She's a very old woman. We can't tell her about our wedding. She wouldn't survive that. So it's a secret. A small country church...'

LEO   But you wanted it!

ROSE   Of course I wanted it. I was twenty-two years old then and stupid. It was all so romantic! Wonderful! It was supposed to last for a few months at most! You promised me that! *(with fury she throws the white dress in Leo's face. He smoothes the material of the dress and hangs it over the back of the chair. He is calm. Fury gets into Rose. She begins to take things out of the suitcases, throws them at Leo. Leo catches them and throws them back. Rose is shouting the whole time.)*

ROSE   Your Mother saved your life, but why should I pay back your debt of gratitude! You travel around the world and I sit here, playing the country bumpkin, a real country girl. I play this bloody nurse and I look after your mother better than if she were my own... Instead of looking after a child, which could be going to school by now, which we could have had ten years ago.

LEO   But I didn't think it would last this long. Do you want me to kill her? I loved you then and I still love you now, with difficulty...

(Through the closed door Mother's shouts are heard.)

MOTHER   Rose! Rose!

(Rose blocks her ears. She calms down, stops throwing everything around. The room looks like a battlefield.)

ROSE   We all love the nurses of our poor old paralysed mothers. Are you comfortable, madam, shall I move your legs? Is the sheet straight? Yes, your Leo is a wonderfully good son.

LEO   You were only that polite for the first year. Then you had a real go at her: 'You keep quiet or I'll stick an injection in your bum.' Do you think I don't hear? Don't see how you stick the needle in, as if it was pig-skin? Don't pretend you're the victim now – you know very well what you're like, and so do I.

ROSE   For ten years I've had to look after what I find most disgusting – a fat old carcass, blood, innards, bedpans, all that

shit, and on top of that, having to listen to that endless going on…
no, if the angels don't take me to heaven alive, then…

MOTHER *(yells)* Rose, Rose, come here at once!

ROSE *(goes up to the door, opens it a little, sticks her head out and shouts)* I'm just coming! Just a minute! *(continues quietly to Leo, her voice strangled with anger)* Master Leo asked me not to wake Madam… Master Leo is really crafty, Madam, he made me into a disciplined nurse – killed two birds with one stone… during the day I do what I have to do for Madam and at night I do what I have to do for him, because what you don't know, Madam, is that Master Leo is a particularly randy little son… his refined, highly-prized fingers range over the octave of all possible kinks and perversions, which is why, Madam, every morning I have black eyes and drained lips.

LEO   But you adore it!

ROSE   I'll go and tell her that, shall I? I'll tell her that for ten years you've been deceiving her. Ten years of samaritan days and nights of excess. Master Leo has everything he wants. In a minute your mother will find out. Before she dies she'll know the truth… I've exchanged my real life among real people for service in the mortuary. *(she moves towards the door. Leo stops her. In his hand he holds some silk handkerchiefs and scarves. He drags Rose to the bed at the back of the stage. Rose screams, Leo gags her with a scarf, ties her up with another one, takes off her fur and begins tying her up with great ease. He pulls her over onto the bed, sits on her. Only his head and shoulders are visible. Rose is hidden by the headboard of the bed. She mumbles something behind the gag.)*

LEO   You're not going anywhere, not to her, not anywhere. Do you think, life in the theatre is something you're suited to? You're too delicate for that. Not today – today you have your day – once a year your brain menstruates… We'll survive this as well. Is this about the theatre? *(Rose burbles something despairingly)* Just a minute – is it about that moulting Romeo, who had to watch out he didn't lose his teeth during his brief displays of eloquence? Who stuffed himself into you in the dressing-room in a hurry, to prove he could still get it up? Surely you're better off with me? Don't lie. *(he is moving rhythmically, like during the sex act. He takes the gag off Rose's mouth, closes her mouth with* *kisses, lifts his head again, rapid breathing, he speaks in a jerky voice)* Maybe you think you'd still be playing Juliet! In the same dress? *(Rose moans)* Do you miss the caress-ing gazes of your audience? That's not for you, Rose, maybe other actresses like it, maybe Eve liked it, but not you, you find it disgusting... *(more rapid breathing)* Now?

ROSE   A bit longer.

(Leo disappears behind the headboard. The bed squeaks horribly. Rose giggles, then moans from both of them, then absolute silence They talk quietly now, intimately, they cannot be seen behind the headboard.)

LEO   Was it good for you?

ROSE   Mmmm *(she purrs)* It was. It was.

LEO   You want more? You'll be the death of me!

ROSE   Not like that. Like this now.

LEO   You like her. I know you like her, even though she's impossible. But she is a human being. And you feel that. During the day you're drawn into the mystery of dying and old fears but at night you have everything you want, is that not enough? Just because you've given up aping the innermost feelings of others? That's good for you... *(he groans with pain)* Don't bite.

MOTHER *(shouts)* Rose! I'm dying!

ROSE   Untie me quickly! I must go to her!

LEO *(unties Rose)* She isn't dying. If she really thought she was dying, she would call me.

Rose quickly puts herself to rights, pats down her hair, throws on the nurse's apron and cap, runs out. Leo is alone in the room. He sits on the bed. He stretches slowly, gets up, picks up Rose's dress, the one in which she played Juliet, throws it over his shoulder, walks around the room looking for something in the wardrobe, in drawers, finds a hammer and nails. He nails Rose's dress to the wall. He crosses it over. One nail in one sleeve, another in the other sleeve, a third in the bottom of the dress, which balloons out, comes out from the wall. Leo moves back and admires his handiwork, nailed above the bed, from a distance. Then he hangs Rose's fur in the wardrobe, tidies up the room. He puts the suitcases on the shelves, finally he opens up the folding doors to the next room, in which a white Bechstein piano stands. He sits at the piano and plays Scriabin's piano concerto in F sharp major.

SCENE 2

It is night. The room is lit only by moonlight. Mother is sleeping on the bed. The patio doors are wide open. Complete silence. Mother breathes noisily. Outside the window we hear asthmatic coughing. A moment's silence and then Mother's heavy breathing again. Then the silence is broken by the sharp sound of a bicycle bell. Mother wakes up. She sits up on the bed, lights the lamp. She is surrounded by a circle of light.

MOTHER   No clock, no calendar. You don't know anything except that it's night and I'm still alive. Even that's too much luck. *(she looks at the travel bag with the present in it. She leans out of bed. She can't reach)* He's placed it brilliantly. Too bad, he's so selfish... I brought him up like that.
(Mother lowers herself with great difficulty onto the floor, dragging her carcass behind her. She falls heavily, with a thud. She reaches for the travel bag. She takes out of it a large, long box made of black plastic, shaped like something between a violin case and a child's coffin. She mutters) A surprise! What is it? A coffin or something? Maybe a violin? Leo's gone mad... Hang on, there's a label, I can't see what it says. Yoko Suki Yaki, the name of a company, I don't know any more than I did before... Japanese trash, what do they all see in Japan, everything's Japanese. *(she struggles to open this peculiar container)* Right now. *(she opens the lid of the box)* Oh my God!
(she takes out of the box a doll the size of a four-year-old child, with a huge head of curly black hair. On the back of the naked doll we can see buttons. When she turns the doll to face the audience we see that the doll has the old face of Leo)
Little Leo! Little Leo! The spitting image! I wonder what this must have cost, it must be made to order... so like him! That Leo!
(She presses the buttons on the doll's back.)
DOLL *(calling)* Mummy, Mummy! Daddy, Daddy!
(It laughs and cries in turn.)

MOTHER   Don't cry, don't cry, my poor little Leo, poor little
naked child, we'll soon dress you… *(she reaches under the bed,
takes out the trunk with little Leo's clothes and carefully dresses
the doll. While it's being dressed the doll cries)* Poor thing's
hungry, you'll get some milk in a minute. *(she pretends to
breastfeed the doll. Silence, the 'satisfied child' stops crying. She
thoughtfully looks into the distance out of the window. We hear
coughing out there, quite near this time. In a moment, as she
freezes in horror - the sound of a bicycle bell)*
Quiet Leo, you mustn't cry now. Who can it be prowling about at
this time of night? They're bound to be coming for us.
*(in a panic she crawls with the doll under the bed. She tries to
hide. The coughing comes nearer, the bicycle bell sounds almost
as if it is in the room. After a while, a clanking noise like old
metal. In the doorway appears an old man with long grey hair
sticking out from under a peaked cap. On his nose are spectacles
with the lenses all shattered. Tattered plus-fours and jacket
complete the outfit, in which we can recognise the elegant clothes
from the portrait. The old man is pushing a bicycle, a rusty and
decrepit vehicle. Hair matted with blood, scratched face, legs
wrapped in cloth puttees, boots hung over his shoulder. In spite of
all this he moves briskly, although he does not see too well. This
is how Leo's father , David, looks. (He is played by the same actor
who played Leo) Mother freezes on the floor like an insect that
senses danger. She shields the doll-Leo. She makes the sign of the
cross time after time and prays noiselessly. The closely held doll
begins to whimper. Mother closes its mouth with her hand, just as
if she believed it to be a living child. The old man coughs.)*

DAVID   Are you here? I can hear Leo crying. I can't see
anything through these spectacles.
*(he blunders around feeling his way, hardly seeing, finds the wall,
leans his bicycle against it, takes a few steps, backs, pushes his
spectacles down his nose and looks over them around the room.
Puts the spectacles back, still not seeing Mother and little Leo.
With uncertain but quite quick steps he crosses the room, until
finally he trips over Mother, who has almost crawled under the
bed. He loses his balance, falls beside Mother)*
Ah, then you are here! I got the right place, I've been circling
around for ages. I heard your voice, I couldn't be wrong. You

often talk about me. It's me, David, don't you recognise me? *(he coughs, his voice is croaky, trembling, but his speech is fast and lively. He rubs his hands together. Mother looks at him fearfully, tries to move away, but can't get any further under the bed)* What cold! It's supposed to be mid-summer, but there's a terrible chill in the air. *(puts his hand out towards Mother)* Aren't you going to greet me at all, not even a kiss or a hug?

MOTHER   No, no, I don't believe it's you. It's a trick. Now? Now you? It's out of the question.

DAVID *(begins to unwind the puttees, hisses with pain)* It's infected … I've been travelling for so long, so many steps, the bicycle's not much good now, the other one was stolen… So many steps I've walked back to you and you don't want to believe that it's me. Look into my eyes, look, now do you recognise me? *(He takes off his spectacles, turns his face towards Mother.)*

MOTHER *(with fear but also curiosity she looks into his eyes)* David had dark violet eyes, and yours are so watery… How can I tell? No, no. David had dark eyes.

DAVID   They shone lights into my eyes for hours on end, to find out my name. Can you imagine? Instead of asking and writing down my name, over and over the same thing… Lights in the eyes and the question. That's why they've faded… The rest of the colour drained away, when I was wandering in the sun through those great deserts… I can prove to you that I'm David, I know your whole life…You were left alone with Leo, when I went to see the tomb of Tamburlaine… you haven't changed at all and little Leo hasn't changed, *(he wants to stroke the doll, but Mother protects it from him)* he hasn't changed at all, and I thought I'd been wandering for so long, but it was only a moment. Obviously time seems longer when you're suffering…

MOTHER   Nearly half a century has gone by.

DAVID   Half a century? I was wandering for half a century to reach this land and you. Yes, yes. It's the unsevered umbilical cord from the motherland which led me like Ariadne's thread. Half a century has passed, but you've sort of frozen in time waiting for me. How is this possible? Half a century? Unimaginable.

MOTHER　　　Yes. Now I recognise you. Unimaginable! That's your word…

DAVID　　　I walked the whole time I was escaping – the whole time I was walking back to you and little Leo. It's God's fault. He didn't warn me that time runs so fast. They took my watch right away. *(he laughs)* But I forgive God, I forgive him everything, because I've found you, even though there's so little time left till death, but what's death to God? He doesn't know it.

MOTHER　　　Don't blaspheme. Of course, God doesn't know his own death, He only knows those who've died. There isn't time now for sorting things out with God. I don't even know whether it's you, or a clever impostor. Maybe you want to get something out of me? Maybe they've sent you…

DAVID　　　I've visited the tomb of Tamburlaine.

MOTHER　　　Maybe you're a murderer? Maybe you've killed David, stolen his bicycle and put on his clothes? We heard a lot about things like that.

DAVID　　　Stop it, I've been living for this day. It's the reason I survived, that and because I learned to howl. Listen, just listen. *(He lifts his head to the window, sticks out his chin and begins to howl frightfully.)*

MOTHER *(cuddles little Leo, who begins to cry)* Stop, stop now! You've woken little Leo.

DAVID　　　Is that really Leo or isn't it?

MOTHER　　　It is and it isn't.

DAVID　　　Your logic. It is and it isn't. Brilliant!

MOTHER　　　Don't argue, you've only just got back and you've started.

DAVID *(bends over the doll, touches it)* It's a doll. I can't deny it's beautifully made.

MOTHER　　　Doll or not, it is little Leo. You can see for yourself how sensitive he is. You woke him up with your howling. It's as if he was alive, that's enough for me. *(suddenly has a brainwave)* Listen! Maybe you're a fake as well? Show me your back, maybe there's some kind of mechanism there? *(he obediently shows her his back. She pulls off the shirt stuck to it)* Oh merciful God! Why didn't you say anything? It's terribly infected! One great sore! My God, David! They beat you! Tell me, did they beat you?

DAVID   They beat me.

MOTHER   Who?

DAVID   Each of them in turn.

MOTHER   We must wash this. Forgive me, David. I don't trust anyone. They've tricked me so many times, I've started to lie to myself. *(she kisses David's wounded back.)*

DAVID   What a relief. If it wasn't for the howling I wouldn't have survived. People there are kinder to dogs than to humans, because a dog won't give you away...

MOTHER   If you're unlucky even a dog will give you away. *(She takes her white handkerchief out from under her pillow, pours water onto it from the glass on the bedside table and delicately begins to wash David's back.)*

DAVID   I used to howl in the bushes and sometimes someone would throw me a piece of mouldy bread. That's my trick. A dog's trick. *(he laughs and coughs)* And that's why I'm here and those who could only be people are lying in ditches somewhere. One false move and I would have been lost...

MOTHER   It's a miracle that you're alive...

DAVID   I only walked at night, I forgot about hunger and thirst...

MOTHER   You're probably hungry! Have an orange. *(David falls on the orange. He bites it with the peel. He shows the audience his back covered with bruised welts and bleeding sores. The doll begins to laugh)* How can you eat so greedily, with the peel? Can't you see, the child is watching, he'll learn bad manners... Give it to me, I'll peel it for you. This is very good for a first meal after hunger, easy to digest. *(He unwillingly gives back the fruit. Mother peels it, puts the segments in his mouth. Just as Rose had done.)*

DAVID   And you, Leo, don't laugh at your father, it's a sin.

MOTHER   He's still too young to sin. *(they sit for a moment in silence. David chews the fruit. He lowers his head)* So tell me, what did you see at Tamburlaine's tomb?

DAVID   What I saw is not important. It's more important that they saw me there. *(he laughs and coughs.)*

MOTHER   But I told you. In plus fours! There in their land! And on top of that the peaked cap!

DAVID *(takes off the cap, hands it to Mother)* It protected my head. It burned down relentlessly. I tried walking at night, but some-times... those open spaces, those deserts... What I saw on the way, indescribable. I saw everything. Even my own grave. I dug it myself, and yet I escaped. *(he says this with pride in his voice.)*

MOTHER   Impossible, no-one escapes that.

DAVID   Not alive. I got out from under a heap of corpses. They didn't count the dead. They thought I was dead...
(He laughs. The laughter becomes a terrible fit of coughing. He is choking, waving his arms around, he leaps up and runs to the French windows, takes deep breaths.)

MOTHER   Put your arms up!

DAVID *(still coughing)* Why, do you want to shoot me?

MOTHER   Oh, David, do you have to make a joke of everything? *(he calms down, breathes deeply. When he starts to speak, he speaks a little seriously, a little pompously, as if he were providing his own counterpoint. He walks around the room.)*

DAVID   All the nations allied themselves to kill me. Yet here I am, a member of the seventh generation of the intelligentsia, weakest of the weak, all those fellows like oaks, those oxen, all left behind dead, and I'm here. I was running away from enemies and I fell into the hands of friends. That was the worst thing. *(he laughs again)* I ran, I ran, I walked a bit, rode when I could... See that bicycle! It's not the same one. They stole mine, so I stole another. They have strong bicycles there. Look, it's still going. *(He gets on the bicycle and begins to ride around the room.)*

MOTHER   Yes, yes, it is you. Unbelievable. The real David. *(He rings the bicycle bell repeatedly. It is the same bell which we heard outside the window. The doll laughs. Mother also laughs.)*

DAVID   This bicycle is a moral defeat. I stole. Mine was stolen, so I stole. I betrayed the principles of my parents. In war and imprisonment different rules prevail. Principles, oh yes. I know it's better to be a victim than the executioner, better to allow yourself to be killed than to kill... but all I did was steal. I swear

on the smoke from my parents that I never killed anyone.
(He gets off the bicycle, leans it against the wall.)

MOTHER   It's a miracle that a thing like that goes at all.

DAVID   It's a bit rusty, it was beginning to fall apart, so I tied
it up with string. It served me well, my squeaky steed.
*(He strokes the bicycle. He is shivering with cold, and his teeth
begin to chatter.)*

MOTHER   Maybe you're ill, maybe you've dragged back some
infectious disease with you? There's smallpox there like the
common cold here. Let's see if you've got any pock marks. I'm
not thinking of myself, only of little Leo.

DAVID   No, it's just this damp chill.

MOTHER   Help me get into bed. I can't use my legs, but I'm
warm, I'll warm you up.

DAVID   You always were as warm as a Russian stove.
What's the problem with the legs?

MOTHER   I don't know. It was the only way I could hold onto
Leo. *(he is weak, he helps Mother onto the bed, and she climbs up
with her hands. With an effort she pulls herself up, David pushes
her, heaves her up. At last Mother is lying on the bed with little
Leo in her arms. David lies down beside her, shivering and teeth
chattering. Mother tucks the duvet round him right up to his neck.
She presses the doll's mechanism, which speaks it's usual words)*

DOLL   Mummy! Mummy! Daddy! Daddy!

MOTHER *(quietens it by feeding)* He doesn't respect my sleep. He
always feeds at night. And he bites, his teeth are strong now.
(hisses with pain) No! Leo! I'll smack you!

DAVID   I'm hungry all the time too.

MOTHER *(reaches under her pillow, pulls out a chunk of dry
bread, gives it to David)* I always have something for
emergencies.

DAVID *(crunches loudly. Puts his broken spectacles up onto his
forehead. Sits up in bed)* I've always been fascinated by infinity.
The bicycle and my spectacles somehow always reminded me of
infinity. Infinity overwhelmed me, even before I began my
journey. I protected my spectacles, protected my bicycle. The
lenses cracked. See the star shape?

MOTHER　　　Wait… a star-shaped crack? That's strange, I was thinking about that yesterday. Tell me, David, when time turns into a star, is that when we'll die? Or maybe I'll be born again then? A terrible emptiness, I kill it with babbling… I drive everyone mad.

DAVID　　　Only fear kills the emptiness. I was so afraid I didn't feel the emptiness and I thought of you all the time. *(she settles little Leo to sleep. She puts her finger to her lips. He speaks more quietly)* Cuddle up to me, you'll see how you lose the emptiness. *(Mother cuddles up to David. She winds her arms desperately round him. They lie locked together.)*

MOTHER　　　At least in those few moments before death, at last I've got you all, you and little Leo and Leo.

DAVID　　　Think, what binds people together? We reject what's different, we leave what's the same, and you know what's left then?

MOTHER　　　I haven't a clue, what you've thought of now.

DAVID　　　Only birth and death will remain. So the only things binding us are what is unremembered and what's unknown. And you're surprised that we're condemned to loneliness? When the only thing that links people is unobtainable? Sometimes, only sometimes, very rarely, a moment like today occurs when a third force links us: love, do you understand? Poor human love.

MOTHER　　　What are you saying, David? You, the cold rationalist, seventh generation intelligentsia…You always ridiculed whatever couldn't be measured, and now you say, 'Love!' *(she gives David another piece of bread and begins crunching on one herself.)*

DAVID　　　You might not believe me, but I never stopped loving. I loved even my bicycle. I should have thrown it away a long time ago, but I won't do that. It saved my life. There are people who don't kill a horse gone lame. I'm proud of the fact that I belong to those people. And if it's a rusty old bicycle? So what? It was with me when I had no-one. I couldn't have friends – they let me down so often, gave me away so many times… I don't blame them – in agony you say anything…

MOTHER   Yes, yes, it's better not to know, I always say it's better to know nothing. *(she lights a cigarette, gives one to David, lights it for him.)*

DAVID   I couldn't get used to that Judas sort of modus vivendi, but for them it was universal. Everyone has to betray someone, because everyone is betrayed by someone. That's how this Judas roundabout goes round, lots of people, more get born all the time, the torturers soon are tortured, and those who hang others will be hung themselves... those are the commandments of their new religion. *(he coughs.)*

MOTHER   It's better not even to think about it. The most important thing is that we're all together again. You mustn't talk too much. It makes you cough.

DAVID *(not listening to her)* All that time, to have no-one around you whom you can trust... That's death. They hang and hang. The gallows' generations of Tamburlaine. Then they stopped hanging and stopped shooting, because it was too expensive. They began to freeze people in thirty degrees of frost...

MOTHER   Stop talking about it – just the words make me cold. I've seen it too, and little Leo's seen it... *(she strokes the doll)* You can sleep easy. Your father's back.

DAVID *(inhales with pleasure)* The first real cigarette for ages... I tell you, when I pretended to be a dog, I got to know this world and its children well. The bicycle and the spectacles gave me an idea about the un-free liberated ones, I measured out unending roads in unending days and nights, waking up with hope and going to sleep without it. Like an eternal traveller I've been everywhere, seen everything, all the evil and despair and I tell you, I only want to see goodness now. I long for sentimental goodness. I have got rid of egoism. I have nothing and I want nothing. I have a crippled bicycle and cracked spectacles. They are the souvenirs of my journey and evidence of existence. *(He coughs.)*

MOTHER   Your throat was always delicate. You talk too much. Put the cigarette out, the smoke is no good for you. *(They both put out their cigarettes on the bed frame and throw the butts on the floor.)*

DAVID   And who am I to tell, if not you, what? I'm attached to these things, and they are attached to me. Literally attached. Do you recognise this elastic? *(he shows her)* You used to tie up your hair with it when you were feeding little Leo. Thanks to this elastic my spectacles stayed on my head. *(he passes her the elastic, she ties her hair back with it)* And this strap, do you recognise it?

MOTHER   What do you think? We used to lead little Leo with it when he was learning to walk.

DAVID   I used to tie myself to the bicycle with it, then I could ride for miles, sleeping watchfully, on the saddle like on a horse, I never fell off. I can't do anything for it. I can only oil it, then it will be a bit easier, when I coat its rusting tin with gentle oil...

MOTHER   You can do it tomorrow, not today. I've got some oil for little Leo, I'll give you some... I can feel you've warmed up a bit.

DAVID   It's almost impossible to believe in the warmth of your own legs, when your feet have always been frozen. I've been everywhere and I'm not moving from here now. I'll never go away again. To visit the tomb of Tamburlaine? It seems irrelevant now.

MOTHER   It's wonderful, this kind of safe, animal old age. Elderly warmth.

DAVID   Mixed up memory. That mix up allows you to live... How did you describe it? That death is a moment turned into a star? Yes, I can accept that, it's a good idea for death. Everyone will have their star...
(They cuddle up together desperately again, like a couple of lost children.)

MOTHER   I'm not so young any more, half a century has passed since I used to cuddle up to you. I expect there were some women there.

DAVID   Maybe there were some women, of no importance, no importance, maybe one of them gave me some bone to gnaw on... We're in our bed now, in our house...

MOTHER   Oh David, something tells me that it's all too late now. We're wasted, burnt out like empty shells. Only a bit of soul left.

DAVID   Isn't that enough? It's everything. If you'd wandered half the world and seen this huge mass made up of individual weaknesses, but solid in a crowd, strong and ready for any murder, then you wouldn't say that a bit of soul is not much – it's everything.

(Mother begins to hum a lullaby, she sings in a low deep voice.)

MOTHER *(sing-song voice)* Warm, you're getting warmer... The warmth is getting into your legs. You begin to think warmly... *(sings again.)*

DAVID *(half asleep)* Sleep is coming over me like sugar takes away strong onion. At last sweet sleep is coming over me...

MOTHER   Do you remember little Leo's lullaby?
(They hum together.)

DAVID   That damned lullaby filled my head and rocked me as I rode along on my bicycle... It extinguished my vigilance. It's so difficult to believe in anything. A moment's rest before the massacre, that's our – *(he falls asleep in mid-sentence.)*

MOTHER *(finishes David's sentence)* ... Life. Amen. Let's thank God for this one moment. I always pray before the night... When I don't forget.

(David waves his hands about in his sleep as if he was intending to fly away, like a bird flapping its wings)

Sleep, sleep. Don't fly away. I know those dreams: to fly high up! They'll reach you in the air, it's better to sit in the burrow, in the earth...at least you don't fall. *(she strokes the old man's cheeks, puts little Leo down in the middle, between his father and herself. She puts her arms around them both and hugs them to her)* It's difficult not to believe, difficult to believe. It's important, this moment turned into a star. Oh God, though I don't understand you *(she prays in a whisper)* I love you above all else, above all creation, because you're infinite goodness... infinite... infinite goodness. *(she kisses little Leo and David on the forehead. She straightens the duvet, lies down on her back next to David. She puts out her hand, turns out the light.)*

The room is filled with a rosy dawn light. In the light of the rising sun, we see three figures lying on the bed, wound up in a deathly embrace. The heads of Mother and David are thrown back. Heavy, tired breathing. A bicycle bell sounds gently. The doll-Leo sits up on the bed. It begins to wail piteously. Through the closed door the sound of a piano reaches us. Scriabin's piano concerto. The doll suddenly stops crying. It falls on its back like a broken mechanism. The piano is silent. The breathing becomes quieter.

There is a total, overwhelming silence. In the silence we hear very close the song of the first bird. The room becomes lighter. Gradually everything whitens.

Into the room comes Rose in a snowy white apron and cap. Her hair and face are also white. She carries a white tray, on which stands a white jug, white plates, a white cup and white sugar bowl. Rose crosses the room. She trips over the bicycle. She puts the tray on the table. She goes up to the French windows. She opens them wide. The room is flooded with brightness, in which everything drowns. The brightness intensifies. We can no longer see anything except a blinding brightness getting ever brighter.

The end.

Krystyna Kofta

Lives in Warsaw. Husband professor of psychology, son biologist. Graduated with M.A. in Polish in 1970. Novels: *The Visor (1978)* - (Faustian themes), *Sawdust (1980)* - (The Stalinist era seen through the eyes of children), *The Small Predator House (1988)* - (a woman gaining her freedom from the power of her mother and then her husband), *No-one's Body (1988)* - (a gothic romance), *In Praise of Witches (1994)* - (on female power), *The Secret Diary of Melanie R. (1997)* - (balancing between the real and virtual worlds), *The Thief of Memory (1998)* - (today and the memory of childhood).

Other work: *The Man who didn't die (1990)* - (a collection of short stories), *How to get, keep and drop a man (1992)* - (a parody of a self-help manual), *Harpies, piranhas, angels (1997)* - (a dialogue with journalist Malgorzata Domagalik on the subject of the lack of solidarity among women).

Film scripts: *I like Bats* (horror), *Femina* (based on *The Small Predator's House).*

Other Plays: *Professor Mephisto's Salon* - (Faust and Mephisto are women).

On-going work for the women's magazine *Your Style.*

Tulip Doctor

by Vera Filo
translated by Mia Nadasi

CHARACTERS
Mama (around 50)
Papa (age 71)
Girl (about 26)
Grandson (say 26)
TV Newscaster (pushing 35)
Bimbo (exactly 28)
Police Chief (45 on a good day)
The Wrapped-up guy (will be 25)
The Second (past 38)
Supporting characters:
Cyber soldiers, pearly, sequiny soldiers
Children
One small kid (I/16, Inter.II.)
An angel
A dragon
Salvador Dalis
Andy Warhol
A nun

Locations: The location is a kaleidoscope:
Act 1. The Cellar. The Room. The Other Room. Around the Rooms. The Street. The Bar, The Police Chief's Flat. A TV (without perspective). An Outside space.
Act 2. Dark, non-functioning kaleidoscope: (broken inside or outside, who knows?)
Sounds: Act I: sounds of the computer. Act II, only after it is indicated.
Note: The blood is green. Except in Act I, Scene 40(a), it is red.

ACT ONE

1. In The Room.

Seven acres of ceiling, One part of the kaleidoscope. Glitter.
Soft footsteps. Some humming is heard. A gun-shot.

MAMA   Who is it?

PAPA *(lifts his head up to listen)* Must be hard working in the dark.

MAMA   How do you know?

PAPA   I have worked for an insurance company.

MAMA   I hope you haven't told anybody.

PAPA   Don't nag.

MAMA   You nerd.

In front of their window soldiers are marching by, 'left, right, left, right'. They have virtual-reality helmets on their heads. The phone rings.

PAPA   It's for you. *(lifts his old index-finger and grins.)*

MAMA   I don't care. I've only been in town for a few years.

PAPA   We have a lot in common, babe.

In front of their window more cyber-soldiers are passing, they are spinning huge CD-s on their fingers and singing: 'Baby, baby' – zombie-euphoria.

MAMA   It's time you got up.

PAPA   We've had a long struggle.

MAMA   Do you remember?

PAPA   I've learnt to shit on my own doorstep.

MAMA *(points to the other room)* Should we do something with
    him?

PAPA   Let's wrap him up and put him on the table.

2. In The Other Room. *(Kaleidoscope-segment) Cobwebs, tulle.*

GiRL	I could go home, if you prefer.
GRANDSoN	We'll bang on the wall a bit. There, how about that?
GiRL	Its significance is only educational.
GRANDSoN	It's our home isn't it?!
GiRL	Good dog, good dog…
GRANDSoN	I won't forget.

3. In The Room.
The kaleidoscope keeps turning, as long as there is someone to turn it. Blood is trickling down the wall

MAMA	You call this fun!
PAPA	It's only a game.
MAMA	I don't see why you make allowances.
PAPA	This guy was in his prime.
MAMA	I don't know, I've only been here a few years.
PAPA	It's late.

4. Around the Rooms.
The one who has blood trickling on him speaks.

THE WRAPPeD UP GUY He didn't tell me how he made his living. And I believed him. I must go to the bathroom. I don't understand why it's wrong to ask somebody what their work is? What did he say? Ah, doesn't matter. Who gets this? I did enjoy life; I have to remember that. Why shouldn't I remember?

5. On The Street.
Glass tubes; in them white mice are running around. Sometimes a lamp flares up. In some places the street lighting is lousy.

POLICE CHIEF You're beautiful. There's no-one more beautiful than you. Do you want to come with me somewhere tonight?

BIMBO   Don't worry, I do fancy you.

POLiCE CHIEF Do you have a weapon?

6. In The Room.

TV NEWSCASTER Dear Viewers! Yesterday another murder was
committed. The culprits are unknown, they've been unknown for
years. I don't know what to say, they've got it down to a fine art. I
know we're all guilty, but I also know that it's only a calculation. I
suggest you keep away from the cellar. And keep your eyes open.
The police are powerless. Buy some explosives. And as I said, be
careful.

PAPA   That was a bit too much.

MAMA   Why are you talking in such large denominations?

PAPA   Same risk, same gain.

7. In The Other Room.

GRANDSoN   You're crazy! You had a job! What will happen
now? What will be your alibi? You have simply too much money.
We don't live in a place where you could keep it secret.

GiRL   There's two of us. *(points to a huge poster)* Your
friends?

GRANDSoN   We just eat together.

GiRL   I adore you.

8. In The Bar. *(The name of the bar: 'The Artist')*
At the tables only Salvador Dalis sit.

POLiCE CHIEF You use masses of eye make-up. Will you come
home with me?

BIMBO   You know what I'd like from you?

POLiCE CHIEF Eye make-up?

BIMBO   No. Oxygen.

POLiCE CHIEF Oxygen. How much is that? Cash is a big event,
you know! It has to be done with a bang.

BIMBO   I usually do it in the dark.

POLiCE CHIEF Unbelievable.

BIMBO   Would you like to see some fireworks?

POLiCE CHIEF A partner is always handy.

BIMBO   Alright. Let's go.

POLiCE CHIEF We could go. Then we'll see.

BIMBO   Careful! The lamp.

9. In The Room.

In front of the window, children are passing. They are making a racket. Flickers of the fireworks are seen. A dragon is flying around. Voices. Another gun-shot.

MAMA *(bald and hunchback)* Do you have a better idea?

PAPA   Do you trust me?

MAMA   I'll go and bat my eyelids outside. *(she starts leaving)* Hey, and do you trust me?

She laughs and goes out.

PAPA   Smart woman. *(looks at the second corpse)* Hey, listen to me!

Mama comes back.

10. In The Other Room.

GiRL   Smart man.

GRANDSoN He must have been in his prime.

GiRL   Just mathematics. *(kissing)* If your protégé was so co-operative, he could have told you where he kept his money.

GRANDSoN Don't worry. It'll be there. *(kissing)* I wonder how different we are.

GiRL   What do you think?

GRANDSoN   I guarantee. But you know how I hate you wearing white socks?

GiRL   You should be so lucky.

11. Around The Rooms.

THE SECoND Ah, doesn't matter, I'm not worried. I could thank them for covering for me. Poor things, they're right. Not to boast, but practice makes perfect. Anyway, life is full of these home truths, travel, time, cast of characters. Fear works wonders. So much for hope. It's only an after-effect. One day everything changes. I shall research a family of rats. Shall I introduce my-self? It's night. I can't play my music. That's the minimum. If you feel like it, call me up.
(he distributes business cards among the audience. Then touches his bloody wound)
Out of the blue. Is this why I studied law?

12. The Police Chief's Flat.
Frog-collection.

BIMBO *(looking at a yellowing photograph)* 'I request the lady solicitor to come and see me'. That was his perversion.

POLiCE CHIEF I should lose 30 kilos.

BIMBO   Nice of you to thank me.

POLiCE CHIEF The way they stood there next to each other, I would even have kicked a nun out of the police station.

BIMBO   She could have said: fuck yourself.

POLiCE CHIEF Shall we have a Johnnie Walker?

BIMBO   That's my organisation.
(She opens her coat and produces a bottle of Johnnie Walker.)

POLiCE CHIEF So, *you're* paying for this.

BIMBO *(shows the yellow photograph)* Solicitor, yesterday, it was.

POLiCE CHIEF *(looks at the photograph, scared)* Of course, nuns don't swear.

BIMBO   What's wrong with you?

POLiCE CHIEF I always see the victim in front of me, when I'm investigating a murder.

BIMBO *(snatches the photo)* Another drink?

POLiCE CHIEF And always after their deaths.

BIMBO   You sure, you see them dead?

POLiCE CHIEF What could be wrong with me?

BIMBO   Get lost.

The TV Newscaster enters. A gunshot.

13. In The Other Room. *Echo*

GiRL   Where the hell are we?

GRANDSoN My father adores the land. Which one, in your opinion?

GiRL   Your father is a legend.

GRANDSoN My home.

GiRL   How old are you?

GRANDSoN You can't say it doesn't stand up.
(love-making) You can't say it doesn't stand up.

GiRL   How old are you?

GRANDSoN My home.

GiRL   Your father is a legend.

GRANDSoN My father adores the land. Which one, in your opinion?

GiRL   Where the hell are we?

14. In The Room

MAMA   Don't talk about it any more.

PAPA   I'm not an angel. Was I ever one?
(In front of their window an angel flutters past, followed by a falling dragon.)

MAMA   What do you think of my proposal?

PAPA   I'll do it. With one condition. That we don't lie to each other any more.

MAMA You don't have to give it back.

PAPA   Are you worried?

MAMA People don't dare come near me.

PAPA   Don't you even trust yourself?

MAMA I'm off.

PAPA   What do you think we should do with him?

MAMA They haven't been the issue for a long time.

(She looks at the second corpse.)

15. Around The Rooms.
A column of smoke.

THE WRAPPeD UP GUY Could I do something to speed up the action? I could sit down between them for instance. If I had a crystal ball, I could be in a glittering state. What for? The trouble is I'm not on speaking terms with them. You see, they don't understand me. Because I'm an emergency measure, I think. Why don't they understand me? Who understands it?

THE SECoND Another dimension.

THE WRAPPeD UP GUY *(frightened)* You and I?

THE SECoND They shot me, because I was searching for my wife's lover. Even though the young ones were keeping an eye out for me. They shot me. Despite me being a lawyer. You know how it is.

THE WRAPPeD UP GUY *(even more frightened)* Did you never cheat on your wife?

THE SECoND I was with a chick yesterday. And you?

THE WRAPPeD UP GUY I was a lodger. I knew nothing. Now, I'm beginning to understand.

16. On The Street.

Green light with red dots. Bimbo hobbles on; she is beaten up.
Tattoo on her face. Mama is sitting brooding. A soldier supports his
injured comrade.

MAMA   Couldn't you close the door?

BIMBO   That's why the wardrobe fell on me.

MAMA   Maybe you should put your records in alphabetical
order. Are you in a bad mood?

BIMBO   Should I have said: 'thank you'?

MAMA   What's this?

BIMBO   It's money.

MAMA   Why did they stick it on you?

BIMBO   It isn't stuck, it's tattooed.

MAMA   Do you know 'The Artist'?

BIMBO   They didn't do it there, though I'm an 'it' girl. I'm
sick of it, I have to say.

MAMA   Why don't you leave? Find yourself a partner.

BIMBO   They just shot him.

MAMA   People are ever so kind.

BIMBO   You're an eternal optimist.

A small kid is skipping in front of them, he has a radio in his hand,
and he is listening to 'Ave Maria'.

17. *The Police Chief walks out of the Police Chief's Flat and walks*
into The Room.

POLiCE CHIEF Good Grief! Hello!

THE SECoND Hello!

THE WRAPPeD UP GUY Hello!

POLiCE CHIEF This is not the real me, you see. Fair enough, I am
an average guy, but I don't want to deceive you. You too…? Tell
me, are there no ladies here?

THE WRAPPeD UP GUY You can't do it here.

POLiCE CHIEF Don't be silly.

THE SECoND Don't ever get married. Watch out instead.

POLiCE CHIEF I haven't got enough. You're wasting your time.

THE WRAPPeD UP GUY Not any more.

THE SECoND For a while still.

POLiCE CHIEF You serious that here you can't…? I feel gutted. Shame because I want to look good. I'm sorry. You really are dead?
(The Second shakes his hand, congratulating him)
You really are dead? I'm sorry. Shame because I want to look good. I feel gutted. You serious that here you can't…?

THE SECoND For a while still.

THE WRAPPeD UP GUY Not any more.

POLiCE CHIEF You're wasting your time. I haven't got enough.

THE SECoND Watch out instead. Don't ever get married.

POLiCE CHIEF Don't be silly.

THE WRAPPeD UP GUY You can't do it here.

POLiCE CHIEF Tell me, are there no ladies here? You too…? Fair enough, I'm an average guy, but I don't want to deceive you. This is not the real me, you see.

THE WRAPPeD UP GUY Hello!

THE SECoND Hello!

POLiCE CHIEF Hello! Good Grief!

18. In The Other Room. *Milk-pouring.*

GRANDSoN Should we make it public?

GiRL Hello! Do you know me? I am the…

(Grandson covers the girl's mouth. Wrapped up and Second wave to him, Police Chief nods.)

GRANDSoN You're the arrow looking for the target.
(An angel looks through the window, takes aim and hits the girl in the back.)

GiRL Where did you get this?

GRANDSoN *(holds money in his hand)* Business is business.

GiRL   So he had it. Which one was it? Never mind. See
    you!

She leaves.

GRANDSoN   See you!

19. In The Room. *Ventilator. (We must not forget that the
kaleidoscope keeps turning.)*

MAMA   That's what they did. Here today, gone tomorrow.
PAPA   I could bash their faces in. Taking me for a ride. By
    the way, I think I'll make a chicken soup.
    *(In front of the window an angel flies past with a chicken spiked
    on an arrow.)*
MAMA   Come along.
PAPA   You look wonderful.
BIMBO   Thanks.
MAMA   What's your name?
BIMBO   I work at Directory Enquiries. I never get jokes.
    Nothing personal.
PAPA   If they touch you again we'll bash their faces in. By
    the way, I know a better tattoo parlour.
BIMBO   How old are you two?
MAMA   That doesn't matter, but we're cool.
PAPA   Could I be alone with her?

Mama leaves.

PAPA   I'll make some chicken soup.
BIMBO   I feel something.
PAPA   I used to work for an insurance company, now my
    son works there.
BIMBO   Was it worthwhile?
PAPA   Too many dead.

BIMBO	A dark one just shot My Guy.
PAPA	Who?
BIMBO	The dark TV Newscaster.
PAPA	The dark one?
BIMBO	You fancy her, don't you?
PAPA	I know her.
BIMBO	How well?
PAPA	That well. My son's lover. She was. Until she found another one. *(he shows a photograph.)*
BIMBO	Adam and Eve, or what?
PAPA	Even stake, even gain. Want some food?

20. On The Street.

Mama suddenly notices the Girl, who pretends to hide in a shop-window. She pretends to look at herself. In one window she sees Mama. Reflections. And soldiers everywhere.

GiRL	Money isn't fame.
MAMA	You took us for a ride.
GiRL	Like he took you.
MAMA	Money isn't travel.
GiRL	Why can't we be the winners for once?
MAMA	You're too young for it.
GiRL	If we gave the money back, could we do it?
MAMA	I'm not paying any more.
GiRL	Money isn't blackmail. That's why you didn't answer the phone?
MAMA	I'm not touching you.
GiRL	Can I go with you?
MAMA	I won't tell you anything. Pay attention!

21. Around the Rooms.

Rattle of gun-fire, pink pus is spraying the walls.

THE WRAPPeD UP GUY One has to face the expected storm. I should have thought of this before. Before all the punctuation. Circus. I knew I shouldn't have poached a wife from her lover... Am I well? Am I getting excited? Well, did she want me? I couldn't even organise a bloody pillow-fight. How was I to know not to become a lodger? Anyway, I thought I was a member of the family. Seriously. I only asked what his work was? There's no water left to wash with.

THE SeCOND I could have called someone.

22. TV. *(No perspective)*

TV NEWSCASTER Dear viewers! On account of technical problems I was unable to tell you that another murder was committed a week ago, actually it was two weeks ago. The police are really completely powerless in these cases. We have to live with it. As ye sow, so shall ye reap... I'm giving a dinner party tonight, if anybody feels like coming, do pop along.
(a gun-shot. Death)
So if anybody feels like coming, do pop along.

23. In The Room.

PAPA   Don't cry, Miss. Nobody's looking for you. Don't pack my clothes. Tell you what we'll do, from now on I'll present the news.

BIMBO   Can I be your agent?

PAPA   Follow me in half an hour.

He leaves. Outside he nearly collides with a bloody soldier.

24. In The Other Room.
The Grandson wakes up, he is naked.

GRANDSoN   I want to know, if I'm well? The secret of success is to go to bed early. I'm glad I can see myself. Should I pay more attention to myself? I want to see father! I should make a habit of going earlier. I miss that girl.

25. Around The Rooms.
The Police Chief wakes up. He is naked (except he has his uniform tattooed on his hairy body). Frog croaking.

POLiCE CHIEF I haven't seen myself for ages. They woke me up.
THE WRAPPeD UP GUY I'd make a speech tonight. The woman.
THE SECoND You'd have a great night.
THE WRAPPeD UP GUY Lucky, I'm so well.
POLiCE CHIEF Lucky, I can't interfere.
THE WRAPPeD UP GUY Lucky, you haven't done it so far.
POLiCE CHIEF Why do they hate me?
THE WRAPPeD UP GUY You've been hand-painted.
POLiCE CHIEF Don't be daft! I passed the medical.
THE WRAPPeD UP GUY Me too, king of King-kong.
THE SECoND Who cares?
POLiCE CHIEF Let's be friends.
THE SECoND OK. But don't come any closer. You can see that we don't play with each other either.
THE WRAPPeD UP GUY Should we talk about money?
(The TV Newscaster enters.)
THE SECoND How about you?
THE WRAPPeD UP GUY *(whispering)* You?

26. TV *(without perspective). Papa on television*

PAPA The good old days. I liked them. I only got five minutes.
ANDY WARHOL Not the fifteen?
PAPA No worries. Imagine, I've been in your town for some years, actually we have been, the family. I was a tough lad at your age. I wonder if I'm past it? Come on! Someone challenge

me! I'm still alive!!! You people must understand. I could be your
father. Someone challenge me!!! I'm waiting.

GRANDSoN It's all finished. I'm finished.

He starts walking off.

27. On The Street. *(in front of their house.)*
The boy steps over bloody soldiers.

GRANDSoN Where can he be? I have to pull myself together. It
can't go on like this. I should do my own thing, not his. It's cold.
Time's passing and I still can't find myself. How can I go on
sleeping? I'd rather die. Nature nurtures me in vain, oh never
mind. I can't say that my body is at the peak of science, anyway I
inherited it. The smoke makes such strange shapes. I'd like a
loudspeaker… for my name day. My father promised me easy
dreams, but he never made it. I hate this cellar. I hate this cellar.
My father didn't make it and he promised me easy dreams. It's
just not possible.

28. Around The Rooms.

TV NEWSCASTER I could hardly find you guys.

POLiCE CHIEF Were you looking for me?

TV NEWSCASTER Presenting, that's what motivated me.

POLiCE CHIEF The TV became you.

TV NEWSCASTER Became?

POLiCE CHIEF Becomes.

THE WRAPPeD UP GUY Should I put a gingerbread heart over
your stripes?

POLiCE CHIEF Who mentioned stripes?

TV NEWSCASTER Do you know who killed you?

POLiCE CHIEF Me, a revolver.

TV NEWSCASTER I killed you, but that doesn't matter. I'm
talking about them.

THE WRAPPeD UP GUY Revolver, too.

THE SECoND Me too.

TV NEWSCASTER You didn't see his face?

THE SECoND Not even his hand.

THE WRAPPeD UP GUY We didn't see anything.

TV NEWSCASTER Don't you ever look at what's in front of you, gentlemen?
(The Second gives her a huge slap on her face, the TV Newscaster smiles at the Wrapped Up, he cowers, the Second does not react.)

POLiCE CHIEF You do know each other? *(silence)* Why so formal?

29. On The Street.
White mice. They are running around in transparent tubes (the ones who don't, are finished). Papa is sauntering back from the TV Studios. Smell of smoke without smoke.

PAPA I'm an honest man. I changed to be changed. But I can't get near to the truth. I was sent to conquer sin by heaven or realism, but I'm still guilty. After all this, I don't know whether I should be instinctive or logical. Every man feels injustice. How far can we go? Reality is different from enthusiasm. It's unreachable. A separate world. Different customs. He doesn't want to know me. I've no choice. I'll have my revenge. The gloves are off! Between ourselves, I tell you, I want to kill my son. I wonder why that chick didn't follow me, half an hour later?

30. In The Room.
Bimbo's face is painted red all over.

BIMBO You're a real hero!

PAPA I like your tattoo.

BIMBO You little golden shaft!

PAPA *(with great tenderness)* I've no more shafting left.

BIMBO You were beautiful!

PAPA Shall I be a wolf?

BIMBO You were making history!

PAPA	Shall I be black?
BIMBO	Shall I take you behind the wings?
PAPA	I don't want to shrink.
BIMBO	I'm really glad I came.
PAPA	Good luck.

31. In The Bar *('The Artist'.)*

One Dali is cleaning windows. It turns black. He gets upset.

GiRL	So he's your second husband.
MAMA	I'm ashamed to say, but he is. I should have driven more carefully.
GiRL	He was the first?
MAMA	He died.
GiRL	Was he covered?
MAMA	He was held.
GiRL	Do you love him?
MAMA	Me?
GiRL	The corpses?
MAMA	We can't be responsible for them. We know.
GiRL	Plan?
MAMA	Action?
GiRL	We have that too.
MAMA	At our expense.
GiRL	Don't split hairs.
MAMA	If they check your account, you've had it. You have too much money and no alibi.
GiRL	Quiet.
MAMA	Do you love him?
GiRL	I do.
MAMA	The main thing is – who is driving!
GiRL	Only, I don't want to risk his life.
MAMA	That truth will smack you in the face.
GiRL	What? Let's go.

MAMA   Let's go.

GiRL   Have you noticed that people avoid you?

MAMA   Have you noticed that nowadays we can't see through the window? Careful you'll knock your arrow.

GiRL   Pardon?

32/a Around the Rooms.

TV NEWSCASTER This will be a time-consuming game. Shall I make a start?

32/b Around the Rooms.

THE SECoND I didn't get a moment's peace from him.

THE WRAPPeD UP GUY Gone, gone, gone.

THE SECoND What's wrong? She was a wife, for sure.

THE WRAPPeD UP GUY Yes.

THE SECoND Couldn't be locked up.

THE WRAPPeD UP GUY Really?

THE SECoND I was tough, nothing. I was soft, nothing. What?

THE WRAPPeD UP GUY Nothing.

THE SECoND We have to learn whose side we're on! 'Don't get mixed up in my affairs!', she said. What affairs? 'What affairs could she have that she had to hide from me?', I asked. Nothing. I checked it out – There! She betrayed me. No sweat, I hear she betrayed her lover too. Imagine! Once she came home covered in blood. I didn't say anything.

THE WRAPPeD UP GUY You still have to communicate. Well, I wouldn't be a cop.

THE SECoND Do you have a profession?

THE WRAPPeD UP GUY I don't.

THE SECoND That's a relief. I'm a lawyer.

32/a

TV NEWSCASTER And I'm a TV series.

32/b

THE SECoND *(looking at the Police Chief's clothes)* Look, paint is
   dripping from him.
THE WRAPPeD UP GUY I told you it's hand-made.

33. In The Room.

BIMBO	Who else lives in this flat?
PAPA	Rats.
BIMBO	I thought you collected frogs.
PAPA	No, bodies.
BIMBO	Why do you live in a cellar?
PAPA	Self-defence.

(A soldier lies on his stomach by the window, he aims his cyber-gun at them. They look at him undisturbed.)

BIMBO	Nuclear?
PAPA	We don't take anything seriously.
BIMBO	You like finishing things off?
PAPA	Are you that clever?
BIMBO	It's not a problem.

*The soldier suddenly turns over on his back, shoots in the air and
runs away.*

BIMBO	What was that?
PAPA	Habit.

A dead frog falls on the stage.

INTERLUDE I.

Light. Everything seems white. Andy Warhol and Salvador Dali shake hands. Everybody claps. On every level and on every side. Suddenly seriousness. There is just tension, no sound. Suddenly everybody claps again. The kaleidoscope is whirling round crazily.

34. In The Room.

BIMBO   I want to eat some frogs' legs.

She leaves. Papa watches without reaction.

35. On The Street. *Moon.*

MAMA   Let's put my money back in the bank account. It's our business. We have to deal with it. We have to stay.
(The Girl gives the money back.)

The sun rises.

36. On The Street.

GRANDSoN   I have to find him.
'I spread my gaze around
I cheat on people who help me.
Boars and rams everywhere.
Mercury.
I don't even know if it's today or tomorrow.
Good Heavens, the Sun is made of the Moon?'
GiRL   They'll kill your father.

The Grandson runs away, The Girl starts crying; she collapses. Red light goes round and round.

GiRL   I've gone lame. Was it now or the last time? Rainbow!!! Where are you? Why wasn't I born lame?

37. An Outside space.
Children with colourful paper whirls, romping.

THE SECoND Shadow flutter, I was betrayed.

THE WRAPPeD UP GUY Stream cry, he betrayed me.

POLiCE CHIEF Women cause creative deaths, creaaaative, creaative, creaaaaative deaaaths.

TV NEWSCASTER Wouldn't it be better if I sang a bitter-sweet song?

THE SeCOND There's no separate female part in it.

THE WRAPPeD UP GUY I could re-write the lyrics.
     (The Second howls, the TV Newscaster laughs loudly.)

POLiCE CHIEF I'm going to look for that chick. I am not dead!!
     (The dead dragon chuckles.)

THE SECoND *(to the TV Newscaster)* If I could, I'd kill you.

38. The Police Chief's Flat.
The frogs are squashed behind glass.

BIMBO   Who did this? Yesterday was still before. I'd like to cry but I don't dare. I was a little girl. My mother used to make me look lovely, little skirt, little ribbon in my hair, girly-scent, and my father slapped her face. 'I wanted a boy! Understand?', he said and put me in a bow-tie. They teased me, they laughed at me, they laughed, they knocked me over... a girl in a bow-tie. I couldn't take it off. It was sewn on. No man could ever give me a love bite. That's why I always wear a scarf. Look, the stitches. Last year my father died. I could finally take my whip off. I did. Then my mother died. I had to work. Went to the Directory Enquiries. I don't understand Hitler. This is the year of the midges. You can't exterminate them. Why do you think I am whispering? When did you come in?

39. In The Room.
Mama is playing on a wind instrument.

PAPA   He hasn't killed for some time. I should visit him.
Do make me a hearty welcome. I don't like repeating my
sentences. *(tears the phone out of its socket)* Not everything is
without a reason. There are no relations. When I die, I'd like to
leave nothing behind except a small explanatory dictionary... and
my son, the murderer.

(A soldier hangs himself.)

MAMA   I'll light a candle.

*The angel flies in, gives a candle to Mama, who places it in front of
the window. The Grandson enters.*

GRANDSoN   Grandfather! Don't kill daddy.

He runs out.

40/a In The Room.
The Girl enters.

GiRL   Where is he?
MAMA   I should hang out the washing.
PAPA   It stinks in here.

*Howling; nobody takes any notice. They look around. Silence. The
Grandson enters. His hand is bloody.*

MAMA   There is no more must.
PAPA   The main thing is to make sense of our sentences.
GiRL   I want to find my sense.
PAPA   I wasn't talking nonsense!

40/b As Above.

TV NEWSCASTER Shall I break the news?
THE SECoND Not for them.

40/c. The Police Chief's Flat.

BIMBO *(having created a dress from the dead frogs)* I'll tell you a story.

40/d As Above.

POLiCE CHIEF If I find you, you can tell me everything.

40/b
The TV Newscaster puts her finger to her lips, indicating "shh".

THE SECoND What's the truth?

40/a

GRANDSoN I just wanted to know what the truth is?

INTERLUDE II.
White light. The soldiers of the past march on to the stage in their pearly clothes covered in sequins with transparent guns. They blow kisses to the lips of the characters, who lived through the tragedy; pink liquid runs down their lips. They cart them off in supermarket trolleys. A little boy enters in bloody, rose-pink and white clothes and sings a nice song (Ave Maria).

The kaleidoscope does not function without lights.

ACT TWO

During the following scenes the characters enter, say their speeches with the wise cynicism of real tragedies, then leave.

1.

PAPA Oh, my soul is yearning for a woman! Here comes one on cue. *(coughs)* Old hag. How old can she be? About 50 but she looks 70. Just like me. Except I'm really 70. Plus one. I'll accost her, no matter how nerve… I get a breakdown, I'll get a grip on myself. *(seriously)* I keep quarrelling with my son. I suspect him. Madam, may I?

MAMA Dear, oh dear. You came just at the right moment. I've just lost my first husband. I was driving. Dear, oh dear. I wanted to be James Dean, but he snuffed it. My soul's crying out for solace. Marry me, please! Don't leave a rickety woman to her sad fate.

PAPA Your words reach my heart. I've made up my mind. I'll marry you.

MAMA Let's walk to the altar right now. I'm so *(coughs)* happy. Here come two soldiers just on cue, let's ask them to be witnesses.

PAPA Young men! A word!

The soldiers shoot into the ground in front of the feet of Mama and Papa, then without laughing walk off.

MAMA Oh, their bullets won't spoil our spirits, will they my dear?

PAPA For sure, for sure. *(coughs)* We'll tie the knot even without witnesses, we were made for each other.

MAMA That's right, my love. *(coughs)* Let's go, the sun is slowly setting, there's nothing to dry our tears.

They smile then they go off suddenly.

2.

THE SECoND I can't take any more why do you torture me? at work I do nothing but think of you I can't be a useful member of society the world can't progress I was forty minutes late again today because all night I was waiting for you oh where can you be? I asked myself why do you torture my soul so full of sadness? why am I such a monumental touchstone for *you* which you wish to smash with the little hammer with the mother-of-pearl handle that I bought for you full-price for your twenty-eighth birthday which was on the second of May you see, I never forget it oh why do you want to break my macho heart, so full of love?

TV NEWSCASTER Where are you going, darling?

THE SECoND I have to get a drink of water.

He returns.

THE SECoND Tell me why? Why do you narrow my world with you?

TV NEWSCASTER I feel I'm widening your world just with that. My thinking is the opposite of yours... on certain things. Let me be free! I'm a little bird. With shiny feathers, a fine tiny beak, charming feet, which you can't put a ring on. I feel like a prisoner in a cage. You're wrong to incarcerate me against my will. I'm not hurting you. I only exist, which makes me happy, which makes you happy, you must be happy. Don't torture me. It's you I love. It's truly you I love. The rest is only insignificance, or silence.

THE SECoND You don't understand. Your freedom is yours, I won't take it. Your slender legs, mmmm, can take you wherever you want to go. Enjoy yourself, live – but don't lie to me. I know the price of this pearl necklace , a boa like this, and your black hair-dye... I know how you got into television, how you became a TV Newscaster. I know all that, and it hurts me beyond belief. Why did you lie to me?

TV NEWSCASTER How do you know all this?

THE SECoND From your drawers.

TV NEWSCASTER You snooped in my ebony drawers?

THE SECoND I wasn't snooping, just looking. I was looking for my earring.

TV NEWSCASTER So you snooped.

THE SECoND I didn't.

TV NEWSCASTER You'll regret arguing with me like this.

THE SECoND I don't want to be against you, I want to be with you. You're my life! Oh, kiss me! Enough quarrelling, throw yourself into my arms!

TV NEWSCASTER You did hurt me but I can't resist your kisses, I'm coming, into your arms!

THE SECoND I hurt you? What are you saying, my love? Why do you leave me in despair? Do you want to fight? You want me to treat you, as you treat me?

TV NEWSCASTER *(sobbing)* Oh, never again, never, this was the last time, I promise. But now I have to dash, I have to present the 7 o'clock news.

THE SECoND What are you saying?

TV NEWSCASTER That there are more and more murders. Public safety is in danger.

THE SECoND But to *me,* what are you saying to me?

TV NEWSCASTER I love you, I have to rush.

THE SECoND One more kiss!

TV NEWSCASTER Yes, a kiss!

Kissing. Soldiers march through the scene, followed by children.

3.

GiRL	What's wrong with you?
GRANDSoN	I'm a depressive.
GiRL	So you stare at the four walls?
GRANDSoN	*Four* walls?! No, leave me alone!
GiRL	I can help you.
GRANDSoN	Nobody can *(he inhales)* help me.*(exhales.)*
GiRL	If you don't let anyone, of course not. Relax!

GRANDSoN   There's no relaxation. It's not up to me. I'm an eternal prisoner. Nobody opens the mouth *(inhales)* of this sack. *(exhales.)*

GiRL   I could open it. Heaven sent me.

GRANDSoN *(doesn't draw breath)* Are you Jesus?

GiRL *(doesn't draw breath)* I'm a girl.

GRANDSoN   Beautiful girl.

GiRL *(rejoices)* At last you looked up. Do you know something that solves everything?

GRANDSoN   Drinking, smoking, gorging. Am I right?

GiRL   I was thinking of love.

GRANDSoN *(rejoices)* That spoils everything.

GiRL   You were born of love.

GRANDSoN   No! Of hatred! My mother abandoned me when I was two! That's it.

GiRL   How terrible.

GRANDSoN   My father's mad. He's on disability pay, but before, he used to work for a cool insurance company.

GiRL *(they are both quiet)* And what's he doing now?

GRANDSoN   He makes kaleidoscopes, he looks at the patterns, or stares into space.

GiRL *(they are both quiet)* Often the mad ones are the sanest.

GRANDSoN   Maybe. As long as they don't come near us.

GiRL   I know a great place! It isn't far from here. There's a quiet river. It's a wonderful place, come!

GRANDSoN   I hate nature!

GiRL   Come on.

(The boy removes the arrow from the girl's back, and spikes something on it from the litter in the street)
Go on, leave it, that's nothing to do with us.

4. The Cellar. *A bell ringing.*

MAMA   Good-day.

THE WRAPPeD UP GUY   Good-day. I came about the advert, about the room. How much is it?

MAMA   The room, let's see… ten thousand plus bills, we'll settle them somehow. Upstairs lives my husband's son, and his son. Sometimes his girlfriend sleeps here too. We live in-between. So the room is downstairs. You want to see it?

THE WRAPPeD UP GUY Ah, now…

MAMA   By the way, second husband. The first… when he was born…

THE WRAPPeD UP GUY Upstairs? But this is a cellar?

MAMA   So what? Why can't there be levels in a cellar? Hell has different levels, so has this. We live in a six-floor house, only they built it backwards. What an idea! No levels in a cellar!? My God! Why don't you grant mankind some mutual understanding? Oh, tell me why?

THE WRAPPeD UP GUY Yes, you're right, I agree with you completely, don't be cross.

A woman sneaks out of the house through some hidden opening. The Wrapped Up Guy notices her.

MAMA   Of course I'm not cross! Have you decided, if you want to look at it?

THE WRAPPeD UP GUY Ah, no… I'll take it. Can I move in tomorrow?

MAMA   If it suits you… come along. I'll make some chicken soup. *(They both look up to the sky)* What were you looking at?

THE WRAPPED UP GUY *Mee*?… I don't know. And you?

MAMA   I was expecting an angel with a chicken skewered on an arrow.

THE WRAPPeD UP GUY Good bye then. See you tomorrow.

MAMA   Bye. Tomorrow.

5. In The Street.
The Wrapped Up Guy runs after the TV Newscaster. After three circles he reaches her.

THE WRAPPeD UP GUY I saw you.

TV NEWSCASTER So, what do you want? Do you want something from me? Good job you don't want me to sleep with you in front of everyone.

THE WRAPPeD UP GUY I really fancy you.

TV NEWSCASTER You oaf! Don't you have any finesse? Why say it like that? Straight out! Why don't you romance me? Even the animals do a mating dance! No hand-kissing, no pearl necklace, what do you imagine!

THE WRAPPeD UP GUY Yes, you're right, I agree with you completely, don't be cross.

TV NEWSCASTER Of course I'm not cross. What do you imagine!

WRAPPeD UP GUY The truth is – I imagine you and me together.

TV NEWSCASTER No way, what do you imagine!

THE WRAPPeD UP GUY Don't say! I really fancy you. Anyway why shouldn't I say it straight out, it's no secret. If I did romance you, you'd know it... now you know it, if I said nothing you'd still know it, don't play games with me please, because it's not possible with me. Shall we go?
(They take each other's arms and walk round three times; towards the end they slow down)
What's wrong with you?

TV NEWSCASTER Why, what's up with you?

THE WRAPPeD UP GUY I haven't moved in here yet, but I only remembered it at the last round.

TV NEWSCASTER As for me, my lover lives here.

THE WRAPPeD UP GUY Really? Don't say!

TV NEWSCASTER So this location is not ideal for satisfaction.

THE WRAPPeD UP GUY Not for our satisfaction.
(Silence.)

TV NEWSCASTER Where are you going to live?

THE WRAPPeD UP GUY In some basement, there are three rooms and underneath those, I don't know.

TV NEWSCASTER Maybe we will... you know?

THE WRAPPeD UP GUY ... do you need him...?

TV NEWSCASTER ... of course, maybe we'll do it just above you. I'll make sure I go underneath, then I can feel I'm with you.

THE WRAPPeD UP GUY Shall we develop the ideology?

TV NEWSCASTER Let's go to your place.

THE WRAPPeD UP GUY My parents wouldn't survive the blow.

TV NEWSCASTER What blow?

THE WRAPPeD UP GUY Me with an older woman... Let's go to your place.

TV NEWSCASTER What's the time?

THE WRAPPeD UP GUY It's past seven.

TV NEWSCASTER Oh, my husband's at home.

THE WRAPPeD UP GUY Oh, you don't say!

TV NEWSCASTER *(produces a yellowing photo)* A modern woman must have a husband, *(shows then throws away photo)* and a lover as well...

THE WRAPPeD UP GUY Are you turning me down?

TV NEWSCASTER Don't interrupt... *and* a pupil... I know a fashionable hotel nearby, let's take aim there, come on!

THE WRAPPeD UP GUY But I'm not fashionable, they just kicked me out of university.

TV NEWSCASTER What were you reading?

THE WRAPPeD UP GUY Aesthetic techniques.

TV NEWSCASTER How exciting! My skin is glowing, my God, it's bursting, my lips are chafing, and oh, they're red, like two cherries without worms... come, be the worm, you're an oasis, because I'm just a dry, but hot, oh so hot desert... for god's sake, what am I talking about and to whom? *(she yawns)* my knickers are all wet. Don't torment me, that's enough! I'll take the risk, for sure. Amazing! Like it wasn't me speaking. Who is panting? Do you hear it?

THE WRAPPeD UP GUY I've lost my voice.

6.

GRANDSoN   I live here. What are you doing here?

THE SECoND My wife's unfaithful. I'm checking up on her.

GiRL   You sensed it?

THE SECoND I did.

GRANDSoN   You want to catch her at it?

THE SECoND Come again?

GRANDSoN   Come again, we'll help you. Here, let's shake on it.

GiRL   Bloody hell.

THE SECoND You don't want to help, or what are you swearing for?

GiRL   I'm game for anything.

7. Love-making, before it and after it as well

THE WRAPPeD UP GUY I don't get it. These people are rich. My electric switch is broken. They've been so nice to me so far, and now they refuse to mend it.

TV NEWSCASTER Oh, my little baby.

THE WRAPPeD UP GUY I'm serious, my little witch's brew. I'm sorry. Do I detect some hostility?

TV NEWSCASTER You imagine things.

THE WRAPPeD UP GUY Don't beat about the bush. What do they live on, I asked myself the other day. But then I found the answer! I stole upstairs and I was gob-smacked. Everything glittering! And the drawers full of money. Just like that, lying about, loose.

TV NEWSCASTER You are snooping around too.

THE WRAPPeD UP GUY No. Your lover doesn't work at the insurance company, like you said. Where's all that money from? And how did you pay for these golden underpants you bought me?

TV NEWSCASTER Don't use such rude words, is that how I trained you?

THE WRAPPeD UP GUY I don't want to be a criminal's pupil. So I'm asking you again: where is all that money from?

TV NEWSCASTER Some people save money and don't spend it. Each to their own.

THE WRAPPeD UP GUY But what's the cost of this?

TV NEWSCASTER What, the money? Don't be silly, the money has its own cost.

THE WRAPPeD UP GUY Don't mess with me. What is he? Or rather who is he?

TV NEWSCASTER Alright I'll tell you.

THE WRAPPeD UP GUY I can't wait.

TV NEWSCASTER He is: Dr. Black Tulip. The Tulip doctor.

THE WRAPPeD UP GUY Pardon?

TV NEWSCASTER Satisfied?

THE WRAPPeD UP GUY It's always so good with you. Something else – your husband saw me yesterday in front of the house.

TV NEWSCASTER Let's start again.

8. *Bimbo walks across the space, picks up a yellowing photograph from the ground, keeps looking behind her. The Second comes in from the right (from Bimbo's point of view). The Wrapped Up from the left.*

POLiCE CHIEF My God! How did you get here? You're dead!

A nun passes by.

9. *The computer noises of the first act start up again.*

THE WRAPPeD UP GUY I'll go in and ask him what he does?

TV NEWSCASTER In my opinion, it's a waste of time.

THE WRAPPeD UP GUY You've got new nail varnish? It's from him, isn't it?

TV NEWSCASTER No, from my husband.

THE WRAPPeD UP GUY I'll go in.

TV NEWSCASTER Don't be stubborn! How did I train you?

THE WRAPPeD UP GUY OK. I won't go in. Only in an emergency.

TV NEWSCASTER That's right.

(A cyber soldier runs across the stage.)

THE WRAPPeD UP GUY What was that?

10. *Mama, Papa and the Grandson are standing by the wall with hanging heads. The sounds get louder and louder. Suddenly silence. The Girl runs in. She stops, smiles.*

GiRL   War's broken out.

Sounds are loud again.

11.

THE WRAPPeD UP GUY Then I'll go in now.

The TV Newscaster smiles. The Wrapped Up Guy disappears into the unknown middle room. Everybody watches him go. The kaleidoscope starts turning.

-3.

PAPA	It's late.
MAMA	I don't know. I've only been here a few years.
PAPA	This guy was in his prime.
MAMA	I don't see why you make allowances.
PAPA	It's only a game.
MAMA	You call this fun!

Blood is trickling down the wall.

-2.

GRANDSoN	I won't forget.
GiRL	Good dog, good dog.
GRANDSoN	It is our home, isn't it?
GiRL	It's only educational.
GRANDSoN	We'll bang on the wall a bit. There, how about that?
GiRL	I could go home if you prefer.

-1.

PAPA	Let's wrap him up and put him on the table.
MAMA	*(points to the other room)* Should we do something with him?
PAPA	I've learnt to shit on my own doorstep.
MAMA	Do you remember?
PAPA	We've had a long struggle.
MAMA	It's time you got up.

In front of their window, cyber soldiers are passing. They are spinning huge CD-s on their fingers and singing: 'Baby, baby' – zombie-euphoria.

PAPA	We have a lot in common, babe.
MAMA	I don't care. I've only been in town for a few years.
	(Papa lifts his old index finger and grins.)
PAPA	It's for you.

The phone (disconnected) rings. In front of their window, soldiers are marching by, 'left, right, left, right'. They have virtual-reality helmets on their heads.

MAMA	You nerd.
PAPA	Don't nag.
MAMA	I hope you haven't told anybody.
PAPA	I have worked for an insurance company.
MAMA	How do you know?
PAPA	*(lifts his hand up to listen)* Must be hard working in the dark.
MAMA	Who is it?

A gunshot. Some humming is heard. Soft footsteps.
The end.

Vera Filo

Whether I try myself here and there, or other people try me now and then, it is to this day – I swear, that is 25 years, (Vera you're getting old – a secret). Do I see things or hear them, or just feel them under my skin or above? It's not at all clear, as my life isn't crystallising either...

I have to work on that – I am not alone in this, am I?

'The worried one
         makes dates
                 Later
                       the future'

I'm quoting myself there but 'it's all the same' whatever you fancy, such is your sensitivity.

Anyway, after directing Genet, Durenmatt, Picasso and Cocteau adaptations, I didn't become modest and took up residency inside myself. After I served up *Tulip Doctor* on the table at the Playwrights and Theatre Practitioners, I wrote *Keresok (Searchers)* which was published in the magazine *Szinhaz (Theatre)* and puzzled over at the Inter-Play in Berlin. The play *Allj-ulve (Stand-sitting)* was published in the periodical *Theleme. Egyenesen (Straight)* won the playwriting competiton of the Miskolc Theatre. Currently I am preparing for the Orkeny Istvan Playwrighting Scholarship by fighting a word and image battle – the working title is *Ariel (Smokestripe)*... my God, why don't you sigh this way a little?

I also draw comic-strips. I write poetry too. These are somehow more accepted by the people here. I don't know why.

The Tender Mercies

The Tender Mercies was written in March 1993. In August that year it was produced by Mania Productions at the Edinburgh Festival Fringe. It won a Fringe First. It was subsequently produced by other small-scale theatre companies in the UK and Germany. Actors and directors who helped me unravel and develop this piece have my deep gratitude.

In 1993 Yugoslav civil war was a definite media hit. I followed the press reports obsessively, trying to understand the nature of events in my former homeland. The hitherto fictional abyss of hatred now had to be accepted as fact. Our former life was pronounced an error and a lie. It was no longer relevant which came first: the words of hatred or the fact itself. The syntax of fear and destruction had stepped off the gutter press page, rolled off the fervent lips and solidified into events of the most gruesome vulgarity. Respectable words like 'civilisation', 'history' and 'culture' were being used daily in support of the orgiastic taking of life.

And there was nothing new about this kind of madness. The world had seen it all before, and mesmerised as it is by human capacity for evil, may do so again.

Sladjana Vujovic

'What marks Vujovic's drama out is the fascinating way it demonstrates how language can become an effective weapon of war.'

(The Guardian)

'This new play in English, by the Montenegrin writer Sladjana Vujovic, must rank as one of the most powerful in recent years.'

(The Scotsman)

'The language buzzes with colloquial fizz as Montenegrin playwright Sladjana Vujovic mimes the mundaneness of evil with playful wit and measured menace.' (The Sunday Times)

'A gripping play.' (What's On)

The Tender Mercies

by Sladjana Vujovic

First produced by Mania Productions at the 1993 Edinburgh Fringe
Festival at the Roman Eagle Lodge Theatre where it was awarded a
Fringe First.
Directed by Sladjana Vujovic

CHARACTERS

Zig	Rob Horton
Rose	Sladjana Vujovic
Alex	Richard Keeling

ACT ONE

*A bare room, except for some boxes and broken furniture. Alex, a
gaunt man in his thirties, is sitting on the floor, propped against one
of the boxes. He looks exhausted. His body is loose, his eyes have a
vacant expression. His clothes are torn and full of blood stains. The
door opens and in walks Zig, a younger man whose clothes are old
but tidy and who looks altogether healthier than Alex.
Zig observes Alex who does not acknowledge his presence in any
way; Zig walks around him.*

ZIG   Marvellous lunch! A very lovely lunch indeed. They
have an excellent chef here - a true artist! *(no reply from Alex)*
I see. No appreciation of finer things what so-bloody-ever! And to
think that *you* could be enjoying them too!
*(Alex remains silent. Zig stops his elaborate movement and sits
close to Alex)*
Well... Well – to that end – let us continue.
*(no sign of life comes from Alex. Zig moves his head quite close to
Alex's and shouts in his ear)*
I said – let's continue! Now!
*(Alex's head jerks to the other side. Zig gets up and walks away in
the same elaborate, school-masterly manner)*

I see... I'll have to do everything myself again, will I? Eh? Eh?
(fractional pause) Who are you?

ALEX   I am a piece of shit.

ZIG   Right. *(he waits for more)*
Is that it? Is that all? All I'm going to get out of you today?
(fractional pause) You seem to have retreated into reticence. It'll
do you no good, you know.

ALEX   I'm a piece of shit. I'm...

ZIG   I'm not deaf. Explain!

ALEX *(with effort, as if trying to remember his lines)* Errr... As soon
as... errr... no sooner was I born... than my mother... gasped... in
shock and despair... It was obvious even then... even to her...

ZIG   Yes, yes, go on, for God's sake, give it some life!

ALEX   ... obvious even to her, that I was sub-human.

ZIG   She knew it instantly? Amazing woman.

ALEX   She was in no doubt.

ZIG   I'd say you paid no heed to her fears. From what I
see I'd say you insisted on growing up. Isn't that a fact?

ALEX   It is. I didn't know what I was doing.

ZIG   Furthermore, I'd say you tend to justify your villainy
with nothing more than a few dubious excuses. A sign of
weakness of character, if ever I saw one. 'Excuse me, I didn't
know what I was doing!' Do you believe that can make up for all
the evil you've done?

ALEX   I should have been put down immediately.

ZIG   Would I be right in saying that this is not what
happened?

ALEX   Yes.

ZIG   You continued living, against all reason!

ALEX   I'm sorry.

ZIG   You had a childhood, boyhood, adulthood, life,
didn't you?

ALEX   I'm sorry.

ZIG   You're a rebellious man.

ALEX   I'm sorry.

ZIG But, the time of reckoning has come! Tell us about your childhood.

ALEX As a child, I was dull-witted. There was nothing to commend me.

ZIG No redeeming features?

ALEX None.

ZIG You're a bad job. I hope you don't expect mercy. Describe yourself, back then.

ALEX Errr... I was... I was... thick... and...

ZIG Unable to use the little potential you had?

ALEX I had no potential. I'm confident in saying my potential was zero.

ZIG *(shouts)* Do you have to sit on the floor like that? No respect? No attention to detail? No manners? Sit up! Up! Up! Up! *(Alex lifts himself off the floor with considerable effort)* Who do you think you are?

ALEX I'm a piece of shit.

ZIG Good! Tell us about your descent into this state of utter crap! How did you become a piece of shit? Did it require effort? Or was it a spontaneous transformation? Tell us facts. Don't hide anything.

ALEX I... I was... I'm...

ZIG You're an inarticulate pile of dung! Brief school memories!

ALEX I... At school, I was despised. Teachers, rightly, tried to beat some sense into me, but I did not understand...

ZIG You refused to understand!

ALEX I refused to understand. Other children spat at me. It was a part of...

ZIG Was that deserved, in your opinion?

ALEX It was richly deserved. I could not serve except as a live spitting target.

ZIG Are you claiming you made a contribution to society?

ALEX Only by accident.

ZIG Not by your own design?

ALEX	Not at all.
ZIG	And your school friends?
ALEX	Some of them became men of distinction.
ZIG	Unlike you?
ALEX	Unlike me.
ZIG	When did you become aware of all this?

ALEX   I became enlightened only recently. About a year ago, when I was introduced to the teachings of The Noble Commandant.

ZIG   And what a happy privilege that was!

ALEX   It was, without a doubt, the happiest day of my life.

ZIG   Have you ever asked yourself why this sort of enlightenment didn't descend on you previously? Why was that? Were you unable to concentrate? Unwilling to exercise reason? Given to non-spiritual pursuits? Tell us. You've got nothing to lose.

ALEX   My thinking was evil, primitive and sadly misguided.

ZIG   How did you deduce that?

ALEX   I was... am... an inferior life form and, as such an affront to all humanity. This makes me poisonous, therefore evil.

ZIG   Good. Now, would you care to apportion responsibility for all this? Where are we to seek the socio-psychological causes of your calamity? The whys and wherefores?
(Alex seems bewildered by Zig's verbosity)
In other words - who's to blame?

ALEX   I am.

ZIG   Only you? Give it some thought. Try again.

ALEX   Errr... the responsibility also lies with my parents.

ZIG   There! Give credit where credit's due. Don't take away what is the most precious privilege of any creature that ever reared an offspring – *guilt*. Tell us about your parents.

ALEX   Which one first?

ZIG   Use your own judgement. And don't ask questions!

ALEX   My father was a police officer...

ZIG   No! That won't do at all.

ALEX   My father was... a... *(remembers)* a pathetic servant of the most perverse regime known to man.

ZIG   Much better. What else?

ALEX   He was a perpetrator of hideous acts against his innocent fellow men, as well as his close family. Even in his old age, he remains quite bestial.

ZIG   What a character! However, your description is somewhat impersonal. Somewhat – distanced, I'd say. I detect no emotional involvement, no sentimental attachment, not to mention any kind of moral or intellectual stand. *(Alex is puzzled)* Well, it's your father we're talking about, for God's sake!

ALEX   He was... is... a piece of shit?

ZIG   Continue.

ALEX   He's a stinking rat.

ZIG   Elaborate.

ALEX   He's a treacherous animal, with a small, twisted mind.

ZIG   Mind is too strong a word! More!

ALEX   He's corrupt and immoral...

ZIG   Too general!

ALEX   He's...

ZIG   Not enough!

ALEX   He's a stinking, treacherous rat... he's an immoral piece of shit... he's a twisted...

ZIG   You seem to believe that repeating a certain number of nouns, or adjectives, or both – will do the job. You think declaiming a set piece will pass for the real thing? What about feeling? *(hits Alex across the chest. He doubles up in pain)* You hope no-one will notice? You trust it'll all go down really well?

ALEX   Nnno...

(Pause. Zig paces up and down the room.)

ZIG   O.K. I'll try once again. Why is he a piece of shit? *(Alex is silent. Zig observes him for a second, then speaks)* You refuse to employ logic. *(shouts)* Logic and methodical stubbornness, together with the relentless pursuit of precision, are the only tools that can help you grasp the truth. But, no! You refuse! You won't budge!

ALEX   I'm no good at logic.

ZIG   Well, it is of little avail repeating that your dear
parent is a piece of excrement, if you're unaware of how and why
you arrived at that particular conclusion.

ALEX   I know.

ZIG   Well, then, what is he?

ALEX   He's... he's a...

ZIG *(gesticulating wildly)* He's a product! A product! A product of
the unsavoury, venomous, malevolent system he served. He had
gone down and down and down, and right through the digestive
tract of that system, and emerged as – a piece of shit, as you're so
fond of calling him. Easy!

ALEX   My father is a product... product of...

ZIG   You don't want to learn it word by word! You have
to master the art of reasoning!

ALEX   My father...

ZIG   Now! To your mother!

ALEX   My mother was...

ZIG   Isn't she still alive?

ALEX   I don't know.

ZIG   You assume she's dead? Your own mum?

ALEX   She was alive when I got here.

ZIG   When you were given the privilege...

ALEX   When I was offered the kindness and excellent
hospitality of our hosts...

ZIG   Your mother!

ALEX   My mother was... is!... is known for... for her...
indecency, vulgarity, treachery... low cunning...

ZIG   Same again. No conviction. Zero persuasion, a
hundred percent miss.

ALEX   She is...

ZIG   A slag?

ALEX   A slag.

ZIG   A woman of easy virtue?

ALEX   Right.

ZIG	Say it!
ALEX	My mother is a woman of easy virtue.
ZIG	A tart. A harlot. A Gorgon.
ALEX	A tart. A har...
ZIG	What sort of a tart?
ALEX	A right revolting old tart?
ZIG	That's nothing. Too tame. It's no good.
ALEX	My mother is a revolting, old, stinking tart. She's... an immoral pig. She talks like a pig. She eats like a pig. She behaves like a pig. She's a primitive life form, she's a piece of shit, she's a filthy scrubber, she's a diseased slut, she's...
ZIG	Does she love you?
ALEX	No.
ZIG	Small wonder. *(brief pause)* What about your sister? I believe you have a sister? *(Alex is silent)* Did you fuck your sister? *(no reply)* Well, it's a plausible question, with all the goings-on in your family! It has to be investigated, and if you're found guilty, added to your catalogue of sins. Well, did you? *(Alex remains silent)* Did you? Did you fuck her? Did you give her one on a more or less regular basis? Did you dip it in there? Did you keep it in the family? How often? For how long? Where? When? How? Was she any good? I bet she was keen. I bet she fucking loved it. Tell me. Did you screw the bitch? *(brief pause)* Or shall I report your silence on this matter?
ALEX	Yes.
ZIG	Yes, what?
ALEX	I did.
ZIG	You did what?
ALEX	I did fuck my sister.
ZIG	I thought so! My God! Why?
ALEX	I'm depraved.
ZIG	She must be depraved, too.

ALEX   She is. We are all immoral and de...

ZIG   Describe her cunt.

ALEX   She's got a hungry, putrefying cunt, the size of a bucket.

ZIG   With teeth?

ALEX   With teeth.

ZIG *(laughs)* Dear, oh, dear! A huge, hungry, putrefying cunt – I'm trying to picture it... Bottomless pit, no doubt.

ALEX   Horrid diseases ravage her body, but it's a small punishment for the wickedness she does.

ZIG   Right! Anyone else fucked her?

ALEX   The whole town.

ZIG   Something will have to be done about your family. We can't have the whole town in jeopardy. No, sir! We've left it too long. Don't you agree?

ALEX   I do.

ZIG *(emphasising each word)* Do you understand, are you able to conceive, do you begin to grasp the enormity of your guilt?

ALEX   Yes.

ZIG   Is there any hope for you?

ALEX   I trust in the kindness of the Good Commandant.

ZIG *(shouts)* Our Most Noble Commandant!

ALEX *(also shouts)* Our Most Noble Commandant!

ZIG *(shouts)* Who we what?

ALEX *(also shouts)* Who we love!

ZIG *(shouts)* And what?

ALEX *(also shouts)* And admire!

ZIG *(quietly)* Why is that?

ALEX   Because he's... errr... he's...

ZIG   What's he done for you?

ALEX   He's been... like... he's a real...

ZIG *(shouts)* What's he done for you, you piece of shit?

ALEX   I've never met him.

ZIG *(exploding with anger)* You've never met God either, yet will you deny him?

ALEX   No.

ZIG *(trying to calm down)* Let's try again. What's he done for you? What has he shown you?

ALEX *(remembering his lines)* He's shown me what a real father could be like.

ZIG   How did he do that?

ALEX   Calmly, methodically, like a true democrat and a beautiful human being.

ZIG   Alas, words are inadequate!

ALEX   Indeed. Like a real human being... like a real... like...

ZIG   The air, the air... What's the air like?

ALEX *(remembers)* The air is sweet with his moral greatness. As we breathe, we think of his glorious deeds.

ZIG   And they are?

ALEX   He created a monumental and historical movement which delighted the masses, giving them strength and new direction.

ZIG   Is that all?

ALEX   He gave us new ethics and philosophy, energy and inspiration.

ZIG   And what are we going to do with all these?

ALEX   Build a better world.

ZIG   When?

ALEX   As soon as The Noble Commandant's army exterminates the enemy, which is us, and cleanses the land of all scum.

ZIG   Exactly! Now, are you able to give us a short history of our Noble Commandant's struggle?

ALEX   Nothing would give me more pleasure.

ZIG   And his glorious army?

ALEX   Our Noble Commandant's glorious army is made up of decent and honest, ordinary men and women, who rose as one, to correct the historical mistakes and injustices perpetrated against them for centuries. Under the wise leadership of The Noble Commandant, they undertook to drive out the enemy, who'd lived by their side for so long, pretending to be friends.

ZIG   Who's the enemy?

ALEX   My own people – we wanted their land, their houses and their superior civilisation. We robbed honest civilians, raped decent women and killed innocent children.

ZIG   You thought you could go on like that forever.

ALEX   Our Noble Commandant, who was but an ordinary, honest, hard working civilian, without pretensions, without academic conceit, without any education, with not a trace of desire for personal power, full of love for his fellow men, just an ordinary guy, a truck driver, in fact...

ZIG   You can leave that out!

ALEX   ... without any desire for personal elevation, rose to battle, driven only by his natural love of justice and peace...

ZIG   What did he have?

ALEX   He had a vision.

ZIG   What vision?

ALEX   A vision of a small and harmonious state, where his people could live next to their own kin, safe in the knowledge that there is no vermin about. No strangers, no foreigners, no perverts, no sodomites, no artists, no two-faced intellectuals. Where the religion will be the same for everyone, and the politics the same for everyone, and everyone will be rewarded according to their loyalty. A vision so unique and original that most of the world cannot understand its greatness. Its greatness... errr...

ZIG   Even though...

ALEX   Even though he's the only true democrat on the whole planet.

ZIG   Can they do anything to stop him?

ALEX   No-one can. He will triumph, because we've got more evil here than anywhere else in the whole world.

ZIG *(shouts)* Do you support him in his efforts?

ALEX   With all my heart.

ZIG   How much?

ALEX   So much, I'd like to be by his side always, to love him and to watch over him. So much, I'd deem my own life worthless, if I hadn't been given the privilege of studying his work and admiring it. So much, I believe that in this world, corrupted by lies, only his immortal words impart the truth. And I shall always love the truth, unless otherwise ordered.

ZIG   Do you mean that?

ALEX   I do.

ZIG   How can I believe you?

ALEX   I wish to spend the rest of my life spreading his creed far and wide.

ZIG   You're not just saying that? To save your skin?

ALEX   I would deem my own life worthless, if I hadn't been given...

ZIG   Is this your deep conviction?

ALEX   It is.

ZIG   You're not likely to change your mind?

ALEX   Never!

ZIG   I wish you were telling the truth.

ALEX   I shall always tell the truth, unless otherwise...

ZIG   I don't know... I just don't know!... All this effort! I mean, we've been doing this for a year now – day in and day out! And for what! Could it be that I've been wasting my time? *(stares at Alex ominously)* You sound somewhat detached. A trifle non-committal. You simply don't convince!... Do you?

Blackout.

SCENE 2

Zig is sitting at a table. There's a tray with a plate of food and a bottle of wine before him. Rose, a woman in her thirties, dressed in a tacky uniform, stands behind him. She has a pistol and a knife tucked in her belt. Zig eats hurriedly. His table manners are quite revolting. There is another chair a little distance from his table. A terrifying scream is heard from not far away, perhaps the next room. Rose doesn't seem to notice, Zig starts munching even more enthusiastically.

ROSE   Pretty hungry, aren't you?

ZIG *(jumps to attention, saluting her)* Yes, sir!
   (Another scream.)

ROSE   Like the food?

ZIG *(jumps again, saluting)* Yes, sir!

ROSE *(laughs)* Stop jumping up and down! Eat! Enjoy it!

ZIG *(sits down)* Thank you, sir.

ROSE   I'm glad you like it. I know how it is.
   (Pause. Another scream)
   I've been there myself, you know.

ZIG   Have you, sir?

ROSE   Oh, yes. That's why I'm here.

ZIG   Oh.

ROSE   Do you have any pride?

ZIG   No, sir.

ROSE   Ever had any?

ZIG   I'm afraid not, sir.

ROSE   I suppose it would get in the way, in your position.

ZIG   You're very understanding, sir.

ROSE   It's because I've been there myself, you see. Three
   months I was there! Every day they brought people to gape at me.

ZIG   Sorry to hear that, sir.

ROSE   They'd bring them in to see a woman soldier.

ZIG   That must have been awful, sir.

ROSE   Oh, no! It was alright. You won't believe this, but
   they didn't even rape me.

ZIG   Thank God for that, sir.

ROSE   A real enemy. Beat me every afternoon, same time,
   right on the dot. I'm talking proper, quality torture. I was treated
   like an equal, like a human fucking being, it was a pleasant
   surprise.

ZIG   War can be an awful thing, sir.

ROSE   Ah! But it's necessary and it shouldn't be
   questioned. That's the thing to bear in mind. It has to be done,
   now and then, to put things right. Throughout history, have you
   noticed that?

ZIG   Yes, yes... I think I have, sir...

ROSE   I'll be frank with you – I read history books a lot. They're a sort of consolation to me. You have to read between the lines, of course. But, when all's said and done, they make you realise that history has to be endured.

ZIG   I couldn't agree more, sir. I'm an avid reader myself...

ROSE   Every morning I was supposed to say: 'Can I, please, have a piece of bread?', and if I got it – 'I humbly thank you'. But, you know me, I just wouldn't. So, they beat me in the morning, too.

ZIG   I'm glad to see you've put it all behind you, sir.

ROSE   I don't need to tell you, it was a waste of their bloody time – they didn't get anything out of me.

ZIG   No, sir, I wouldn't expect them to.

ROSE   There was just one tiny confession to make. I made it. Unfortunately.

ZIG   That was... unfortunate, sir.

ROSE *(stares at Zig intensely, infuriated)* Do you have to agree with everything I say?

ZIG   Yes... yes, I believe I do... sir!

ROSE   Well it gets on my bloody nerves, I can tell you that much! I mean, don't you feel that there's so much we could discuss? Debate, exchange views and all that... I find there's very little real communication here.

ZIG   I'd be more than... That is more than kind, sir, I'm flattered and I...

ROSE *(but she's already lost interest)* They caught me up north – we were trying to cleanse the area, and I got a bullet through the leg. My fault entirely, I just had to be first in the firing-line, so, it served me right, I suppose.

ZIG   Oh no, you didn't deserve that, sir.

ROSE   Oh, yes, I did! I was miles ahead! Got carried away. Got lost, would you believe it! Had to hide in a shed behind this house and wait for our lads to appear 'cos your people were quite close, only I didn't know how close. Anyway, I had to be really quiet.

ZIG   I suppose you must remember quite a few such things, sir? Suffering and fear and, er, not that you would feel any fear normally, I mean...

ROSE   Suddenly, the door opens and a little girl is standing there. Out of the blue! I am staring at her, she's staring at me, lovely big eyes, like a picture... And then she screams. It was all the blood on my leg, I suppose. I tell you – I didn't know what to do! She went on forever – you know what kids are like. Anyway, I grabbed her, cut her throat, but – too late! The whole bloody family rushed in – what can you do – had to shoot them, and that was it. Your guys were just round the corner. Wasted a few of them, too, before they got to me... I fully expected them to kill me there and then.

ZIG   Well, they wouldn't shoot a lady, sir...

ROSE   Do you know what that is? That is unfair. To spare me on the basis of gender or sex, or whatever you want to call it, that is upsetting, to say the least! Did I spare the little girl? No! Always hated that. It's so humiliating. Anyway, it turned out they were going to exchange me in the end... *(pause)* That was the confession, you see. *(she laughs. Zig attempts to laugh, rather unsuccessfully)* You didn't get it, did you? There was nothing to confess, it was there, for all to see!

ZIG   Yes, I suppose it was, sir...

ROSE   Mind you, I did reveal one secret. It became something of a controversial issue – the rusty knives theory. I'm sure you've heard about it.

ZIG   I'm afraid I haven't, sir.

ROSE   Where do you live, for Christ's sake? It was in all the papers! Oh, do eat, don't pay any attention to me. I seem to be overwhelmed by memories today. And when it comes to memories I do tend to be a bit sentimental. Please don't interrupt your dinner on my account.

ZIG   Thank you, sir.

ROSE   In short, we found that, if you stab a person with a rusty object, later on, when the body's decomposed, if there's ever an autopsy, that is, it seems like they died of tetanus! It was a simple, but a mind-blowing discovery. Nature's way of sorting things out. So, A – you save a bullet, and B – there can be no talk

of atrocities and all that, when they died a natural death in the
first place. Clever, don't you think?

ZIG   Very clever, sir.

ROSE   How's the food?

ZIG   Errr... as good as always, sir. Excellent.

ROSE   There's nothing like small pleasures. They smooth
out all the creases of life.

ZIG   That's so... so... poetic, sir.

ROSE   Thank you. We need a bit of poetry. A bit of calm
and beauty in the middle of all this.

ZIG   Its power is underestimated, sir.

ROSE   All the things you have to do, it's all routine, if you
ask me. I'm not complaining, you understand, but sometimes... I
wonder about, well, the whole thing, really...

ZIG   Quite, it does make you wonder...

ROSE   I mean, why me? I'm not cut out for all that.

ZIG   It can't be easy for a lady... I mean, for you, sir...

ROSE   It's because I used to work in an office, I suppose.
People can't see beyond their prejudices, it's sad, but that's how it
is.

ZIG   That's so true, sir.

ROSE   Do you know what I had to do today? The whole
morning?

ZIG   No, sir.

ROSE   Filing!! *(waits for his reaction – he acts amazement)*
I'm not kidding. That's what I had to do. And, in case you were
wondering, it's not the first time either.

ZIG   Oh, sir, that's so... well...

ROSE   I mean, you have to bury them in some order, you
have to have some paperwork, I understand that. I'm a reasonable
person and a very accommodating one. I understand the wider
implications of our situation. All these international groups and
inspections and God knows what – you never know where they'll
poke their noses next. And journalists – you can't shoot them...
all... I suppose. But, such attention to detail, when there's so
much mess! It's like – head there, leg missing, tits cut off, eyes

gouged, no names... I mean, I have a brain, and I want to use it,
I'm not a bloody clerk!

ZIG *(apprehensively)* Nnno, no, no, sir.

ROSE *(quite worked up now, walks up and down angrily)* Your side
print awful lies about us in their so-called press, don't they?

ZIG   Yes, sir.

ROSE   Vicious lies!

ZIG   Incredible lies, sir.

ROSE   Atrocities and all that!

ZIG   What can I say, sir?

ROSE   They say we roast little children. Can you believe
that?

ZIG   No, sir, no, I can't.

ROSE   Slit their little throats, stick apples in their mouths,
and roast the little buggers! Do you think there's anything in that?

ZIG   No, sir, of course not.

ROSE   How do you know?

ZIG   You wouldn't do that, sir.

ROSE   Oh, yeah? How's the meat? Young and tender?
(Pause. She observes Zig, then bursts out laughing)
Good one, eh? I'm just teasing, killing time! You know my wacky
sense of humour.

ZIG   Sense of humour, very important to keep it, sir.

ROSE   Is that your opinion on the subject of humour?

ZIG   Well, only... metaphorically speaking, sir, I didn't
mean anyth-

ROSE   You are not here to laugh.

ZIG   No, sir.

ROSE   You are here to perform an honourable task.

ZIG   I'm honoured, sir.

ROSE   You're here to show us that change and progress are
possible.

ZIG   I have changed, sir. I know I have, sir!

ROSE   I know, I know. What about your friend, though?
Are you working on him?

ZIG   I am – he's making progress, sir.

ROSE   I hope so.

ZIG   He's a little slow, sir.

ROSE   Is he? Or is it you?

ZIG   It isn't me, sir.

ROSE   It's him, then. He's no good.

ZIG   He's proud, sir.

ROSE   That's the problem with all of you. Pride. You
haven't got any! You haven't got any bloody guts, either! You
haven't got any dignity or anything, have you? And yet, you
believe you can win!

ZIG   Oh no, sir. We don't. We don't want to win. We're
not soldiers, sir.

ROSE   You're nothing – don't you forget that now.

ZIG   Most probably, sir... It's just that... We don't hate
anybody, sir.

ROSE   Why not?

ZIG   I don't know, sir.

ROSE   You've got an identity problem, that's why.
(observes him absent-mindedly) I've been meaning to tell you –
you remind me of somebody.

ZIG   Do I, sir?

ROSE   Yes... He was one of yours. You remind me of a lot
of people. You all seem the same after a while. It's the identity
problem. *(pause)* I've been here too long, you see. They think I
haven't quite recovered yet.

ZIG   Maybe it's... for the best, sir. *(pause.)*

ROSE   Any word from your parents?

ZIG *(puzzled)* Errr... nnno... no, sir.

ROSE   Are they well?

ZIG   I... don't know, sir. I hope so.

ROSE   So do I. So do I. How come you're so ignorant?

ZIG *(attempts a smile)* I've been here for a long time, too... sir.

ROSE   But, not for much longer, eh? Hopefully.

ZIG   I hope not, sir.

ROSE   Would you like me to visit them? I mean, your
parents. Your mum and dad.

ZIG   That's too kind. No, thank you, sir.

ROSE   Give them your regards?

ZIG   No, thank you so much, sir.

ROSE   Tell them you're doing well?

ZIG   Oh, no, really, sir...

ROSE   Why not? Don't you love them? Don't you recall
their faces in your solitude? Don't you think they've had enough
of sitting all alone by the fire every night? That's providing they
have any fire. Providing they're even still alive. All alone, night
after night, thinking of you, their son. Don't you think you owe
them something? A little affection, by proxy, if not in person?
You surprise me.

ZIG   They live very far, sir. Very tricky getting there. It's
very kind of you, but...

ROSE   Well, forget it, I was only trying to help, to show
compassion, but you make it clear it's none of my business.
(pause. She looks at him mischievously) Shall I tell you a secret? I
think I know where they live. A cherry tree in the garden. Right?
(Zig is quiet. She grins. He seems hypnotised by her gaze)
Near the railway station?

ZIG *(quietly)* Yes... sir.

ROSE   Don't ask me how I know. I won't tell you that.
That's between me and your dear parents. I will say this – it's a
small world.

ZIG   Indeed... sir.

ROSE   I mean, we might have never met, at all. You and I.
Not to talk about me and your dear parents. And yet, I'm sure we
did meet, a thousand times, before. So close, and yet so far. So far
apart, and yet as close as hell. Never to be separated! Do you ever
think about that?

ZIG *(still mesmerised)* Oh, yes, I do, sir. It's a very interesting
philosophical problem... *(pause.)*

ROSE   Can I trust you?

ZIG   You certainly can, sir.

ROSE   Honest?

ZIG	Honest, sir.
ROSE	Even though we did away with so many of your own people? Your own kin, so to speak. You don't mind that?
ZIG	Not in the least, sir.
ROSE	You're a remarkable man. You wouldn't be lying?
ZIG	Me? No, sir!
ROSE	You must be a man of principle.
ZIG	Thank you, sir.
ROSE	That's why we've been kind to you. Me and the Commandant.
ZIG	I'm grateful, sir.
ROSE	We want to give you a chance.
ZIG	I humbly thank you.
ROSE	It isn't something we do, normally.
ZIG	I know, sir. It's a great honour.
ROSE	It's a considerable risk. I hope you won't let us down.
ZIG	I won't, sir.
ROSE	You're not like your friend.
ZIG	No, sir.
ROSE	He's a disappointment. Not a man of your moral fibre.
ZIG	He isn't, sir.
ROSE	He won't see sense.
ZIG	You're so right, sir.
ROSE	Maybe it's down to you.
ZIG	I swear it isn't, sir.
ROSE	Maybe you reckon you're buying time. Not doing your best. Not even trying.
ZIG	I am, sir.
ROSE	I wonder.
ZIG	I'll do better. I'm nearly there.
ROSE	I bet you think they'll come and free you any day now.
ZIG	Never crossed my mind, sir.
ROSE	You don't even hope?

ROSE *(shouts)* There's only a few bastards left out there, anyway!
Shooting the guns you sold them!

ZIG   We... we... we didn't sell guns, sir.

ROSE   What then?

ZIG   S... soap powder.

ROSE   Very few. None really! Our lads have seen to that.
Our lads don't rest.

ZIG   Excellent soldiers, sir.

ROSE   Well said!

ZIG   Very fine soldiers, sir!

ROSE   What worries me, is that I can't join them. Because
you've decided to take your time. Because you won't get on with
it. Because you refuse to do your bit. Now, is that fair?

ZIG   It isn't, sir.

ROSE   However, we made a deal, and we'll stick by it.

ZIG   I'm grateful, sir. I appreciate that.

ROSE   Only a couple of days more.

ZIG   Quite... sir.

ROSE   Are you looking forward to it?

ZIG   I can't wait, sir.

ROSE   We'll see. I'm not going to pre-judge you.

ZIG   Thank you, sir.

ROSE   We try to be fair.

ZIG   Very fair, sir.

ROSE   We give everybody a chance.

ZIG   You do indeed, sir.

ROSE   We don't like messing about. With us, you know
exactly where you are. You're not required to think. You're
required to do. It's not difficult. It's easy. Do you get me? Do you
know what I'm talking about? *(pause)* Shall we have a game of
chess?

Blackout.

SCENE 3

Alex and Zig are busy marking the 'stage' area. Walking away from it to take yet another look, pushing the boxes around, putting them together to form a raised 'stage', and generally pottering around. Alex is very apathetic, while Zig seems excited and full of enthusiasm.

ZIG *(walking away from the 'stage' to take another look)* It isn't ideal, but it'll have to do.
(Zig regards the boxes. Alex sits down)
What you can't have, you can't have.
(no reply)
Right?
(Alex stares at the floor. He doesn't seem to hear)
Do you think this is really central?
(Alex looks at him with contempt)
What do you say? Central or not?

ALEX Central enough.

ZIG *(walks towards the boxes, and then back again)* The audience will be... here... I wonder if this is the right distance. *(no reply from Alex)* Oh, well, it's the best we can do.
(he walks up and down, sometimes stopping suddenly, as if lost in thought) I don't mind telling you, I'm rather nervous. I'm almost shaking... Funny... *(stops and looks at the boxes)* I'm not sure if that stage is really central. *(paces to both walls on either side of the boxes, counting the steps)* Seems all right. Best to be philosophical about it.
(Alex begins to look mildly amused)
Oh, well. Each life has its climax... When things reach that... that critical point. That's how it should be. And then, there's peace... hopefully... *(turns to Alex, obviously eager for communication)* Don't you agree?

ALEX   How can I help it?

ZIG   I'm not certain. I'm not certain and that's not at all like me. No, no, in fact, that's not quite right – it is like me to doubt – I mean, my God, with my intelligence, I'm always reassessing, endlessly, I never stop, but... that's beside the point... *(Alex begins to nod off)* There's no space for uncertainty here, it's

as simple as that, not now, this is it, no time for it, none at all.
(he paces up and down, getting quite worked up)
I'm simply at odds with everything. Is this the famous creative
process – my God – utter crisis... I'm not at all certain about that
last scene. It's potentially controversial. *(no reply. Alex seems
asleep)* You exasperate me! You brainless piece of shit! Tell me
what you think! *(Alex looks at him, irritated. Zig rushes around in
despair)* You can't tell me you're indifferent!
*(he rushes over to Alex, grabs him by the shoulders and shakes
him vigorously)* Don't you dare be indifferent!

ALEX   Alright. I'm not indifferent.

ZIG   You're not, hell!

*(Zig walks quickly, without direction, trying to calm down. He sits
on the boxes, near Alex.)*

ZIG   I need your help here. I need your full cooperation.

ALEX   I know.

ZIG   I can't do it on my bloody own. It won't work.

ALEX   Right.

ZIG   You hate me now, you doubt me ... I understand
that.

ALEX *(sarcasm)* Yeah?

ZIG   But, you must help.

ALEX   Right.

ZIG   This is all we're doing today.

ALEX   Is it?

ZIG   It is.

ALEX   What's this, a new game?

ZIG   I promise you, this is it.

ALEX   How come?

ZIG   We need to prepare. Mentally. Or just rest, if we
want to.

ALEX   What about... the routine?

ZIG   You might call it our day off. I requested it. I
requested it and it was granted.

ALEX   Good for you.

ZIG   I explained it would be good for the morale. Yours,
     of course.

ALEX   Whatever... it's good. *(he tries to lift himself off the
     floor.)*

ZIG   So, please, talk to me. *(Alex makes a few painful
     steps)* I mean, anything... just talk to me. Open up. We haven't
     talked in years. *(Alex does not respond)* Feel free to say anything.
     Get it out, you'll feel better. Criticise me!

ALEX   You're pulling my leg, right?

ZIG   I'm imploring you.

ALEX   What do you think I am, stupid?

ZIG   We need to clear things up. Clear our minds. We're
     off duty.

ALEX   So what?

ZIG   It's our last chance.

ALEX   The last joke.

ZIG   It isn't true. I disagree.

ALEX   You're full of crap!

ZIG   Things are not what they seem to be. *(pause)* There's
     a pattern here, a purpose. They wouldn't keep us here for ages and
     then kill us.

ALEX   Why not?

ZIG   You don't think logically, that's your problem. What
     would be the point?

ALEX   A bit of fun?

ZIG   No, it's all a part of something, a plan, you'll see.
     They want to make sure, that's all... Some sort of training, we'll
     know soon enough.

ALEX   Bollocks.

ZIG *(observes his left hand)* Look, I've cut my finger *(Alex pays no
     attention)* moving things around.

ALEX   Maybe it's all a part of that plan.

ZIG   You... you... I don't mind telling you – you've
     changed. You're not the person you used to be. You... you've
     grown old.

ALEX *(sarcasm)* No??

ZIG   Oh, yes. You look old. Very. *(Alex ignores him)* You've let yourself go.

ALEX   So sorry.

ZIG   You've lost all ambition. There's nothing you want to do. There's no hunger in you any more.

ALEX   Don't make me laugh!

ZIG   You actually want to die.

ALEX   I want to wring your neck!

ZIG   You've let your intellect go. It's the worst thing.

ALEX   What, like I don't read enough in here?

ZIG   I haven't let myself go.

ALEX   Jesus!

ZIG   It's the easiest thing to do. The easiest way, I assure you, is the way down.

ALEX   You ought to know.

ZIG   I still have my faculties intact. I believe they've actually improved, despite, or rather, because of adversity. I still have my looks. I still have my optimism.

ALEX   You still get three meals a day.

ZIG   Food is not the issue. I have an open mind, that's all. And flexibility. You lack both.

ALEX   *You* haven't changed.

ZIG *(false modesty)* I didn't say that. My role has changed, so...

ALEX   You've always been a cunt.

ZIG   I have adjusted. I didn't choose the circumstances, I simply adapted.

ALEX   One day...

ZIG   You detest it, I detest it, but it could have been worse.

ALEX   ... I'll wring your fucking neck.

ZIG   Well, why don't you keep that energy for the performance? Channel it into your delivery! It'll make the whole thing so much better. *(pause. They both stare at the floor)* I was surprised to find out how talented you are.

ALEX   I can't tell you what that means to me.

ZIG   I wonder if he'll come.

ALEX   I guess not.

ZIG   On the contrary. I'm convinced he'll make an appearance.

ALEX   Why is that?

ZIG   He'll want to see it for himself.

ALEX   You reckon he likes a laugh?

ZIG   The final decision will be his, after all.

ALEX   Who says he's here at all?

ZIG   Who says he isn't? He must be.

ALEX   Cunt!

ZIG   You don't believe in anything.

ALEX   So what?

ZIG   So, I have to believe for you, too... 'cos, we were friends once.

ALEX   What?

ZIG   I said we were friends.

ALEX   Not that again.

ZIG   You reject me. You despise me. But, I understand your suffering.

ALEX   You do what they tell you.

ZIG   They're not my masters. I play my own game.

ALEX   You've sold your little soul and for what?

ZIG   For you as much as for myself.

ALEX *(grabs Zig angrily)* You grass on me and then you go eat your fucking dinner! You eat your fucking dinner and you listen to them beat me! What did they promise you? Eh? You don't have to do this. I don't see anybody beat you!

ZIG *(clearly frightened)* I hurt for you, I bleed for you inside, all the time...

ALEX *(puts his arm around Zig's neck, squeezes)* What's the deal? There's got to be a deal. Talk to me. Open your fucking mouth. Go on, you can tell me, we're friends.

ZIG   I collapse inside when they beat you. I scream inside my head...

ALEX *(tightening his grip)* I could kill you. But, you aren't worth bothering with! *(pushes him away, Zig falls.)*

ZIG   I haven't let you down! You'll understand that, soon. You'll thank me. I'm the one who's fighting here! If I stop, maybe...

ALEX   Maybe what?

ZIG   You don't understand, you refuse to help me, you don't see I never rest, I never sleep, it's always with me, exploding inside my head! The thought of it, the idea that this is my life, only this and so weak...

ALEX   Shut up!

ZIG   Don't you see – there's this, just this flesh, and – nothing? I cannot imagine nothing. Can you? No-one can. It's not within our power. *(slight pause)* It keeps coming to me. I don't want it to, but it does, without mercy. I see a knife, not a real knife, more the idea of a knife. It slides into me, slowly, and I see it go right into my stomach, and it goes in and up and deep inside, just like that, no pain, just a trickle of blood. I see my whole body, it's solid, it feels substantial, but that trickle of blood is doing its job, and that's it, that's where nothing begins. I shout – no, it's a mistake, I say – it's only a small cut – what the hell, I've been hurt before, only a bit of blood; I try to cover it, but it's too late. All my guts burst out, gush out forever, like they're laughing at me, and I am small and empty. I try to stuff them back inside, but they're slippery, they're alive and no longer mine, I'm changing colour, I'm turning into nothing, nothing creeps all over me, it's like worms. I cry. *(he sobs)* I weep and wail like a slaughtered pig, I cry for my life, but it's no use...
(Pause. Zig is slumped on the floor, shaking uncontrollably.)

ALEX   Look...

ZIG *(trying to recover)* I can't help it.

ALEX   It's alright.

ZIG *(crawls towards Alex, distraught)* That moment... when you know you're dying... What do you think about then?

ALEX   I reckon you don't.

ZIG *(gets up)* I'm not gonna think about it any more!

ALEX   No use. Think about some bird if you've got to think.

ZIG	As of now!
ALEX	Good.
ZIG	It can't happen to us!
ALEX	Right.
ZIG	Say it.
ALEX	What?
ZIG	Say we're not gonna die.
ALEX	Jesus!
ZIG *(shouts)*	Say it!
ALEX	We're not gonna die.
ZIG	I depend on you.
ALEX	Leave it out.
ZIG	We're more than friends now. We're one body.
ALEX	You're out of your mind.
ZIG	You can't have forgotten.
ALEX	Don't remember a thing!
ZIG	We've been through thick and thin.
ALEX	We've been through shit.
ZIG	We had a life together.
ALEX	It never happened.
ZIG	You were the one who made it happen. *(pause.)*
ALEX	Sometimes I try to remember it.
ZIG	I haven't forgotten. I know I owe you everything.
ALEX	I remember it all.
ZIG	I owe you my first break.
ALEX	I try to hang on to it.
ZIG	The most exciting time of my life...
ALEX	Most of the time it isn't there.
ZIG	So rich in possibilities... full of poetry.
ALEX	The names get me. I can't remember them.
ZIG	I can. Oh, yes.
ALEX	I miss all that.
ZIG	You miss the action. You've always been the one for adventure.

ALEX	I didn't mind a bit of action.
ZIG	Not like me. I'm a thinker. Forever a melancholic.
ALEX	You're a cunt.
ZIG	I don't mind you saying that. I appreciate your honesty.
ALEX	The faces, yes. But the names – they drive me up the wall.
ZIG	Me, I remember everything.
ALEX	Do you?
ZIG	I'm more fond of some memories, than of others, of course.
ALEX	It was all crap, anyway.
ZIG	It was creative.
ALEX	It was like everything else.
ZIG	It was living by one's wits, never knowing what the next day may bring.
ALEX	You didn't do it for the derring-do.
ZIG	It was a new world.
ALEX	You did it for the dosh.
ZIG	I took the money. But, it was incidental. I liked the hazard – living on a knife's edge, walking on a tightrope...
ALEX	You were shitting yourself.
ZIG	It was a sort of courage. You were used to danger, you didn't respect life.
ALEX	I respected mine.
ZIG	I was gentle, unaccustomed to strife. I was an artist.
ALEX	You were a bum.
ZIG	In terms of material possessions, perhaps... I was down on my luck.
ALEX	You were down in the gutter, with all the other bums.
ZIG	Many people lost their jobs, all of a sudden.
ALEX	You never had one!
ZIG	I was unable to compromise. Integrity wouldn't allow it.

ALEX	It didn't stop you stealing.
ZIG	I wouldn't call it stealing. It was... liberating. It had a sort of... dignity.
ALEX	What, nicking and cheating and all that? Smuggling? Black market? Do me a favour.
ZIG	It's inherently romantic. Manly, poetic, cinematic...
ALEX	Pathetic! Not a patch on what I did before the war. You can't beat narcotics – it's clean.
ZIG	Well, I was moved by it all. Running arms, it just seemed... heroic.
ALEX	We only ever sold a few hand grenades.
ZIG	It was the idea of running arms.
ALEX	I believe we nicked them off some twelve year olds.
ZIG	What about those guns we stole from the police?
ALEX	Yeah, that was good.
ZIG	And then, there was the money.
ALEX	There was a fair bit of that. Not that you cared.
ZIG	It had a purely symbolic value.
ALEX	Never saw you spend any.
ZIG	Errr... the interest rates went up like mad... I... I invested it. *(Alex laughs)* We were a good team.
ALEX	Soap powder went well... and cigarettes.
ZIG	And those police goods.
ALEX	Everybody went for that.
ZIG	Remember that night we raided their stuff?
ALEX	We had a hot tip-off...
ZIG	Chocolates, guns, everything...
ALEX	And that fat copper walked in.
ZIG	I wondered later if you went too far.
ALEX	Had to teach him.
ZIG	It was fascinating. I was impressed.
ALEX	It had to be done.
ZIG	You had potential. You were quite unique.
ALEX	I was a social misfit.
ZIG	I always admired you.

ALEX *(amazed)* Why?

ZIG   For your energy, dynamism, your single-mindedness.

ALEX   My parents weren't impressed. Never understood why I turned out this way.

ZIG   Well, they're decent. Almost too respectable. *(pause)* I was in love with your sister. I think I can tell you now.

ALEX   I knew.

ZIG   Never did anything about it, of course, being your best friend.

ALEX   Never stopped trying to get into her knickers, you mean? But, she wouldn't go out with you, 'cos she didn't like scum!

ZIG   I attempted an intellectual exchange with her, on a few occasions, that's all.

ALEX   I told her you'd got the clap. *(he laughs, very amused.)*

ZIG   You what?!

ALEX   And just to make sure, I issued a few minor death threats in her direction.

ZIG *(lost for words for a few seconds, then collects himself)* I appreciate your sincerity. I mean, it took courage to tell her you disapproved of me.

ALEX   That's not what I said. I said: 'I see you out with that git, you're dead meat'.

ZIG   What... what was her reaction?

ALEX   She's a good girl. Very well-behaved. My dad being a copper and all that.

ZIG   I know she's your sister, but you owed her more respect.

ALEX   Nothing personal. I had her reputation to think of. And the family's. You've got no sister, you don't understand.

ZIG   Well, no, perhaps you're right... Maybe I found a sort of... brother in you... back there. Someone to look up to.

ALEX   How's that?

ZIG   I always admired you, ever since school. I used to see you, hanging out with all the tough kids – they respected you, too. I was a lonely child, friendless, frightened. Highly sensitive, searching mind... Not like you.

ALEX   You were weird.

ZIG   I was quiet. Wrote poetry.

ALEX   Did you? What for?

ZIG   Some of it pretty good, actually. *(waits for Alex's reaction. Alex remains silent)* And then, we met again.

ALEX   In *'The Lion's Den'*.

ZIG   I'd been having a quiet drink. I was about to leave.

ALEX   You were about to have your face smashed in. You hadn't paid for your booze.

ZIG   There was fighting in the villages already. Money had lost its meaning.

ALEX   Not to that barman, it hadn't.

ZIG   It was an act of defiance.

ALEX   It was an act of a bum.

ZIG   Lives were being lost. The rest was immaterial.

ALEX   Yeah, yeah...

ZIG   You were sitting by the door, with someone.

ALEX   Yeah... I wonder who?

ZIG   I decided to approach you; you – not anybody else, sensing, as I did, that you were the only person there with any dignity, with any understanding of human suffering...

ALEX   With any money.

ZIG   I said: 'Friend...', I called you a friend immediately and without intent, I said: 'Friend...'

ALEX   You said: 'Sir...'

ZIG   I said: 'I apologise for disturbing your peace and your conversation...'

ALEX   You said: 'Can you spare some change, please, sir?'

ZIG   I said: 'I like to pay my way, and never forget a debt.'

ALEX   You said: 'Please help!' That barman was about to knock you down.

ZIG   It was clear to me this was more than a chance
encounter. I knew this would be significant.

ALEX   Never liked that barman, he was always a bit of a
cunt...

ZIG   You took me under your wing, and I was safe again.

ALEX   I grabbed him by the throat and his eyes popped out.

ZIG   You said: 'See this line here?'

ALEX   'This side of it is life, the other side is me!'

ZIG   'You take another step...'

ALEX   'You'll meet the Prince of Darkness!'

ZIG   Then you asked me to join you.

ALEX   I ordered another round.

ZIG   I was revived, my dignity restored.

ALEX   You were pathetic.

ZIG   Then, you recognised me.

ALEX   It wasn't easy. It took a bit of time.

ZIG   Immediately, you decided to use me. I became your
disciple.

ALEX   I didn't decide anything. It was a bit of fun, that's all.
Didn't think you'd be of any use.

ZIG   I learned fast.

ALEX   I was surprised.

ZIG   I didn't let you down.

ALEX   You were a natural con-artist. You could talk your
way out of anything.

ZIG   We became friends.

ALEX   You have a thing about bloody friends!

ZIG   I was your best friend. You were unaware of my
quiet influence.

ALEX   I couldn't get rid of you. You moved into my house.

ZIG   Your quality of life improved beyond recognition.

ALEX   I never asked you to do anything. I gave you work
out of the goodness of my heart, and the next thing I knew – you
moved in... and started cooking and cleaning... like I got you
pregnant, or something! *(pause. They both laugh.)*

ZIG　　　Look... shall we... shall we go through that final scene, just once? *(Alex looks at him, alarmed.)*

ALEX　　　I can't do this any more.

ZIG　　　You... we have to do it. You know it. It has to be done.

ALEX　　　They'll kill us anyway.

ZIG　　　No! We're getting out. In a couple of days... They'll let us go. We've done enough.

ALEX　　　Bollocks!

ZIG　　　We'll be out in the streets. We'll breathe fresh air.

ALEX　　　We won't.

ZIG　　　We'll walk down the main street and the guys will wave to us from the bars.

ALEX　　　We'll never see the light of day!

ZIG　　　We'll walk like we used to and they'll all want to drink with us.

ALEX　　　Never.

ZIG　　　They'll want to know where we've been and what happened to us.

ALEX　　　We'll die.

ZIG　　　They'll say they knew we'd be back.

ALEX　　　There'll be no-one there.

ZIG　　　It must be summer again. July, I reckon.

ALEX　　　God.

ZIG　　　There'll be a warm wind as we go out in the evening.

ALEX　　　Never again. Never.

ZIG　　　We'll go to your mum's to eat. There'll be a feast for us there!

ALEX　　　If they're still alive.

ZIG　　　We'll take your sister out!.. She'll wear her red dress, with small white dots. Better still, we'll buy her a new dress! All the guys will look at her!

ALEX　　　God, please, let them still be alive!

ZIG　　　We'll stroll down to *'The Lion's Den'*. The news will spread fast.

ALEX	I'd give anything to see them again.
ZIG	Everybody will be there, waiting. We'll walk in, like we've never been away.
ALEX	Just one day. One minute! They'd never catch me again!
ZIG	Everybody will want to talk to us!
ALEX	Always did.
ZIG	They'll buy us drinks!
ALEX	We'll buy our own.
ZIG	We'll go from bar to bar, all night. We'll take your sister to a dance! We won't worry about anything!
ALEX	We'll rest for a few days.
ZIG	I'll stay with my parents. They'll fuss over me.
ALEX	Yeah, I guess they will.
ZIG	We'll lie low for a while. Then, we'll set up a business!
ALEX	Import-export.
ZIG	We'll be good at that. We've had experience.
ALEX	We can pick up where we left off.
ZIG	There'll be a lot of demand. The economy will be starting again.
ALEX	There'll be no stopping us. All legit!
ZIG	We'll have everything to live for! *(pause.)*
ALEX	We'll have things to do.

Blackout.

SCENE 4

Alex is sitting on the 'stage', while Zig paces up and down, tidying his clothes and glancing at the door. It opens abruptly and Rose walks in, smiling. Both jump to attention and salute her. She carries a long truncheon and still has a gun and a knife in her belt. She wears a brand new uniform. As she shuts the door and walks over towards front stage, the two prisoners still look at it, expecting the Commandant to follow.

ROSE Glorious day! Weather first class. *(pause. Alex and Zig stare at her. Zig looks at the door again)* Such a shame you can't see it. There'll never be another day quite like it... Well, what's all this? You're very quiet.

ZIG Sir...

ROSE What?

ZIG Well, maybe we ought to...

ROSE Haven't you prepared? Well? What is it?

ZIG We were wondering...

ROSE Yes?

ZIG We just thought... shouldn't we wait for...

ROSE For who?

ZIG Our Noble Commandant?

ROSE Naw!

ZIG *(devastated)* Oh, we thought... It's his decision and everything...

ROSE No. He won't be coming, I'm afraid. Too busy. *(Zig glances at Alex, who stares ahead, expressionless. They seem suspended in space)* I've been thinking. I've got used to you. I don't know what I'll do without you. I really don't. Oh, well, I'll just miss you, I suppose. But, there you go. That's life. You lose people all the time... Still, you've got to go on... Any songs? To warm us up?

ZIG *(lost for words for a few seconds)* Songs?... errr... Yes, yes, we have several songs. I've written them myself... sir...

ROSE If the lads like them, you'll have left something behind you. For postcrity, so to speak. What more can you want?

ZIG What, indeed, sir. Nothing, absolutely nothing.

ROSE It gets boring. Singing the same old songs. Every day. Every bloody night. I hate repetition. Begin! *(pause. They seem to be at a loss as to what is expected.)*

ZIG *(begins to sing, timidly)* I'm a patriot, what can I do...

ROSE Stop! What's that? Together! *(to Alex)* What's the matter with you!? Where's the team spirit?

(Zig glares at Alex, giving him a signal to start.)

ZIG & ALEX   I'm a patriot, what can I do?
                   My guns are mighty, my blood is blue,
                   I slaughter foes and rape their wives,
                   Come close and you will feel my knives.

ROSE   That's very good.

ZIG   Thank you, sir.

ROSE *(to Alex)* You don't say much.

ALEX   Suppose not, sir. Thank you, sir.

ROSE   That's all right. Tell me something. Do you believe
     in God?

ALEX   I... I don't know.

ROSE   That's what I thought. You should consider the idea.

ALEX   I will... sir.

ROSE   Define God.

ALEX   Well, he...

ROSE   Why he?

ALEX   I don't know, I'm not very religious... sir.

ROSE   I'd like you to learn. You can't go through life
     without knowing your Lord. You cannot get on in this world and
     not know your master. You cannot serve your purpose without
     any enlightenment. Can you?

ALEX   Suppose not... sir.

ROSE   It'll come to you. I'm in no doubt. I just want you to
     expect it, to look out for it. It's my concern for you. For your
     spiritual well-being. I remember days when I was as ignorant as
     you. Not a care in the world. The days before we took our
     destined places in life. I didn't know about God, either. I didn't
     know who, what ruled my life. That's all there is to it. Who rules
     yours? Think about it, will you? It's not too late. For you, I mean.
     It's too late for me. I already *know*, you see. So, it isn't easy for
     me. Not at all easy, oh no. Having to, and being able to, well,
     decide. To order, to forbid, to caution, to even yield to a whim or
     fancy sometimes, and know that the consequences will affect the
     world. To see it go on. All right here, in my very hand as it were.
     To make things happen or not happen, as the case may be. It's not
     a joke. I want you to know that.

ALEX   That's very considerate of you, sir. Thank you.

ROSE *(to Zig)* Well now! Is there more? *(they both nod)* Go on, then.

ALEX & ZIG   Enemies are rats, a poisonous breed,

We shall not let them change our creed,

We'll cut off their legs and cut off their arms,

Dig out their eyes and burn their farms.

ROSE *(laughs)* You're good! Born bloody comedians! Ha, ha, ha! Go on!

ALEX & ZIG   Strangers and all who come to steal

Our land, our jobs, will have to kneel

Before our mighty superior lads,

Who'll dance on their bodies and cut off their heads.

ROSE *(laughs, very amused)* Dear, oh, dear! What a silly tune! What a laugh!

ZIG   There's more, sir… where that came from, as they say. Lots more.

ROSE   My God, it'll be boring without you. You may not think so, but it gets very monotonous round here. Too quiet. Same old routine, day in and day out, makes you restless.

ZIG   Oh, you'll manage, sir.

ROSE   I know I will, but it won't be the same. You're a part of my life now. You bring memories, too. The minute I see you, I start reminiscing. Can't help it somehow. You remind me of the people I used to know. Friends, oh, yes, even family.

ZIG   Thank you, sir. It's nice to hear that.

ROSE   All dead now. Still, you've got to laugh… It's very strange, when you think about it. All dead.

ZIG   My condolences, sir.

ROSE   You won't believe this, but I hadn't even reached eighteen, when they started dying out. Just like that. The war was a long way away when they began to expire. One by one, without any warning! You couldn't keep count. *(pause. Prisoners stand still)* My parents died one day. Cancer.

ZIG   Awful. How awful for you, sir.

ROSE   Then five people from my school died.

ZIG   Five? That's a lot of people dead.

ROSE   Maybe it was six. Or seven. Do sit down, for God's
sake! Don't drive me mad! *(they sit down)* My brother was the
funniest. He died in a car crash. Drove his car right into a camel.
*(waits for their reaction. Zig shows amazement, Alex slight
amusement)* Well, it was in the desert. No-one expected it.

ZIG   Tragic, sir, tragic.

ROSE   That's what I thought. Of all the things you can
think of! When you're small and you lie in your little bed at night,
and you think: 'Please, God, don't let this or that happen to me',
you never even think of saying: 'Please, God, don't let me drive
my car into a camel', do you? I don't believe anybody does.

ZIG   Absolutely not, sir. Never.

ROSE   My best friend got trampled on by a horse. Can you
believe that? Fell off a horse, and it kicked her head in! Which is
very unusual for horses, I don't know how much you know about
horses, but...

ZIG   Oh, next to nothing, sir...

ROSE   ... but, they normally step over you in such cases.

ZIG   Do they really?

ROSE   Another friend went to the country and got bitten by
a snake. That was it for her.

ZIG   Didn't they give her any serum?

ROSE   She was allergic to it. That's what killed her. We
never saw her again. *(pause. Zig makes a move, as if wanting to
say something)* My sister came next. Sweet, ordinary girl, she
was. Not like me at all. People were always commenting on that.
On how different we were. You know what people are like... Got
on a bus and the bus went into a ravine. Everybody got killed.
(Zig gets discouraged and sits back again) Two friends died of
some disease or other.

ZIG *(apprehensively)* That's eight already.

ROSE   One O-D-ed. Only two died a natural death.

ZIG   Immensely sad, sir...

ALEX   Tragic.

ROSE   And that's without the two who tried to commit
suicide and survived. Not that they count.

ZIG   No, sir. To take your own life – I don't understand that.

ROSE   And to think that I was one of those two, and nearly died myself. *(pause. She stares at Alex)* I used to be very impressionable. *(she smiles to herself, musing, then suddenly seems to come round)* It's just occurred to me, I'm wasting your time! My mind's wandering. It isn't easy to stop it, once it starts. I believe this is a common problem. It's as if your mind was a different person altogether. Doing things quite independently from you, and doing things to you, too. And yet, it's your own mind; always found that pretty confusing. It's like a major con, don't you think?

ZIG   Quite... quite right, sir... It is an interesting problem.

ROSE   Where were we? Is there anything else?

ZIG   There's a whole performance, sir, you remember, along the lines you yourself suggested...

ROSE   Do you know any jokes? *(they shake their heads)* Wouldn't you like to share a joke with me, just a tiny one?... Never mind! I'll tell you one. I must warn you, though – I'm crap at telling jokes, but, what the hell! This one's so good, not even I can spoil it. Listen to this. Some international inspection group comes to snoop around and finds two heaps of your people's bodies. Dead as a doornail. One heap is just dead, in the other everybody's got a hole in the head. They go: 'What's happened to these?' Our guys say: 'They ate poisoned mushrooms.' They go: 'What about these? They've got a hole in the head.' Our guy says: 'Oh, well, those – they refused to eat the mushrooms.'
(she laughs riotously. Prisoners try to laugh with her)
Oh, dear. *(she recovers a little)* Oh, dear... You were saying something about... something?

ZIG   The performance, that's what you said you wanted, sir. The performance, both artistic and instructive, we've worked on it...

ROSE   Ah! The play! I remember now, yes...

ZIG   It was supposed to show progress, the change of heart, as it were, that we're now ready...

ROSE   Please try to surprise me. I'm dying to see it.

ZIG   ... so that you could decide... if we're ready...

ROSE   Let's get on with it, for God's sake! We haven't got
all day!

ZIG *(trying to hide his panic)* Yes, yes, let's start... Let's start.
*(he moves around Alex, not knowing where to start. Finally, he
signals Alex to move towards one end of the boxes, and arranges
his body in a hunched, down-trodden pose)*
Yes, let's start!
*(Zig climbs onto the boxes and stands above Alex. He looks into
the distance, as if about to address a large audience. He makes a
big theatrical gesture, pointing to Alex)*
The enemy! You might have wondered what they look like, these
people you thought you knew, these monsters you had been good
to, these messengers of death you found by your side. What does
the enemy look like? How can you distinguish between an enemy
and a friend when they are just like us? They wear our clothes,
they look through our eyes, they speak in our voices, they live in
our towns, they play with our children, they're well acquainted
with our joys and sorrows! Feast your eyes upon a dreadful
example of this universal truth – *(points to Alex, who raises his
head only to meet Rose's gaze and dreadful smile)* here he is, the
enemy by his own admission and his own deeds! There is, you
might think, little to be scared of, from this pitiful heap of flesh.
But, beware! This is the enemy! The enemy of everything! The
enemy of life itself!

ROSE *(applauding)* Well said!

ZIG *(catapulted out of his trance, looks quite confused)* Thank you...
sir... The enemy of life itself...

ROSE   But it does go on a bit.

ZIG   Sir... it's...

ROSE   It's all those words.

ZIG   Errr... it's only the introduction...

ROSE   Not that I know anything about theatre. Is there any
action?

ZIG   Yes, yes, yes, of course there is... Lots of action, sir.
If you let me explain... Under normal circumstances, we'd have a
programme... but here...

ROSE   I'm all for action. In the end it's the action that
counts. Words are no use. Nothing's ever been done by talking.

ZIG   Quite... There's a lot of action, sir. Interrogation, confession, punishment...

ROSE   Like, if he's the enemy of life, what are you doing about it? This is the question that comes to my mind. What's to be done about him? And when? Whether 'tis nobler in the mind to suffer etc., or take up arms, that's what I want to know.

ZIG   I know what you mean, sir, and that is absolutely the central idea of the whole piece. What's to be done? *(seems quite puzzled by this question)* Errr... The impossible – that's the answer, metaphorically speaking, sir.

ROSE   If it's impossible, what's the bloody use of doing it?

ZIG   If we can just show you, sir...

ROSE   Well, that's why I'm here. Let me see for myself. Let me enjoy the fruits of your joint endeavour, please. Show me, by all means. I'll make up my own mind. Don't point me in the right direction. Surely, I can be given that much respect. Don't waste my time. You know who I am.

ZIG *(to Alex, rearranging his position again)* Who are you?

ALEX   I'm a piece of shit.

ZIG   We've always known that. Now you yourself have realised the dreadful consequences of your sins! What's to be done with you?

ALEX   I should be put down.

ZIG   Is there any hope for you?

ALEX   I trust in the kindness of the good...

ROSE   I don't get this.

ZIG   It leads towards an important revelation, sir...

ROSE   Is it modernist, or something?

ZIG   Errr, well... no, sir... If we, maybe, show you another part, a part with a significant message...

ROSE   This is all a bit sketchy, I must say... disappointment is sort of creeping in on the whole thing, but alright, I don't want you to think I'm narrow-minded...

ZIG   Thank you so much, sir, I'm sure, well, I hope, you'll like this. The progress he's made, the genuine change of heart, truly amazing; naturally, it took a lot of work... *(Rose shows signs* *of impatience)* Well, anyway... *(to Alex, shouting)* Brief history of Our Noble Commandant's glorious struggle!

ALEX   Our Noble Commandant's glorious war was inspired by his concern for all decent people and their peace, by his desire for justice and harmony...

ROSE   Honestly! I know all that! I'm not here to hear what I already know, thank you very much. I'm here to explore! And to see results. To see action. To see the end results of your action against the enemy. Are there any results?

ZIG   Oh, yes, quite sir, of course there are, plenty of results, you see, we have that later, towards the end, as a culmination. The end - crime and punishment sort of thing, re-education...

ROSE   That's all right, then. Can we possibly see it at the beginning? I always read the end first, anyway. If the end's any good, then I may read the beginning. Most beginnings are not worth touching at all. They are just a waste of space.

ZIG   Quite, but there's all the process of understanding one's guilt first, if you remember, sir, particularly for him *(points to Alex)*, and then the process... *(looks at Rose, realises that she's not listening.)*

ROSE   You're beginning to bore me. Don't get me wrong, I'm not angry. I'm all right when I'm angry. Tedium, however, tends to create a tension inside me. It's because I've got things to do. There's a whole world out there to put in order. And here you are, selfishly putting yourself before anybody else. And boring me to death. I don't think you realise what an awesome amount of discipline I have to summon up simply to remain calm. And not to do something... radical.

ZIG *(frightened)* Right. The end.
(Signals to Alex to help him move the boxes out of the way.)

ROSE   Give me a good ending any day, that's what I always say. Then, I'm happy.
(Zig whispers some instructions to Alex, while rearranging his body yet again)
Then I'll feel we've achieved something. Spare me the beginnings. They beat around the bush too much.
(Zig rearranges Alex so that he now stands erect, his hands above

his head. He looks as if he were holding some weapon or tool, ready to strike.)

ZIG This may need a bit of explanation, sir.

ROSE If you must.

ZIG It's just because it's... a sort of improvised... stylised story... well, history, almost. Not as we planned it, but still... Of your victorious struggle... sir.

ROSE Yes, yes, let me see it.

ZIG To which you were provoked... of course...

ROSE There's nothing new in life any more. It all just goes on forever.

ZIG Of course, this should be at the end. That's the only problem, sir.

ROSE It never comes to any conclusion.

ZIG So the continuity may be lost, the whole point of the performance gone, that's what worries me, sir...

ROSE There's too much continuity in life, believe me. The only thing that matters is the end result.

ZIG Well...

ROSE *(shouts)* Get on with it!
(Zig retreats and bumps into Alex. He drops down on his knees, in front of towering Alex, and assumes an innocent and rather idiotic expression. He stares into distance looking serene. Alex pretends to hold some weapon or tool in his hands above Zig's head.)

ZIG *(solemnly)* The noble citizen is attacked by the scum of the earth.
(Alex mimes a slow motion blow on Zig's head. Zig drops onto the floor, again in slow motion. The scene looks quite clumsy and grotesque. Alex bends down and pretends to steal Zig's possessions which he then stuffs into his own pockets.)

ALEX We robbed honest civilians, raped decent women and killed innocent children. *(he moves away from Zig's motionless body)* We thought we could go on like that forever.
(Zig starts lifting himself off the floor in slow motion.)

ZIG The noble citizens rise as one to correct the historical mistakes and injustices perpetrated against them for centuries.

*(He walks towards Alex whose back is now turned towards him
and throws himself at him. Alex frees himself from Zig's grip,
turns around slowly and assumes a ready to fight position. Zig
puts up a guard for a second, then attacks. They exchange a few
stylised punches to the chin, in slow motion, missing each other's
faces. Rose is amused.)*

ROSE   Faster! *(they repeat the same exchange at a faster
pace)* Faster! *(they quicken the pace. Rose waves her truncheon
at them, laughing, encouraging them)* Move it! Faster! More!
(They move faster. She shouts at Zig) Hit him properly!

ZIG   Sir, it's only...

ROSE   Hit him!

(Zig slaps Alex's arm rather reluctantly) Well done! More!
(Zig slaps Alex's other arm) Hit him! I said hit him! Go on!
*(Zig becomes more energetic. Alex stands still. Rose raises the
truncheon as if to hit Alex, shouting)* Hit back! Hit back, scum!
(Alex starts slapping Zig) That's it!
Move it! Give it some life! *(Rose starts moving away from them
shouting encouragement, as they become more vigorous)*
Go on, move! That's good! Excellent! More!
(the fight begins to look real)
More! More! Hurt him! I said hurt the bastard!
(Zig becomes more and more overwhelmed by Alex)
Harder! Harder! Harder!
*(Zig is suddenly pushed away and staggers backwards, bumping
into Rose. Alex and Rose stare at each other. She pushes Zig
forward towards Alex who stands still, looking at Rose)*
Get him! Get the enemy!
(Zig punches Alex in the stomach. Alex doubles up in pain)
Hit his fucking head! His head! Go for the head!
*(Zig attempts to do this, Alex grabs his raised arm, twists it and
pushes him onto Rose again. She catches him, all the while
looking at Alex, turns him around and throws him at Alex, who
stands bent forward, his legs wide apart. Zig kicks him between
the legs. Alex drops on the floor. Rose runs around Zig waving
the truncheon at his head and shouts, looking quite insane)*
Kick the bastard! Kick him again! Smash his head! Break his
fucking skull! Drink his fucking blood!
(Zig kicks prostrate Alex rather indecisively a few times; stops,

turns round to Rose, tearful, as if imploring her to stop. She pushes her truncheon in his hands, still very amused)
Get the fucker! Get the fucking enemy!

ZIG   Sir, I... please...

ROSE *(playfully)* C'mon, you can do it. Hit him properly, just this once. Just for me. Go on!
(Zig strikes once, softly and clumsily, then drops the truncheon, scared and stares at Alex's body. Rose is delighted)
Well done!
(she picks up the truncheon and offers it to him again. He seems unaware of this and keeps staring at Alex. She throws the truncheon at his feet and walks away, smiling)
Now, kill him.

ZIG   Sir...

ROSE   You can do it.

ZIG *(begins to sob)* I can't. I can't. I can't.

ROSE   I said kill him. *(Zig cowers in the corner, whimpering)* I said kill him.

ZIG   No, no, no... I can't... no...
(She walks over to him and tries to straighten him up. They struggle.)

ROSE   Yes, you can. Everyone can! Why should you be worse than anyone else?

ZIG   No, I can't, I won't...

ROSE   Yes, you fucking will!
(She grabs the truncheon and makes him hold it)
Kill him! Kill him! Kill him!
(Zig is beside himself with grief, wailing and pleading inarticulately. She takes out her gun and points it at him)
Kill him! Kill him! Kill him!
(Zig lifts the truncheon. The gun is pointed at his head)
I said fucking kill him!
(Zig shuts his eyes and strikes, screaming. Rose shouts with delight. He hits Alex frantically; Rose screams and laughs like a child. Alex's body jerks with each blow. Zig drops on his knees and strikes repeatedly for a long time. Alex's body becomes motionless. With the final blow a stream of blood shoots up in the air. Zig stops abruptly, as if struck, drops the bloody truncheon.

Then he cries quietly, his face disfigured with pain. Rose wipes the sweat off her face. She looks at Zig and smiles, tenderly, gratefully, for a long time. Then she points the gun at him quickly and shoots him through the head. He falls. She grows serious, looks around the room. Then she goes to Zig, kicks him gently a couple of times. As he shows no sign of life she starts taking off his boots.)

Blackout.
The end.

Sladjana Vujovic

Sladjana Vujovic is a Yugoslav-born writer, theatre director, producer and actress.

An honours graduate, her academic background includes studies of English, drama, mathematics and archaeology. She moved to Britain in 1984.

She has worked in a number of theatres in the UK, and toured in Yugoslavia, Slovenia, Germany and Switzerland.

Nascendo

Nascendo was written as a passionate and almost musical piece of work for an ensemble of women playing the chords of the human soul. It did, of course, emerge out of personal experience, but also as a result of some meditation on the condition of my people, my city and my country.

Targu-Mures is a city in Transylvania. It has two communities, almost isolated from each other: a Romanian one (mostly dating from the 60's as a result of communist mass moving) and a Hungarian one (a historical minority). Sixty kilometers away there is a unique fortress and a town that was deserted by the people who built it – the Saxons, who went back to Germany, the home of their ancestors. The town and the neighbouring villages are now inhabited by Romanies.

I wanted to tell a story with characters I was familiar with, and they turned out to be mainly women. Ina, the Hungarian musician, tender and proud, Rita, the Romany bursting with life and loving life, so positive and so playful, Dutza, the Romanian teacher rearing four children and suffering from paternalist prejudices she is not even aware of, Valentina, the Saxon doctor, building herself a career but forgetting the little girl inside herself, Marta, the saint. The only male character is Manole the dreamer, the jerk and the poet, the son-of-a-bitch and the hurting artist – the very spirit of Romanians.

Nascendo is my fourth play, and the first one to be so strongly rejected as a feminist play. It was the first time I'd written about women and I was quite shocked at the accusations. I didn't feel *Nascendo* was more feminist than my other plays; the only difference between this play and the others was the story. (There were also accusations of anti-feminism). The play was produced mainly because some actresses who read it, wanted so much to do it. And in the audience, it was the women who were the most impressed by the show. However, the play is about women *and* men, about what they have in common: their sexless spirits.

New writing, regardless of gender, is hardly encouraged in our theatre culture. There are a couple of exceptions, and I'm really proud to have championed one of them – *The Romanian New Writing Project*. Three of the five new writers this project has developed so far, are women. And there will be more...

Alina Nelega

Nascendo

by Alina Nelega
translated by Alina Nelega and Cheryl Robson

First performed at The National Theatre of Targu-Mures (Studio) on
September 22nd 1996.
Directed by Gavril Cadariu.

CHARACTERS

Ina a failed piano soloist, between 30-35, jaded, tired and
Hungarian.

Valentina the doctor in charge of the ward, same age, impeccable,
rigid, authoritarian and Saxon.

Dutza a teacher in a distant village, having her fourth baby.
Romanian and proud of this.

Rita 15, a Romany, outspoken, vulgar, warm, earthy.

Marta a midwife, between 50-54, calm, experienced.

A young man

*December 1989, in a Maternity Ward, in a small town, somewhere in
Transylvania, Romania.*

PART ONE

*A room with four beds, in a Maternity Ward. Rita, in the foreground
bed. Ina, miming playing the piano on the edge of her bed. She hums
the scores of the other orchestra instruments.*

RITA	What's this?
INA	Tchaikovsky. *(she plays on.)*
RITA	Oh, yeh? I play a bit myself, the harmonium. I think I told you that. I'd have liked to play the violin, but we already had two fiddlers in the village. Besides, I'm a girl... I once nicked my father's harmonium... you don't wanna know what happened when he caught me...

INA   Piotr Ilici Tchaikovsky. He composed it more than a hundred years ago. It was winter... like now.

RITA   Oh, yeh? I bet he wasn't wrapped up in blankets, like us.

INA   Russia is not a warm country.

RITA   Neither is ours. *(laughs)* A family from our village was given a flat in the Cold Valley District and – you know what they did? They took up the floor to make a fire, 'cos they couldn't stand the freeze. Then they danced and danced *(laughs)* until they almost set the whole block on fire. *(seriously)* Then the militia came... put them in jail... *(laughs again, enthusiastically)* Then one night they escaped and ran – our people were waiting for them with horses and they all ran to Germany. They crossed the border at night...

INA   Rita...

RITA   It's true, I tell you... I saw it with my own eyes... they got to Germany and opened a trading firm. Two of the sons are sales directors, the girls are secretaries. The grandfather is a silversmith and he's opened his own little shop there, in Frankfurt...

INA   Rita.

RITA   What? You don't believe me? You see this bracelet? And the locket on this chain?

INA   Rita! Tell the truth.

RITA   It's a fucking waste of time. You'd better teach me the singing. I'll take my baby and run off with it.

INA   Where?

RITA   Outside. In the street.

INA   You'd go begging?

RITA   Ha – that's what you think. I make myself blind. *(she rises from the bed, pretending she can't see)*, I wrap him up and carry him in my arms... *(she enacts this and starts singing.)*

Look at me, you people
look at my bad luck
there's no light in my eyes
I'm back on the street

> Virgin Mary have pity
> Pity on the homeless
> Bless me, sweet Jesus
> Take us up to heaven

INA   Cut it out.

RITA *(she continues)*   The sky is high above
> Dirt goes right up to it
> Look at me, you people
> No light in my eyes

INA   Cut it out now, d'you hear?

RITA *(she continues)*   Sweet Jesus come and take me
> Take us up to heaven
> Don't let babies die
> Except for mine.

(She stops with her hand stretched out.)

INA   Stop it, stop it, stop it! Stop it!

RITA   Maybe you don't like me singing, huh?

INA   Your singing is out of tune

RITA   And ladies hate false singing, ladies hate our music, folk music... they love Shaikovsky. Well, I'd better read your cards then. *(takes out a pack of cards from under her skirt)* Or maybe you'd prefer me to read your palm? Come on, let me read your future. A Romany can read the stars, that's what she can read, the cards and the palms. The future. I can tell your future. *(quick reading)* A man's coming at night... beware of the knave of hearts and his sweet tongue, and the queen of spades 'cos she wishes you evil. A great misfortune's coming, but you'll get by and make love to a knave of clubs. Do you have a wedding ring? Give it to the gypsy and she'll tell you more!

INA   I don't have a wedding ring, Rita. Do you?

RITA   What do I need one for? But you should have one, since you've got a man.

INA   And you.

RITA   Me? I don't have a man.

INA   Your child does have a father.

RITA   This baby is one thing, a wedding ring is another.
My Zaki's gone, they took him away for the army, and when he's
back I'll be with somebody else.

INA   You'll leave him for another man?

RITA   If I go back home my father will marry me off.
That's why they want to take my baby away, to put it in an orph-
anage, 'cos you know, nobody will fucking marry me unless I'm a
virgin.

INA   What do *you* want?

RITA   I want you to teach me to sing. I'll take my baby and
run away. Till they catch me…

INA   How old are you?

RITA   Sixteen… I think…

INA   You're not even old enough to get married.

RITA   Oh, really? In our village, girls marry at twelve.

INA   But you're under-aged. There are laws, the militia…

RITA   The militia? My father would fucking kill me.
Besides, they don't bother with the likes of us…

INA   Then maybe you'd like to stay in here for longer?

RITA   Fucking right. I've been here three weeks already,
and the doctor says she needs the bed for other *(very important,
showing that she knows the word)* pregnant women… you
know…

INA   Maybe they need… someone to clean the toilets, to
wash the floors, to–

RITA   That's what I've been doing since the second day I
came here! But they don't like it. They say I don't do it properly…
I think the doctor's had enough of me and my poor little fatherless
baby…

INA   I could talk to her, if you like. I know her, we used
to go to the same school…

RITA   Sure, you fucking ladies, you all get along together.
Marta tried, but no way… and she sometimes listens to Marta…
*(She searches under her folded skirt, takes out a cigarette and
lights it.)*

INA   Put it out! Marta will be here in a minute with the
baby – remember all that fuss she made yesterday.

RITA   So what? Open the fucking window, it's warmer outside, anyway... and nobody will know. Besides, the doctor smokes, I saw her dragging on a fag...

INA   In her office.

RITA   Yeh, and drinking coffee, like a lady, and not ersatz. The real thing. With you and the other... ladies.

INA   I don't drink coffee. Or smoke – I can't. Because of the baby. It hasn't moved and I've been on medication for two months. And cigarette smoke makes it worse.

RITA   Alright, alright, one more drag and I'll put it out. *(she pretends to put it out, but she hides the cigarette behind her)* You lot! Cigarette smoke makes me puke, food makes me puke, the smell of gypsies makes me puke. What about the prick you used to make the kid – didn't that make you puke?

INA *(disgusted)* You're out of order.

RITA   How come you make such a fuss over this baby and it's not happening? You don't even fucking force yourself in the loo – afraid you might drop it. We don't worry.

INA   You're different.

RITA   Oh, yeh? We're both women. You think because you went to college and your mother's been fucked by a baron, you're better than me?

INA   You make me ill.

RITA *(laughs)* Everything makes you ill. *(she holds her belly)* Your fucking la-de-da baby hates dirty words. The little prince, a kis herzeg[1], who will come out speaking three fucking languages and humming Shaikovsky. Oh, oh, oooooh,oh,oh...
(Ina turns her face to the wall. Pause. Rita stops, disarmed.)

RITA   Ina... *(she touches her.)*

INA   Take your fucking hand off me.
(Rita withdraws. She smokes passionately.)

Enter Marta supporting Dutza.

---

[1] In Hungarian in original, meaning: 'the little prince'.

MARTA   Put out that cigarette right away!
(Rita drops the cigarette and extinguishes it with her foot) Wait until the doctor comes – she'll throw you out – you and your... child!

RITA   Cigarette? What cigarette? Do you see any cigarette? I wasn't smoking, cross my heart...

MARTA   I'm calling her now! And then you'll see...

RITA   No, Marta, please, don't call her. Don't tell her. I won't do it again, please, Marta, I swear on my baby, I'll never smoke again, never in my life, on my mother's grave...

MARTA   Alright, alright, calm down. We'll leave the door open, the smoke will go out. But if it happens again...

RITA   Never! I promise...

MARTA   I'm not joking. She's waiting for a good reason to throw you out. And she's right – your baby's almost crawling and you're still here...

RITA   Dear Marta, good Marta, if you do that, I'll hang myself...

MARTA   Oh, shut up and sit down. And no more filth. Look, you've upset her.

RITA   Yes, yes, I'll shut up. But you won't tell on me...

MARTA   Shut up. *(to Dutza)* You sit here, and wait. If you feel anything, send her to call me. She doesn't have anything else to do, anyway. *(menacingly, to Rita)* Does she?

DUTZA   Yes.

RITA   No.

MARTA   You should be in labour in two, three hours. If not... we'll wait for the morning.

DUTZA   And if in the morning...

MARTA   Then we will induce it. Trust the doctor, she's the expert...

DUTZA   I'm two weeks overdue.

MARTA   We'll have to induce it... or you might die, and the baby too.

DUTZA   I... is it – safe? I mean...

MARTA   There's nothing to be afraid of. How many deliveries have you had?

DUTZA   This is the fourth.

MARTA   So you've had children before? It will be like a normal delivery. No big deal, the doctor is good. Inducing a delivery is different from abortion.

DUTZA   I've had some of those...

MARTA   Ssshhhut up. Don't mention that, or you'll be in trouble. Where do you think you are?

DUTZA   Yes... of course... you're right, what am I saying?

MARTA   It's a deal, then. You sit here calmly and call me at the first sign.

DUTZA   I'm still afraid. I don't feel it moving. What if–

MARTA   I've seen a lot like you, dear, in my time. Be patient. The baby will come and everything will be alright. Are you hungry?

DUTZA   God forbid!

RITA   I'm hungry!

MARTA   You're always hungry.

RITA   With the mush you give us. I never get enough.

MARTA   Have you seen us eat anything else? What do you eat at home? Oranges and bananas?

RITA   I did see an orange once! At the old bulibasha's place, when he came back from the Congress...

MARTA   What congress, you idiot?

RITA   ...'cos he's a deputy. He'd just come from Bucharest.

MARTA   Rita!

RITA   They were that big, and he kept them in a briefcase, like a real poli-ti-tician. We fought over the peels – me and the other kids. They smelled so good, and were so sweet.

MARTA *(disgusted)* You're lying again. Sit down there and shut up. The food will come soon. Ina?

RITA *(hypocritically)* She's asleep, poor thing, 'cos she's fuck–
...she's tired.

MARTA   You must have told her another one of your dirty stories. Ina...

RITA   You always come and tell me to shut up. Don't I
have the right to speak?

MARTA   Ina... you alright? *(to herself)* She *is* asleep.

RITA   See? *(to Dutza)* And she doesn't believe me, she says
I'm lying.

MARTA   Cut the crap – I've had enough of you.

DUTZA   Nurse...

MARTA   What now?

DUTZA   Nothing... an extra blanket...

MARTA   There's none left. Take the one from the other bed,
and if another woman comes in we'll put her directly in the
delivery room. They should bring blankets from home...

DUTZA *(acidly)* I'll tell my husband to bring me one, too.

MARTA   Yeh, why don't you? Did you think you were coming
to Monte Carlo? This is a hospital, not a health club!

She exits.

RITA   Mi az Monte Carlo? *(to Dutza)* Mit jelent Monte
Carlo?[2] *(Dutza pretends not to hear and does her bed)* You've no
idea! Ina – what is Monte Carlo?

INA *(without turning)*: A place that doesn't exist.

DUTZA   That's silly – if it didn't exist it wouldn't have a
name!

INA   Lots of things that do not exist have names – love,
wealth, tolerance, happiness...

RITA   Oranges.

INA   Children. They have names, even before they're
born. *(to Dutza)* What's yours called?

RITA   Zaki.

DUTZA   It's – but my child exists. It's inside my body. I felt
it.

INA   Are you sure?

DUTZA   Yes. No... Yes, I'm sure. Alive or dead, it exists.

---

[2] In Hungarian in original, meaning 'What is Monte Carlo?'

INA   The other things exist as well. Inside me. Love, kindness... alive or dead, who can tell? Happiness exists too, somewhere, far away. Like Monte Carlo. My talent has a name – I feel it. But it exists only on the edge of my bed, mimed, with my fingers, without the piano. Bring me a piano *(she rises)* bring me a real piano, to give birth, to bring this pain to an end. The edge of my bed can't play, will never play, never... why do I have Liszt, Chopin, in me, I hear them – but life? Where is life? Where is the truth? Where is my piano, my grandmother's piano, out of tune, dust on the keys, dust rising when the trucks drive in the street, through the sashes of my window, it comes in, covers everything, cement dust from the blocks of flats across the road, the noise of the crane drowns out the music, breaks it, there's nothing left but a heap of laquered wood and some old keys quietly humming with the dust falling... *(pause)* And outside – the roar of bulldozers, the workers shouting, noises that make the crystal chandelier in the dining-room shatter into pieces of Murano glass... give me back my piano, and the child inside me will have a name. *(pause)* It doesn't exist yet. I don't feel it, its heart doesn't beat, *(to Dutza)* yours has moved, has lived, mine exists only in my mind. I say to myself: 'It's alright, it is there, it will give me a sign in a few days. I will feel it, it will grow, it will live.' But my child doesn't exist, like the withered fruit in the orchard... and I play on the edge of my bed. The scores of all the instruments, and the piano inside me. And I play. And give birth. And give birth. And play. Nothing's heard. Symphonies lost in the barkings of stray dogs... Give me back my piano! Give it back to me, give it back...
(She stops, sits. Silence.)

RITA   Oh, come on, I didn't fucking take it. But, if you like, I can get hold of one, just say when!

DUTZA   I felt the same when I finished school. The Teaching Institute. I used to play too – the clarinet. 'What a strange instrument for a woman', they said, laughing and making jokes... you know men... Then, I got married, had no time for music. I sing old *doinas*[3], songs I'd learned from my grandmother, like you... sang

---

[3] Slow melancholic and plaintive Romanian folk song, expressing feelings of yearning for love, freedom, home, etc.

them when I was holding my daughters, when I put them to sleep.
I have three daughters, you know. Sometimes, when my man is
cross with me because he has no sons I say: 'You're like the old
emperor in the fairy tales. He had three daughters. The eldest was
wise and obedient, the second was beautiful – a regular peach, the
little one was hard-working and sweet-tongued. Like my
daughters. What do you want a son for?' *(pause.)*

INA   And?

DUTZA   And – nothing. He just wants one. And me too.
Actually, we need a son. But now, I'm afraid. I haven't been so
afraid since our wedding night, when he came over to me stagger-
ing and mumbling and I... didn't know, didn't understand what he
wanted. I did know, of course, but I thought, felt... that it wasn't
the way it was supposed to happen... it wasn't... what...

RITA   But then you get used to it.

DUTZA   Yes. Why am I telling you these silly stories? What
do you care?

RITA   And if it isn't a boy?

DUTZA   It's not possible. I prayed so much... it has to have a
willy. *(she laughs a bit embarrassed.)*

RITA   Mine has.

DUTZA   Good for you! Your kind are always lucky.

RITA   I couldn't care less 'cos I can't keep it, anyway...
They'll take it away from me. You have what I want, I have what
you want. If I were you, I'd give your husband as many sons as he
wants.

DUTZA   Really? Talk is easy...

RITA   Yeh, for some people it is...
*(she abandons her in favour of another idea that has just come to
her mind)* Ina, write me a letter, please, to my Zaki, the big one.
'Cause the little one is like me. *(laughs)* Doesn't read, doesn't
write.

DUTZA   And thank God it doesn't speak!

RITA   Tell him to come and take us away, wherever he
wants to.

DUTZA *(suddenly interested)* I can teach you to write, if you want.
In two days, with capital letters. That's my job, at home. I taught

half the village children to write – I couldn't get the other half to come to school. It was no use trying… with my husband, Gitza, he's a teacher too, a history teacher… and with the militia man – we used to fine them, they come to school. Three days, then, off again…

RITA   Why would I want to fucking learn to write? Look at me – I get by perfectly well without writing. A letter – that's something anyone can do for me. Why should I bother? Zaki can understand all the same, whoever writes the fucking letter.

DUTZA   That's why nothing works in this country! Because you don't bother. You want everything done for you. No order, no discipline, you don't want to work, only to steal. Let me see you working, not making babies! Digging ditches, not playing the piano!

INA *(feels the dig)* Everybody has a right to live.

DUTZA   Yeh, but not how they want to. In music there is a discipline, people don't play as they want to, without thinking.

INA   In music there is no discipline. Just harmony.

DUTZA   Nonsense. *(to Rita)* Well, do you want me to teach you? Look at you, you should be going to school, not having babies!

RITA *(pokes out her tongue)* I'm going for a piss.

She exits.
Lights fade to black.

SCENE 2
In the blackout, Marta is heard coming in, with a huge trolley. On the top she has placed about ten babies. On the bottom: plates with food for the women.

MARTA *(lighting a candle)* Why is it so dark in here? Don't you have any candles?

DUTZA   We didn't know they put the lights out in here. *(sarcastic)* Or else I'd have brought some with me.

MARTA *(irritated)* Put it out, put it out. Of course they do. Don't we live in the same country? Hold this, and look in your bedside table – you have a little saucer there.

(The light grows diffusely, while Marta is counting the babies)
Women in other rooms have come here better prepared... five,
six, seven, eight, nine. All of them. Why don't you grab a couple
of plates and put them somewhere? Like that, yeh... and now the
babies. Here we have Rita's, yes? *(she takes a baby and places it
in Dutza's arms.)* Where could his mother be? One minute whining with hunger, and then she's coming onto men, in this
darkness!

DUTZA   Men? What men?

MARTA   She could find a man on the moon! She's... you
know... with all the male doctors – until 'The Doctor' throws her
out. And that day is coming, believe me!

DUTZA   He's a beautiful baby. So white, you wouldn't think
he was a gypsy.

MARTA   As if you could tell white from black these days.
What about you – still nothing, huh?

DUTZA   Nothing. It's not moving, nurse Marta. It's not
moving at all. If you know anything, you have to tell me. It's
dead, isn't it?

MARTA   Don't be stupid. How would I know? Wait, that's all
I can say.

DUTZA   I don't believe you. You know everything. You
haunt this hospital, silent, helping, delivering, giving away plates
of food and babies to their mothers. You're in the middle of
everything, so you must know everything.

MARTA *(icily)* In your dreams. I know nothing.

DUTZA   Oh, no, oh, no, sister, please, have pity, do something. Talk to the doctor, I'm so long overdue and so afraid of dying. As if I had a stone inside my belly. I cuddle it, I talk to it, but
it's still a stone. Not a baby at all, I don't know what will come
out. I used to feel it before... it was a joy, fretting, waiting for it –
the two of us. Now I'm alone and with this stone inside me. I have
to get rid of it. As if it's hanging from my throat, not inside my
belly.

MARTA   Come on, relax and put down that baby before you
drop it. Not on your bed, on Rita's! We'll think of something. But
you have to wait.

DUTZA   I can't take it any longer, you hear me? You said it could be done...

MARTA   What?!

DUTZA   Induction, or whatever you call it...

MARTA   It can be done, yes. But it's not ideal. What is meant to be, will be.

DUTZA *(very agitated, extremely nervous)* I've been waiting for months, hoping, every moment, going to sleep and waking up, thinking of it, of *him*, what would *he* look like, who would *he* take after, I was hoping, madly hoping that *he'd* come to life in nine months, alive, in one piece, mine. My boy. My redemption. But now *he's* not moving any longer, it's hopeless! Will *he* ever be born? Maybe it's not a baby – it's a tumour, a huge cyst, a fake! Maybe it's my bowels – a heap of loathesome flesh, stinking cancer, death. What if instead of life I'm carrying death, swallowing more day by day? Marta, help me, please... I must know. I must be free! I must deliver!

MARTA   Just be patient.

DUTZA   It's fucking hopeless, I know it is.
(She blows out the candle. Pitch dark.)

MARTA   What's going on? Dutza, where are you?

DUTZA   I can induce my own delivery. *(moaning)* Like this, with this candle!

MARTA   Dutza, wait, listen, stop, don't! Don't do it! *Wait!*

DUTZA   Yes, yes, I will know. *(moaning harder)* Oh, it hurts, it hurts... I will know! I must know! *(screams)* Ooooh, it broke, nurse, the water's coming, it's coming, the baby's coming, nurse. Help, help me, help me...

MARTA *(trying to find the door)* Doctor! Ina, wake up! Light a candle, for God's sake! Doctor!

INA *(lighting a candle, calmly)* I'm not asleep, I heard it all. And I think she's right.

MARTA   Doctor! Where is the emergency doctor? Ina! Doctor! She's dying, somebody get someone!

She exits in a hurry. Ina gets up very slowly, takes the trolley Marta has abandoned and pushes it downstage. A strange light.

INA   They called this one Andrei, this one András, this
one Andrea. This one is Ana, the other Anna, this is Johann, and
this is János, and Rita's Zaki... *(very loud)* This is Marius, Horat-
io, Trajan, Caesar, Virgil, Remus...

DUTZA   God! Help me, God! Have mercy, sweet Jesus. Help
me!

INA   None of the women cry: 'Mother' when in pain.
Strange. Men do, when they die... They have the right, to be the
sons of mothers and we women – mothers of the sons but never
daughters? They call us endlessly, but not as lovers, or sisters, or
daughters... only as mothers. Why? *(she is startled)* Oh! God,
Istenem[4], it's moved. Oh thank you, thank you Holy Father, it's
moved. I hear. I feel. I hear. I hear the piano, the winds and the
violins, I hear the piano. Nascendo plays the piano. Nascendo.

Blackout.

SCENE 3

*The trolley has disappeared, and so have Dutza and the baby on
Rita's bed. Ina is sitting on the edge of her bed, stroking her belly.
She hums. Enter Valentina.*

VALENTINA   Látod? Veled is megtörtént.[5] It's happened to you
too, after all.

INA   When I'd almost given up hope. How is Dutza?

VALENTINA   She's in the delivery room. With Marta. She'll be
alright, I hope...

INA   You hope? I thought you knew.

VALENTINA   Either we know, or we pretend to know...

INA   Unpredictable, isn't it?

VALENTINA   Yes. Rita's the expert in reading the future. You
know, she read my cards. She said my life would change.

INA   She told me the same.

---

[4] In Hungarian, in original ,meaning: 'God'.
[5] In Hungarian in original, meaning: 'See? It's happened to you, too.'

VALENTINA She probably says that to everybody. And people believe her. They want to believe. We're all waiting for a change. *(she takes out some chocolate from her pocket, unwrapping it)* Do you want some?

INA *(helps herself, enthusiastically)* Chinese chocolate! Delicious! Christmas is coming... 'O, Tannenbaum...'

VALENTINA ...wie grün sind deine Blätter[6]... I haven't had a real Christmas since I was a little girl. Since my father left.

INA We thought you were the stuck-up neighbour with Western clothes... me – the poor child of a reformed reverend, playing the organ...

VALENTINA *(laughing apologetically)* I'm not stuck-up any more. Poor Elsa, remember her?

INA The crispy cookies she made! She's the one who taught me German. She wouldn't give me any cookies, unless I spoke German to her, and you always ate faster than me!

VALENTINA That's not true! Come on, you were such a pig! Look at the size of your belly now!
(They both laugh, like two naughty little girls.)

INA And you? Still on your own?

VALENTINA You know perfectly well. I made my bed, now I have to lie in it.

INA Sometimes I think you did the right thing. I wanted the moon, and now what I've got?

VALENTINA A baby. Security.

INA At last! But the price I've paid – so much worry, so many things put off!

VALENTINA *(a bit embarrassed)* Listen, Ina, I have to tell you something...

INA I know. He's defected. I knew, the moment he left. We fought for so long over it, but he had to escape. There was no future for him. A soloist in a miserable orchestra in the regions... as if he'd been buried alive...

VALENTINA They'll take your house away.

---

[6] The beginning of a very well-known Saxon Christmas Carol.

INA   Maybe they will. Maybe they won't. You never
know. Maybe I'll go too one day. *(bravely)* Right now, I'm not
sure what I want.

VALENTINA At least you've lived.

INA   You think so?

VALENTINA All in the name of this ungrateful profession, where
women are second class. That's what they say. Because the
strangest thing is – women prefer to be assisted by men – they
feel safe, protected. Even if they're incompetents who know nothing about giving birth, except from books, and most of them feel
sick when they actually see it happen.

INA   It's quite difficult to like it. All that pain and blood...

VALENTINA It's not just the blood. It's not spilt for nothing.
There's always a reason. Even if reality is ugly, abject. Inter urina
et faeces...

INA   Didn't a man say that? Saint Augustine, perhaps?

VALENTINA Probably – from a safe distance. *(laughs)*

INA   You know what, Valentina? I've been thinking about
you – about this hard shell of a career woman, hiding the soul of a
little girl–

VALENTINA *(interrupting)* You're wrong...

INA *(goes on without paying attention)* Not the soul of a child, but
of a little girl. It makes all the difference. So few can make it,
after all... A girl, small and brittle, in a corner of her room, with
the doll they gave her when she was born. They put it in the
cradle, as an omen.

VALENTINA And?

INA   What if you did have a baby?

VALENTINA I've been thinking about that too. The biological
clock – it doesn't care about career, communist meetings or rules,
doesn't give a shit about anything else. It wakes you up at night,
sweating and panting. The curse.
*(a pause while she reconsiders her sincerity. The next lines are
said in an outburst of passionate duplicity)*
I actually think I hate babies. I can't stand them. When I see them
clinging to their mothers' breasts, regurgitating milk, puking up...
The idea of a child, yes. I like the idea – but me? To swell up, to

have my genitals poked and prodded by all those doctors, to have
a baby sucking at me... No, I'm sorry. I work with my brain, not
with my... body. Sorry – they're not for me.

INA   Or men either.

VALENTINA *(the same bravado that makes her very unsympath-
etic)* Oh, I do like men. They can be used, you can take revenge
on them occasionally. I like them the way I like a new coat, a
piece of jewelry, a new perfume. But I never become attached to
my possessions. I wouldn't sell myself for the sake of a child.

INA   What about love?

VALENTINA Love? A euphemism for social conventions, an
empty word for fucking, orgasm, parturition. There is no greater
pleasure than to have all those horny males eating out of the palm
of your hand every morning at the start of the rounds.
(She can hardly stop herself from bursting into tears.)

INA: *(sympathetically)* Valentina...

VALENTINA No, please. Stop it. I have more than you'll ever
have. Career, lovers, power. My two books on obstetrics.

INA   And a lot of compromise.

VALENTINA Oh, shut up! I think Rita's smarter than you. At least
she jumps over the fence from time to time. And I will throw her
out. Tomorrow. I've had enough of her tricks. I need the bed. We
can't afford to turn this hospital into a hostel.

*Rita comes in, alert, her hair and clothes in disorder. She sees
Valentina and stops intimidated.*

RITA   Evening ma'am...

VALENTINA Where have you been? You've been out and about
again?

RITA   I was –

VALENTINA *(shouting furiously)* What are you doing busking in
your condition? Tomorrow you're out! I've said all along I'll have
you thrown out and now the time has come! We've got one in the
delivery room, your baby crying for milk and you're out tramping
about... You think you're still living in some gypsy camp where
everybody does as she pleases? You think you know better than

us? Just you wait! I will have order in here, once and for all! This
disruption is over!

Valentina exits furiously.

RITA   Disruption? What do you know about it? *You* just
wait and see – it's barely started! *(to Ina)* Do you hear? Can't you
hear it?

INA   You'd better cool off, ok? Look, you've missed out
on dinner...

RITA   Oh, fuck dinner! Who cares? Come on, come with
me! *(she pulls her by the hand downstage)* Can you hear it?

INA   Hear what?

RITA   It's started! It's started and it will go on and on!
(she begins to dance) It's started and it will last forever! Everybody can do what they want! It's over! No us and them. Down
with the snobs! You can have your piano! We can have oranges!
*(she takes out some clothes from under her large skirts – the
clothes that the women will wear at the beginning of Part II –
and a small Chinese toy piano)* Look, look what I've found!
*(She also takes out Christmas ornaments, tinsel and gold thread
and turns herself into a Christmas tree.)*

INA   Rita! Where did you get these from? Take them
back, right away!

RITA   No way! We're alive, we're alive! Let's go out in the
streets, shout, die, dance! We are doing what we've been longing
to do at last, at last... Olé! Olé! Olé! Olé! People, hear me... Olé!
Olé! Olé! Olé! Olé! *(she stops her dancing and takes out a bottle
of champagne. She spits out the words)*
Olé! Olé! Olé! Olé! Olé! Ceausescu's dead and grey!

The door opens and Dutza enters, supported by Marta.

DUTZA   I've had the baby!
MARTA   It's alive.

Blackout.

PART TWO

*The room is decorated for Christmas with little fir branches, colour-
ed ornaments, even a few candles and candies. In the middle, the
trolley Marta had used to carry the food and the babies. Two of them
are on the top, and near them, a bottle of champagne and four tin
mugs. Rita, Dutza, Ina and Marta are dressed as follows:
Rita is in tails and a bow tie, like a concert soloist; Ina is wearing a
large gown like those worn by pregnant women, embroidered with
Romanian folklore designs on the sleeves and inset; Dutza is wearing a gypsy woman's large folded skirt, low-necked and bare should-
ered blouse, a golden coin necklace and long earrings, tinkling
bracelets at her wrists; Marta is wearing a long black dress, her
head covered with a black scarf like a nun.
Marta is praying, Dutza is admiring her necklace, Ina is pensively
stroking her belly.*

RITA *(playing with the toy-piano)* Now I can go back home. My
home, my house... warm and cosy. The bulldozers have gone. The
chief of the construction site is delivering milk to the old people
in the area. Tinkle-tinkle, the sound of bottles. Tinkle-tankle – the
sound of the great chandelier in the dining-room. And I hear – the
piano. It's my own piano, it's not stolen. Ta-ta-ta-ta... ta-ta-ta-ta...
ta-ta! Says the baby. And pokes out his tongue in the mirror. Paa-
pa! I take him in my arms, I give him an orange. He loves
oranges. Takes after me. Ta-ta! No, not like that, I tell him.
Listen: ta-ta-ta-ta... ta-ta-ta-ta...

INA   I've come back to the village. The school is clean,
whitewashed. There's plenty of wood for the fire, the stoves are
roaring full. The pupils are waiting for me, disciplined, at their
desks. I come in, with my register under my arm. A little pest in
the second row whispers something to her friend. 'Yes', I say,
'don't look like that, I'm having another baby. He'll be like you,
he'll learn here, at these desks.' I open the register. My husband,
Gitza, comes in. He apologizes, approaches my desk.. 'Aren't you
too tired, my dear? It's your fifth lesson today. Why don't you
have a rest, and I'll do it for you? What's on today?' he asks the
children. 'History, oh, that's my specialty.' I go out, pass through
the village. In the café, two old men drink coffee. 'Is it *real*
coffee?' one says. 'No', the other one beckons, disappointed. 'It's

instant.' 'Come on, it's ok', the first one says. 'No, the other one was better', the second one grumbles. I get to my front yard, I'm very careful not to step into puddles. There are still some places left unpaved. The girls are playing with Tex, the German shepherd. The sun is setting. I put the pots on the stove. Cheese pancakes with cream sauce. 'Mummy,' the elder one comes in – she goes to high school in the town, 'can you help me with my French homework? We have Rabelais today.' 'Fais ce que voudras', I tell her.

DUTZA   There's no-one waiting for me at the big hospital gate. I take my baby and go out, my chin up, my eyes looking straight ahead. I stop a taxi. 'Yes ma'am,' the driver says. 'Where shall I take you?' 'To the hotel,' I say. He stops, I get out, I pay. I tip him heavily, I am generous. At the desk, they give me a single with a big bathroom. I send the maid to buy milk for my baby. He's asleep. I write to Zaki, I give him my new address. I tell him to come and take me away. He asks for leave, he finds me. We embrace in the elegant lobby of the huge hotel. He takes me to his mother. She lives in a new flat. 'You can stay here as long as you want', the old lady says. 'I'll help you with your baby. But you have to go back to school.' I want to go to college. I want to become a secretary. I study, I take my exams. Zaki comes home from the army. He becomes a taxi driver. You see, that's why the guy who drove me from the hospital was so nice to me. He knew Zaki. And I am his wife.

MARTA   I am old. I am so old that I don't even know my own age. The children have grown up. I've buried my husband. I'd like to die in peace, to stop seeing women giving birth. Only God is left for me now. I get off the train and walk there. It's among the hills, you can see the shiny red-tiled roof. White and tall, flowers at the window sills. I knock on the door… Mother Superior opens. 'Welcome, Marta, it's been so long'… the bed is hard and clean, the sheets are coarse. 'At your age the skin is rough, it won't hurt. Go, Marta, she says, go. Pray for us.'
(Silence. The women look at each other as if awakening from a dream.)

RITA   Maybe we're wrong. They're still shooting, aren't they? They're shooting, I know it!

MARTA   Don't worry, you'll be alright.

DUTZA   And the tanks, do you hear them? Don't pretend you don't hear them. They're marching under our windows. The soldiers... they're shooting...

MARTA   Don't worry, it's not the soldiers...

RITA   Of course not. Poor Zaki, he couldn't do it...

DUTZA   But who? Who is shooting? Who?

MARTA   They've calmed down now. Just a shot now and then.

DUTZA   What's going on outside?

INA   Let's go out and see!

MARTA   No. It's too dangerous.

DUTZA   What do you mean? If they've stopped, how can it be too dangerous? What do you know that you're not telling us?

MARTA   I don't know anything.

DUTZA   What are they doing now?

INA   They're celebrating. It's another birth.

MARTA   Just shut up, will you? Rejoice and shut up!

DUTZA   When people rejoice they don't keep quiet. I'm afraid. I'm always afraid. What can I do to get rid of this fear? I've been afraid ever since I was a child. Of my father, of my husband, now of what's outside...

MARTA   Come on now, your baby is perfectly ok. What else do you want?

DUTZA   It's a girl. Another girl, besides the other three. What will my husband say? What will we do with another girl?

RITA *(laughs)* You know what. He'll fucking jump on you and ho! and ho! Maybe a boy next time!

DUTZA   Shut up! It's over, no more babies! From now on I don't have to get pregnant!

MARTA   Let's not argue. It's Christmas Eve. Let's open the champagne. I'll call Valentina... *(she exits.)*

RITA   That bitch? Who wanted to throw me out in the streets? Serves her right! Now she's the one who'll get thrown out! No longer the boss, how about that?

DUTZA   She left me alone to deliver with Marta. What if there'd been complications? Serves her right!

INA   Leave her out of this! She's depressed enough...

DUTZA   That's right, take her side. You're both the same.

INA   What do you know?

DUTZA *(looking down on her)* I know. My husband is a history teacher, if your memory's still working. I know everything! About you and your Asian, barbaric, loathesome ancestors! And her Teutonic roots – none of you belong here, you're both pommies!

INA   You don't even know your own history! You belong to a people who never tell the truth! Thieves, liars, cheats...

DUTZA   Arrogant, cruel, kinky, suicidal, greedy, drunkards...

INA   What!

DUTZA   Yes!
(They gradually start to push each other and almost fight.)

RITA   Hey, ladies, relax, have you gone kinky? You – let go of Ina. Vedd le a kezed róla, me én is ütök[7].

INA   Stay out of this! Ne szólj bele, nem a te dolgod. Maradj veszteg[8].

DUTZA   Stop talking gibberish! *(she pushes Ina away, takes off her necklace, bracelets, earrings. To Rita)* You can take your bits of tin and you – give me back my dress 'cos you stink! *(she pulls at the dress Ina is wearing, but Rita has hardly waited to fight.)*

RITA *(tears away her bow tie)* What a shit! Revolution, I say.
(to Dutza) Here - shove them down your...
(The three of them take off their clothes, throw them to each other. They are left in long, white nightgowns.)

INA   Take it back. You think you can take everything, but one day things will change, I promise you!

Valentina and Marta come in, supporting a man. His trousers are blood-stained. Rita and Dutza are petrified, Ina jumps up to help.

INA   Oh, God, he's hurt!

---

[7] In Hungarian in original, meaning: 'Take your hands off her, or I'll smash you!'

[8] In Hungarian in original, meaning: 'Don't interfere, it's not your business!'

MARTA   Shut up and help us lay him on the bed.
(They lay the young man on Ina's bed. Valentina retreats too, towards the door.)

MARTA   Come, doctor, let's get him undressed.

VALENTINA I'm going to get some bandages and disinfectant.

MARTA *(tearing off his trousers)* They're full of blood.

VALENTINA I can't operate on him here. Call the porters to take him into the delivery room.

MARTA   You can't do that. It's full. They're all giving birth now – in the wards, on the streets... the world's gone mad. Doctor, please look at him!

VALENTINA*(mechanically)* I'll get the bandages and the disinfectant.

MARTA *(raises her voice)*: Come and see him! You haven't even looked at him!

VALENTINA *(mechanically)* I need instruments. Catgut, scalpel, bandages, disinfectant, cotton...

MARTA *(shouts at her)*: You are the doctor! This man must be seen by a doctor. He's loosing blood!

VALENTINA I can't look at his blood... I'm sick, I'm very sick. I can't stand the sight of blood.

MARTA   Come on, stop talking nonsense. You see blood all day long. Come over here!

VALENTINA The blood of birth is different from the blood of death. It's life. It's Nature, it purifies, it makes you well. It doesn't flow without reason, it brings the baby...

YOUNG MAN *(subdued voice)* Mother... mother...

VALENTINA His blood is thin, watery, it flows for death, not for life. It's not the same thing! It's not, you hear me? It's not the same thing! *(she exits furiously.)*

YOUNG MAN Mother... mother...

MARTA   He's calling for his mother. Like a child... and he's dying, dying before our eyes.

RITA   Oh, what the – I'll do it. I'll help you, Marta.

MARTA   Jesus, sweet Jesus, help your servant whats-his-name and don't let him be taken to your eternal kingdom, oh, God...

Valentina comes in, with the bandages, the disinfectant and the instruments.

MARTA   Give them to me. Rita – come here! Hold them and give them to me when I ask. *(Rita obeys.)*

DUTZA *(takes the two babies, hers and Rita's, in her arms)* What am I supposed to do?
(She unbuttons her gown and feeds the babies)
Oh, little ones, you must have been so hungry... Mummy's little darlings... dear little poppets...

Marta treats the young man. She asks Rita to pass her the instruments, bandages, disinfectant, syringe, cotton. Rita gives them to her, making mistakes from time to time. Ina is holding Valentina's hand.

The lights slowly fade to black.

SCENE 2
The young man lies in bed, apparently asleep.

MARTA   There was no bullet.

DUTZA   Then where did all that blood come from?

MARTA   I don't know. He was covered in it, but he's safe and sound. It wasn't his blood.

INA   And now he's sleeping. As if he didn't have a care in the world.

VALENTINA He said he'd been shot.

DUTZA   By who?

VALENTINA *(nasty voice)* How should I know? People are dying – they're shooting out there. *(sarcastic)* You must have heard that much.

INA   Who's they?

VALENTINA I'm tired. And I've no wish to answer stupid questions. Or ask them. There's only one man who's really been shot in this country.

RITA   They shot him? It served him right!

DUTZA *(terrified)* The Russians will come, listen to me – maybe they're here already.

RITA What Russians? Shaikovski – that one?

DUTZA The Russians will come and then the devil will take us! They'll bring order into this country! Harasho, harasho[9]!

RITA Mishto[10]!

DUTZA Mishto, my eye! We'll all speak Russian, drink vodka, and eat blinele!

RITA That's alright, if we can get enough of it!

DUTZA You'll see for yourselves what's in store for us! You wanted oil and flour, bananas and oranges, fine soaps and passports, they'll give you – more than enough! It's been cold here alright – now you'll see how cold Siberia is!

RITA What's she on about?

DUTZA And what about him? What's he doing here? Wake him up, let's hear him talk. Does he even speak Romanian?

RITA He said: 'mother'...

DUTZA Big deal! That's not difficult! *(she goes to his bed)* Wake up, tavarishi Sovietki[11]! *(shakes him)* Wake up, you!

MARTA Leave him alone, he is a human being.

DUTZA He is not. He's a 'comrade'. *(shakes him harder)* Wake up!

YOUNG MAN What... what do you want? Who are you?

DUTZA Who am I? Who are you ?

INA *(triumphantly)* He is Romanian, see? He speaks Romanian.

DUTZA Don't jump to conclusions, speaking is one thing, feeling is a different one! His heart – see if it's Romanian. Come on, tell us – who are you?

YOUNG MAN *(yawning)* My name is Mihai.

DUTZA Where do you come from?

YOUNG MAN I live on the street of Happiness, number eight. Near the railway station.

---

[9] In Russian in original, meaning: 'Good!'

[10] In Romany in original, meaning: 'Good!'

[11] In pidgin Russian in original, meaning: 'Soviet comrade'.

DUTZA   There is no such street!

YOUNG MAN Oh yes, there is. It's the shortest street in the city. It has ten houses, but none faces the street. The gardens face it. Large, nice, with flowers. No door, just the gardens and the backs of the houses. If you want to go in, you have to go round the other side. The entrances are all on other streets.

MARTA   He's delirious.

DUTZA *(rudely)* Don't be silly – he's fine.

YOUNG MAN I'm telling the truth. That's where I live. That's my address. I've already told you my name. What else do you want? *(He tries to turn his back and go to sleep again.)*

VALENTINA We want to know what's happened.

YOUNG MAN I don't know. There was a signal. It must have been a siren we all heard. Then we came out. We jumped over the fences, behind the houses. Right into the street of Happiness.

RITA   I'm always jumping over fences!

YOUNG MAN Somebody set off the alarm bells.

VALENTINA Who?

YOUNG MAN A passer-by. Occasionally, somebody goes past.

INA   I don't believe it. Everything must have been planned, thought out, organized.

YOUNG MAN That's what you think. But there was nothing. Only the siren, and then the train stopped.

VALENTINA But the train whistles and then it leaves again.

YOUNG MAN Once the passengers have got off. Those who've reached the end of the line.

INA   The end of the line? You mean we've got nowhere left to go? That everything that's happened was all for nothing? That the train has broken down and we have to walk? In the dark? To the final stop?

YOUNG MAN Oh, well, it was bound to happen. If there's no station, that's ok. We'll build one. If the train's stopped, no problem, it's the end of the road.

INA   You mean that… when the lights go out, the fuel's run out, and somebody pulls the emergency stop, that's where the stop is? Who says so? Who?

YOUNG MAN The stops are only by chance, trains have to stop from time to time.

INA I don't understand. And I don't want to understand!

DUTZA Bollocks! he's lying. Why did you say you were shot?

YOUNG MAN Me? I didn't.

DUTZA So you weren't shot?

YOUNG MAN: What if I wasn't? Others were, around me, in the crowd. People got hurt, some even died... it's not enough to pull the alarm, someone has to lie on the rails.

VALENTINA You let us bring you here, treat you like a wounded hero, drove us mad with worry, crying for your mother. Why? Why did you lead us on?

YOUNG MAN Why, why, why! You wanted to believe and I – I was crying for my mother. So? Don't I have the right to cry for my mother? You said I was hurt. Why should I argue with you? I was tired. I'd slept long enough on benches, in parks, spent so long the militia would take me away in my sleep.

INA But you said that... on the street of Happiness –

YOUNG MAN I didn't say I slept there! Come on! Did you believe *that? (he laughs)* You thought it was true?
(He laughs more and more.)

RITA Ok. Fuck off!

YOUNG MAN I don't want to. I like it here. Is there anything to eat?

VALENTINA Go, or I'll get the porters to throw you out.

YOUNG MAN 'cos you ain't capable, are you? You can't do it. Poor little women *(change of tone)* – no pity for a poor man... you pretending you cared for me, pretending you had a heart, but no... *(he rises)* You commies – you stinking filthy commies! *(to Valentina)* you commie doctor, bitch – they'll find you in a ditch!

VALENTINA *(pathetically)* Out! get out! *Now!*

YOUNG MAN *(mocking them, acting again, as he has done all the time, but then he becomes deadly serious, then mocks again shortly after)* Outside? In the streets? They're shooting out there, can't you hear? They're shooting. They'll kill me – mother – you're sending me to death, you bastards. Who's shooting who?

You commies are, your secret police, at us, the people, who've been carrying them like trained horses, and you shoot at us, you – who else is to blame? You are, and those like you, those who stay indoors under their warm blankets peeping out, crying for the dead and never interfering – saying they've something better to do – like looking after babies. For two thousand years you haven't interfered, simply made babies and then killed them, and cried for them saying others were the murderers. You're the ones – it's your fault.

VALENTINA It's easy to blame others. But who made you the way you are? Look at you – you weren't born like this – with your back always bent.

YOUNG MAN My mother, of course. She's to blame. She should have fucked an American marine, not a Roman slave. You cunts! Do you think your sons are any better? Do you think you're not guilty of bringing them to life? You think it will be any better now? We built, and we built and we built. Stations, a future of light – what for? Who for? The same people will stay at the top. *(pause)* Why should I die? Why should I let them shoot me? There are no heroes, only the dead who mean nothing, nothing at all… I'd rather live. Anyway, anywhere, they give me a plate of catfood, I'll be happy. Let the Germans come, the Americans, the French, let them bring us petfood – they owe it to us. It's because of them we've come to this. Their re-spon-si-bi-li-ty!!! Theirs! Let the foreign aid come! And let's have a party! Let's eat, drink, fuck and be merry! Five days after the Revolution! Six days after the Revolution! Seven days after the Revolution! Seven days and three hours. And let's sing! Wake up, Romanians…yo, heroes… *(he raises his fist)* And let's make statues for them — let's cast them all in cement. A bust for the beloved leader, a bust for the national poet, a bust for mother, 'cos she gave me life. And another one for, 'cos I deserve it. I'm not dead yet. So what? I'm immortal, like the Phoenix… and I stand here, at the crossroads of Europe, with my belly full, pointing one accusing finger to the West, and another one to the East. Me? I'm really sorry, I'm not to blame. I'm not, you hear? It's them – the Russians, the Turks, the Americans, the Germans, the Hungarians, the Jews, the Gypsies! Not me! Not my fault! I am what I am – it's not my fault that I was born here! *(long pause)* But if you've got a lump of sugar, you can let me have it – French sugar, English sugar, Baptist sugar… it's been a long time since we used to make Romanian sugar. We make statues. So what? We have jobs. We work, we work hard. Look, look how hard we work… Build, demolish, build, demolish! My name is Meister Manole, the builder[12], hear me? I work all day long, and at night it all comes down. I work during the day… at night I'm busy. I dream. I dream, yeh… I dream I'm in the San Pietro Cathedral, in the Basilica at Sophia, in the Eiffel Tower. They were all built at night… but I don't work at night. Let others build cathedrals at night… in the mornings I wake up crying because even my foundations have crumbled. Manole is my name, do you hear me? Meister Manole! *(pause)* And I only believe in what I dream – in what I see around me – never. I don't believe people are being shot outdoors, I don't believe the commies have disappeared, I don't believe the world changes.The world changes at night, but unfortunately I'm sleeping then. Wake up, Manole! Oh, yeh… We all sleep at night. It's our right – a human right, isn't it? And I won't raise a finger, except to ask for my human sleeping rights. To sleep! That's my right! And I'll sleep here now, in your beds, 'cos it's noisy outside.

(He lies on the bed, pulls the blanket over his head. Silence.)

INA   What are we going to do with him?

VALENTINA I quit. I'm only filling out the discharge forms. For both of you. For all three of you, if you want… *(she exits.)*

DUTZA   Yes. I want to go. I want to go home… poor Gitza, who knows what's happening?… with three children…

INA   I want to go, too. Now that I'm better.

RITA   What am I going to do? I'd rather stay here .

MARTA   That's no longer possible.You have to go, Rita. Me too – I'm old enough to retire. What should I stay for? It's over. Over.

---

[12]   Manole is the hero of a famous Romanian folk poem. He was asked by the Black King to build the most beautiful monastery in the world, and to sacrifice his loving wife, Ana, who was pregnant. She was buried alive in the foundations. When Manole proposed to build an even greater monastery, the King ordered the staircases to be removed and all the masons died trying to fly from the roof, with wings they had made from the shingles.

RITA   But what should I do with the baby? What should I do with him?

DUTZA   The borders are open. Maybe a rich German will come along and buy him from you. You could get a lot for him.

RITA   Sell him? For money?

MARTA   Why not? We've been selling our souls for nothing. For illusions. For dreams. *(she exits.)*

RITA   I'll be rich! And I'll make another one and sell that one too. For good money! I'll make ten more and sell them all! A hundred, a thousand! I'll populate the world with them! And I'll buy you all! I'll drive a Mercedes and throw oranges at you! I won't eat sunflower seeds anymore. I'll spit orange peel from the window of my big black Mercedes! I'll buy you all! All of you! From my Mercedes! All of you! *(triumphantly)* With cash! *(she takes out a handful of sunflower seeds from her pocket)* Like this! Like this! *(she scatters seeds over the audience.)*

Blackout.

SCENE 3

The women are ready to leave. Ina, Rita, Dutza. Rita and Dutza hold their babies. They're sitting on their beds. Ina, her hands on her belly, feeling it from time to time, as if it were a piano. She hums Tchaikovsky's 'Napolitan Song'.

YOUNG MAN *(speaks easily, at first, then with more and more difficulty, and grim, panting and choking, until the final word. He is bleeding again. When he walks, he leaves traces. He looks at his hands, obviously he has a wound. But no-one cares, the women ignore him)* This is Radio Romania. Here is the news. Today, at ten o'clock, in the Palace Square, three people died. A cross was quickly raised, candles were lit. We foresee a good year for the domestic candle industry. Also at ten o'clock, three generals committed suicide. No comment, in alphabetical order. Candles were lit, brass fanfares sounded the national anthem. At the funeral, the national poet made a speech: 'The entire Romanian People thank you!' Then the most important of the generals rose from the dead and replied: 'The Fatherland will be grateful to us! We serve the Fatherland!' Death toll: Timisoara – constant; Brasov – increased 10 bullets; Sibiu – decreased by two feet of earth; Jassy – decreased five coffins; Craiova – increased two babies; Bucharest – constant and dangerous increase.

INA *(stops her imaginary piano playing)* What's he on about? He's delirious again!

DUTZA *(disdainfully)* Fuck, he's putting it on…

YOUNG MAN *(more and more difficult)* We now have more important information. A truck with aid from the Netherlands has stopped at the first corner, in Cluj. Blue jeans, peanuts and chocolate are being distributed. In the main square in Calafat, another two trucks – Belgian. They're distributing vacuum-packed coffee and second-hand refrigerators. The people were also given special parcels containing Caucasian pullovers with Norwegian designs and export-refused Korean scarves made of red Shetland wool. All the maternity hospitals have been sent out-of-date powdered milk. You can find Bulgarian cigarettes at 12 lei 50 in all the tobacconists, you can find colour TVs and hand embroidered curtains in all the shops in the centre of every town in Romania.

RITA   Where did he say? I need some of those.

YOUNG MAN And now you can hear the Free Romanian Television programme. Today: Live talk show at 4 o'clock. Live transmission at 6 o'clock. Live transmission of Railway workers' strike at 8 o'clock. Live transmission of the Miners' march at 9 o'clock. At half past nine, for the first time on Romanian Television, Channel I, *Superman III*, at 23.00 exclusive Bruce Lee, at 1 o' clock, *The Red Dictator's Shoes*, a previously banned film. We shall now broadcast a very important announcement for the whole country, coming from the Central Front: 'You needn't worry. We are free. We have won. We are free. We have won. We are free. We have won. We are free. We have won. We are free. We have won… *(he stumbles, falls, snorts, moans. Nobody cares. Rita lights a cigarette.)*

DUTZA   You smoking again? Fucking drop that cigarette right now!

RITA   Really? I don't think anyone can stop me now! I'm free to smoke whenever I want to!

DUTZA   Can't you see there are people around you?

RITA   What the fuck do I care?

DUTZA   We don't bloody like it, that's why.

RITA   Why don't you fucking go home? You're free, so am I. If you don't like fags, why stop me?

DUTZA   Because I say so.

RITA   That's no fucking freedom. It's fucking dictatorship!

INA   Please, put it out. I'm asking you nicely. Of course you may smoke, but in the corridor, or outside but not here.

RITA   You mean I'm allowed to be free? What fucking kind of freedom is that – with conditions? *(Ina makes a begging gesture)* Alright. I'll put it out. Just one more drag...
(She puts out the cigarette on the floor.)

DUTZA   You little slut! Where do you think you are? At home in your fucking tent?

INA   Oh, no, please, please, don't start again! I've had enough!

DUTZA   Oh, the lady does not quarrel, the lady does not swear. The lady is educated.

RITA   Now we're equal! And I talk when and how I want to.

Valentina enters.

VALENTINA What's going on here? Calm down now!

DUTZA *(menacingly)* Here's somebody else wants to give orders!

VALENTINA *(authoritatively)* Stop it! Now!
(they stop, intimidated) I've brought your discharge papers. Here! And let's wake him up, he can't stay here. Hey, you, Mihai Manole, or whatever your name is – wake up! *(she pulls the blanket away from him)* Wake up, it's time to leave! *(shakes him)* Come on, don't play dead... cut the crap!

INA   Maybe he's not pretending.

VALENTINA Meaning?

INA   Maybe he *is* dead. Really dead this time. He was saying something... and we didn't listen.

VALENTINA *(bending over)* I don't think so. *(she stands, petrified. Pause. Tired)* He's not breathing. And he's covered in blood.

DUTZA   God... he really?

VALENTINA It looks like it. He must have been sick, very sick.

DUTZA   ...some unknown illness...

RITA   ...that doesn't even exist...

VALENTINA ...nor does he.

DUTZA   Yeh, right. He doesn't exist. He's never been here, the son-of-a-bitch...

INA   We've killed him.

DUTZA   Shut up! Nobody's killed anybody.

VALENTINA *(mockingly)* It was an accident.*(laughs)* Nobody will believe it. I'll call the militia now.You killed a hero, a young man who was asking for your help, a miserable boy who depended on you... So?

INA   Another hero on the lists of unknown heroes. One more or less... what difference?...

DUTZA   No! Don't! Courts, militia, prison! I have four children. *(she clings to Valentina's white overall, bursting into tears)* Who's going to look after them?

RITA   Why, Gitza, of course!

DUTZA   I'm not going to prison! I don't want to. Do something, do something, please! *(she cries)* Tell us what to do.

VALENTINA Go home! Now – at once! Leave him here, you know nothing. You haven't even seen him. He's a foreigner. Nobody knows who he is – he's a tramp, a vagabond...

INA   What does one more grave matter?

DUTZA   What about her? She'll drop us in it. She can't wait to get her own back.

VALENTINA She's not going to talk, either. She hasn't raised a finger to help him – she's as guilty as we are! Personally, I feel my conscience is clear.

INA   Your conscience! The cupboard where you've kept all your corpses, Valentina! That's what you've done all your life – hide them away. Will you hide him away, as well?

Marta comes in.

VALENTINA Marta! I thought you'd left!

MARTA *(her eyes on the fallen Young Man)* I've come to say good bye. *(she stares at him)* I couldn't leave like this, without a word. *(she speaks to the women, but continuously stares at the man)* I've been through all the wards, I've said goodbye to all the corners, to all the beds. To all the seventeen thousand women I've helped to deliver their babies, to all my babies. To all the doctors. *(she bends down, touches him)* You've died, haven't you? Poor love, this has been your destiny. To leave the world, where others begin. *(she caresses him, and discretely begins to weep.)*

INA   What's going to happen to us?

RITA   Come, let the Romany read your future! Your future is in your own hands! *(she takes their palms, in turn)* Just a hundred to find out your future! You'll find romance at night with a knave of hearts, but don't trust him, 'cos you never know what's ahead... you'll marry three times, but the last husband's your true love... I can see two boys here: one is very clever, the other one's a blind fool, but I don't know which one is gonna live... you travel a long way and get sick – you don't die, but don't know if you survive either... you'll earn a heap of money but don't know if it's you who'll spend it... you'll have a huge house, but don't know if you're gonna live in it, don't know, the Romany don't know...

(The four women are petrified. They speak their monologues alternately, then in parallel, culminating in a symphony.)

VALENTINA I take my doll, my childhood doll that I sleep with every night and I get on the first train. I run, I have no luggage, I don't want to take anything with me. The train eats up the rails, I get to the border.

INA   Now I can go back home. My big house, with warm rooms. I walk in the street, I call on a neighbour. We have some tea.

DUTZA   I go back to my village. The school is clean, white-washed. There's plenty of wood for the fire, the stoves are roaring.

MARTA   It's among the hills, you can see the shiny red tiled roof. It's tall and white, with flowers at the windows.

VALENTINA A soldier takes my doll. He laughs. Its head is broken. 'What have you got hidden in its belly?' he asks. 'Nothing,' I feel like crying. But I never cry. He tears her belly open with his bayonet. 'And now?' he says. 'Aren't you going to cry now?' My doll, my doll. He throws her on the floor. He treads on her with his boots.

INA   I see my piano again. It's full of dust, but it looks al-right. Maybe it's not out of tune. I sit, raise my hands.

DUTZA   At the pub, two old men drink coffee. 'Yuk,' one says, the chickory one was a lot better!

MARTA   Mother Superior comes to me. 'Welcome, Marta,' the cell's waiting for you...

VALENTINA I pick up my baby from the floor. The stuffing falls out and a broken voice-box says over and over: 'mama-mama-mama-mama-mama-ma...' I crush it with my heel. And I run. I run and never come back to / *(they speak simultaneously)*: ...the cold, the dirt, the humiliation, the dark.

INA   I play. But not a sound comes out. The music is inside me./ *(alone)* And it makes me forget. I forget about myself, my loneliness, music speaks no tongue. I forget what tongue I speak./ *(overlapping with Dutza)* I don't think any more, I feel. And I hear the piano. Forcefully. Powerfully./

DUTZA   My daughters have grown up. Now I have grand-children. And I forget / *(alone)* I forget I've ever delivered babies, that I didn't want them, that I'm afraid. I forget who I am./ *(over-lapping with Marta)* It's only the muddy courtyard, the slops for the pigs, and the washing-up.../

MARTA   The sheets are coarse, but I'm old. I pray and I forget. I forget about this world./ *(alone)* I even forget about God. 'Remember, Marta,' says Mother Superior. 'Stop praying. Remember!'

(The Young Man rises slowly to his feet.)

YOUNG MAN And you? Did you believe? Oh, come on!
(he laughs) Did you?

(He laughs again and the laughter gets louder and louder.)

Blackout.
The end.

Alina Nelega

Born in 1960, December 18, in Targu-Mures, Transylvania. Graduated the Cluj/Kolosvar University in 1984. She has had short stories,
plays, essays and reviews published in various literary and theatre
journals. She is currently running a theatre quarterly founded by The
University of Journalism of Bucharest and an alternative group of
critics, based in Bucharest and Cluj.

At present she is the Artistic Director of the *International New
Writing Festival Dramafest* and runs *The Romanian New Writing
Project*. She is an associate lecturer at the Theatre University in
Targu-Mures and runs the *International Department* of the *National
Theatre* in the same city.

The Chosen Ones

In 1994, *The Chosen Ones* won joint first prize in the first European playwriting competition held in Kassel, Germany. Successful productions ran in Moscow, Tallinn and Minsk. *Life's Small Pleasures* is running successfully in Dresden. *Korytsin's Life* and *Farewell to the Homeland* did well in two competitions for playwrights in Belorussia and are now running in a Belorussian version in Minsk and Vitebsk.

I was haunted by shadows of the past for many years. Then, one day, I closed my eyes and I saw a huge old apartment, time-worn and almost empty, in which a heap of old junk was all that remained of former glory. A mad old man was wandering about the apartment, crying out from time to time. And then a beautiful woman appeared; there was something in her eyes which reminded me of Italian madonnas. That was the beginning of *The Chosen Ones*, a play about a family crisis and the fall of a State.

My characters tread their own paths of penitence and atonement; but they are normal people and like all people they are victims of circumstance. They deserve our pity. The force and meaning of this feeling should not be underestimated. It unites us and makes us better people.

There was no fairness in the old system – there was no miracle of loaves and fishes, it was not all happiness and equality... There is no fairness now either, yet, somewhere far in the future, Truth and the Ideal are beginning to stir and glimmer. There is a Path to them – perhaps a number of paths. The path is endless. It is, in fact, life and the meaning of life. The most important thing is to go forward, knowing that life itself, apart from its dogma and social demands, this quivering, fluttering, thrill, trepidation, trembling of Being is wonderful.

Elena Popova

'... a modern drama... honest, truthful, without ornamentation, but with sympathy towards its characters, whose destinies are controlled by Time in all its ruthlessness... the first night ended with standing ovations and a stage covered with flowers... the actors in love with their characters, however strange and pathetic they seem...'

Moskovskaya Pravda, N. Balasheva.

The Chosen Ones

by Elena Popova
translated by Sandra Harvey

The play was first performed on 7th September 1995 at the Pushkin
Theatre in Moscow. It was produced by Elena Dolgina.
Subsequently produced as part of the Bonner Biennale in 1998 and
by Vitaly Barkovsky at the Russian Theatre, Minsk.

CHARACTERS
Irina
Nastya
Vanda
Olya
Slava
Reutskii
The Old Man

ACT ONE

*A flat in a block built in the late nineteen forties or early nineteen
fifties. It is large, echoing and grand in design. On stage we see a big
hall, an entrance lobby, which connects a number of other rooms,
and a kitchen. Nonetheless, the overriding impression is one of
neglect. The walls are discoloured and long due for redecoration.
The corners are cluttered with boxes and all those other objects
which build up in a human habitation over the years. The coat rack
is piled haphazardly with clothes; its base is heaped with old shoes.*

*The Old Man enters the lobby. He is putting on his overcoat, fumb-
ling for the sleeves. Irina and Nastya are sitting in the kitchen opposite an uncurtained window. Irina is wearing a man's dressing-gown.
She is Nastya's mother, but at this hour of the morning, before they
have washed and with puffy, unmade-up faces, they look more like*

*sisters. They are drinking coffee in silence from unmatched cups.
Each is lost in her own thoughts. Suddenly, Nastya moves towards
the window sill and throws some crumbs out to the pigeons.*

IRINA *(lazily)* Don't! When you're not here, I'm the one who has to
clear up the mess they make on the windowsill.

NASTYA   A sparrow's come down! *(she calls the sparrow)* Oh,
he's so sweet, the cheeky little chap – he's not scared of us at all!

IRINA   True to his working class nature, then.

NASTYA   Not like your upper class pigeons... Look, they're
too lazy even to chase my sparrow off. The doves of peace! Oh,
but, no, it looks as if there's going to be a fight... it looks like it...
will they fight or not, what do you think?

IRINA   They won't fight.

NASTYA   Right as usual, Mum. He's taken the best bit and
flown off. *(she jumps back from the window sill and drains her
coffee cup.)*

(A noise comes from the lobby. The Old Man has dropped a box.)

NASTYA   He's up and about again, is he?

IRINA *(after a pause)* God, I'm so tired.

NASTYA   Well, you shouldn't do so much. *(after a pause)* I
don't think there've been any curtains here since spring.

IRINA   Don't exaggerate. It's been a month at most. Vanda
took them down to wash them.

*(The doorbell rings. The Old Man raps at the hall door with his
stick.)*

OLD MAN   Who's there? Who's there?

NASTYA   He's terrorising people again. Who is it?

*She gets up lightly, runs into the lobby, opens the door and
disappears behind it. She returns with a telegram.*

...where are you off to, Grandpa? It's still early.

OLD MAN   I'm going.

NASTYA   Look at the time! It's too early!

OLD MAN *(looks at the clock)* It's ten twenty two. I told them. I *said* I'm going.

NASTYA   Come on, Grandpa, be reasonable. Come on, let's get your coat off. Come on now. Let's just…
(Nastya quickly takes off the Old Man's overcoat, takes him into his room and comes back to the kitchen)
…the telegram's for you. No harm done, the postman knows him.

IRINA *(looks at the telegram)* No, it's not for me.

NASTYA   It's got your full name on it.

IRINA *(reading)* Arriving sixteenth. Aleksandr. No, it's not for me.

NASTYA Don't give me that! It's got your name on it, see? Try and think back. I know what you're like!

IRINA   I don't remember anyone called Aleksandr…
(pause) Do you want some more coffee?

NASTYA   No, I'm all shaky as it is. It's Valerka… My imagination starts working overtime.

IRINA   That's no bad thing, sometimes.

NASTYA   Do you know what he said to me the other day? 'Put on weight and I'll dump you! You're already on the heavy side…' Am I on the heavy side? I'm not exactly fat.

IRINA   Of course you're not fat!

NASTYA   I've got broad shoulders.

IRINA   You've got normal shoulders. Be proud of the way you are.

NASTYA   I've heard that kind of advice before: 'Be proud of the way you are … and sit at home on your own'. You were the pretty one in our family.

IRINA   And you're pretty too.

Slava comes out of his room. He is wearing a faded tracksuit which has gone baggy at the knees. He lights a gas ring on the cooker and puts on a pan of water.

SLAVA   Good morning.

NASTYA   Hi, Dad. *(Slava goes out)* Are you two still not speaking?

IRINA   You could say that. There's no need.

NASTYA   Well, you should find one.

Slava returns and puts two eggs into the pan. He watches dejectedly as the water boils. Then he glances at the clock, puts the eggs onto a plate and goes out.

NASTYA   Bye, Dad. I'm going.

SLAVA   Cheerio.
               (He disappears into his room.)

NASTYA   Poor, neglected man.

IRINA (*wraps herself tighter in the dressing-gown*) You feel sorry for him.

NASTYA (*pause*) Of course, it's awful that he's been living here all this time. He upsets you.

IRINA   Personally, I couldn't care less.

NASTYA   Maybe not, but that doesn't make it any better. Do you want a cigarette? *(they smoke. Nastya stubs out her cigarette)* I can't even smoke! It's time for me to go, Ma.

IRINA   When will you be back?

NASTYA   I don't know. When I can get away. Don't look like that! Maybe that Aleksandr will turn up!

IRINA (*uncertainly*) I don't know anyone called Aleksandr…

NASTYA   Try and think back. I can see it in your eyes – you've already remembered! Oh, Ma, who are you trying to kid? Anyway, I'm off. To run about all day, and for absolute peanuts. I've had enough of it. Give me a ring.

Nastya leaves. Irina lights another cigarette, picks up a broom, goes into the lobby and starts cleaning. Slava comes out of his room. He is dressed smartly and with care in a well-pressed suit. He has a brief-case. He stops in front of the mirror and tidies his hair.

SLAVA   Are you in this evening?

IRINA   Possibly.

SLAVA   I've got guests this evening.

IRINA   That's your business.

SLAVA   I'm just letting you know.

IRINA   Alright.

SLAVA   Have you turned Nastya against me too?

IRINA   No, I haven't turned her against you.

SLAVA   I'm the one who's brought her up since she was six – amongst other things. I've given her a lot!

IRINA   She calls you Dad… What date is it today, do you know?

SLAVA   It's the sixteenth. *(pause)* I've got guests this evening…

IRINA   So you said. *(she sits very straight and smokes. She does not look at Slava. Her indifference probably annoys him more than anything else. He turns on his heel and closes the hall door slightly more loudly than usual. Irina picks up a box from the floor)* Oh, Dad, what have you done now?

The doorbell rings. Irina opens the door as she is – a cigarette in one hand and the broom in the other. Reutskii is standing in the doorway. He is expensively, stylishly dressed. He has a habit of brushing the sleeves of his jacket. The Old Man comes out of his room, rapping his stick.

OLD MAN   Who's there? Who's there? *(he raises his stick sharply, aims at Reutskii and fires)* Bang!
(Reutskii makes a startled movement backwards and knocks his shoulder against the door post.)

REUTSKII   Ow! Damn!

IRINA   Dad, go to your room… *(she takes her father back into his room)* He's here to see me, not you. Go on… *(she shuts the door behind him.)*.

REUTSKII   Er, ye-es…

IRINA   So it is you after all, Reutskii. How funny.

REUTSKII *(rubbing his bruised shoulder)* Yes, very funny!

IRINA   You appeared so suddenly…

REUTSKII   You mean you didn't get my letters?

IRINA   I did, actually… At New Year and on the eighth of March last year…
(There is the sound of a key turning in a lock. Vanda comes in)
But here's Vanda Petrovna!

VANDA *(crossing the lobby as if in her own house, tidying as she goes)* I go out for five minutes and the whole place goes to pieces. Look at the mess they've made, just look at it!

IRINA   I'm cleaning up, Vanda Petrovna.

VANDA   I know your kind of cleaning. You might as well not bother. What's he had to eat?

IRINA   He hasn't had anything yet. He's waiting for you. But yesterday I did some dumplings.

VANDA   All shop-bought. And you know what shop-bought food's like. That's why he doesn't eat when he's with you. Well, he does with me – he eats everything I put in front of him.

IRINA   Yes, Vanda Petrovna, what would I do without you? *(pause)* And this is Reutskii. Aleksandr Reutskii! *(pause)* We were on holiday together a few years ago, in the South.

VANDA   The South – that's nice.
(She goes into the Old Man's room and then into the kitchen.)

IRINA   Yes, in the South it was wonderful! *(pause)* Are you here on business?

REUTSKII   Partly on business, partly to see you. I did promise.

IRINA   How long for?

REUTSKII   Until tomorrow evening.

IRINA   It's funny…

REUTSKII   Why?

IRINA   It's just that… Time's passed…

REUTSKII   Does time mean that much to you?

IRINA   Time means that much to everyone.

REUTSKII   Not to me, it doesn't!

IRINA   So you're the exception.

REUTSKII   I remember your words… you said: 'If we meet a year from now, it won't be me. It'll be me plus a year.' So now are you, you as you were then in the South, plus four years?

IRINA *(pause)* This is my daughter's room, but she doesn't live here any more. I'll put some clean sheets on the bed.

REUTSKII   Shall I throw my bag down here?

IRINA   I can give you a key.

REUTSKII   Won't you be here later on?

IRINA   I should be, in theory…

REUTSKII   If you aren't here, I'll wait. I'm not in a hotel, I've come to see you. *(pause)* I'll be back in a few hours. Wait for me.

Reutskii goes out. Vanda appears, stirring something in a pan.

VANDA   He seems very energetic.

IRINA   We were on holiday together. In Gagrakh.

VANDA   I've never been to Gagrakh. I've been to Sakakh and Berdansk. A friend of mine lived in Berdansk. The fruit there was exceptionally cheap.

IRINA   It was nice in Gagrakh, too…

VANDA   After that I told everyone, if you go down there, go to Berdansk.

IRINA   We went everywhere, we had a wonderful time… We went to Sukhumi, Novii Afon… it was the beginning of May… there was hardly anybody there… the colours were so fresh – holiday colours. And the sea was a stunning blue, a sort of aquamarine. There was the sea, that fresh greenness, the waterfalls… I had some leave at the end of April, I thought I was going to die of boredom. I got out of the train – it was early morning and the platform was empty – it was drizzling in a depressing sort of way… and then Reutskii gets out of the next carriage and takes hold of my suitcase *(she laughs. Pause)* How funny…

VANDA *(with feeling)* Plums were only a few kopeks!
(Irina starts to rummage in a chest of drawers)…what are you looking for in there, Irina Nikolayevna?

IRINA   I want to put up some sort of curtains in the kitchen.

VANDA   I'll bring them tomorrow. I keep forgetting.

IRINA   Tomorrow's all very well – I want them today!

SCENE 2

*The evening of the same day. The door of Slava's room flies open
and Slava and Olya stumble out, dancing. They move around the
entrance lobby and the hall, bumping into furniture and laughing.
Olya is squealing. Slava takes some long-stemmed glasses from the
cupboard. He plays a tune from Carmen on the glasses and hums
along. (CARMEN) Olya laughs.*

SLAVA   Shhh! You're not at home now! (*Olya laughs even
   louder)*…I said be quiet! Sshh! *(he drags Olya back into his
   room.)*

*Vanda is watching them through a crack in between the doors. She
comes out quickly with the Old Man. She puts on her coat and pulls
the Old Man's overcoat on. Irina comes in from the street.*

IRINA   What's this, are you off to Moscow?
VANDA   Off to Moscow, off to Moscow… It's the second
   time we've been to Moscow today. *(she sits the Old Man down)*
   To Moscow!
   *(Irina goes through to the kitchen and comes back with a sand-
   wich. She is humming)*
   … You've got visitors, by the way.
IRINA   Yes, he said.
VANDA   A blonde. Very loud.
IRINA   He likes blondes.
VANDA   They put the tea on then got the wine glasses out.
IRINA   Oh, for goodness' sake, let them!
VANDA   Last time, he broke a glass. It was a Venetian one.
   You should have told him not to use them.
IRINA   What was I supposed to say?
VANDA   Of course, it wasn't you who worked so hard to buy
   them. That took years – but they're gone in a day. Nikolai Nikol-
   ayevich bought those glasses in an antique shop in Vienna.
IRINA   Dad loved glass. He loved all beautiful, delicate
   things. We had some Christmas toys, unusual ones. They got
   broken.

(The Old Man is becoming upset. He is starting to fidget in his chair. He raps his stick.)

VANDA *(rocking the chair vigorously, as if rocking the cradle of a grizzling child)* Shhh! There, we'll be in Moscow soon! It's cold in Moscow! We'll have to put your fur hat on. *(she puts the Old Man's fur hat on)* That's it. We've put your fur hat on.

IRINA   You won't get lost, will you?

VANDA   No, they're sending a car to meet us from the train. We shan't have to walk... we shan't have to wa-alk *(sing song)*... Come on then, shall we get into the car? *(she sits the Old Man down in another chair. Pause)* Can you hear them? Music... They're dancing!

IRINA   Oh, let them do what they want!

VANDA   If it was me, I'd be furious. I was jealous with all my husbands. All of them. Even now, when I think of it, I get jealous.

IRINA   Well, I'm not. I'm not jealous of anyone.

VANDA   That's because you're a cold woman. Cold-hearted.
(The doorbell rings)
Well, that's your young man! You go and meet your young man. And we'll be off to the Kremlin, won't we? Off we go good as gold to the Kremlin... good as gold. *(she takes off the Old Man's overcoat and fur hat and puts them back onto the rack. She takes the Old Man away.)*

Irina opens the door and Reutskii comes in, loaded down with packages.

IRINA   What's that you're carrying?

REUTSKII   What do you mean, what is it? Food!

IRINA   All that?

REUTSKII   You're not going to feed me on dumplings!

IRINA *(pause)* And naturally you want me to go into the kitchen and do something with all of it?

REUTSKII   Don't you want to?

IRINA   I've just eaten. *(pause)* Can I get you a sandwich or something?

REUTSKII   I wouldn't say no.
(Irina takes Reutskii's shopping into the kitchen and comes back with a sandwich.)

IRINA   I've put it all in the fridge. We'll have it when we feel like it.

REUTSKII   Don't you feel like it now?

IRINA   No. I've already told you – I've just eaten. There's no need for people to eat so much.

REUTSKII   But they have to eat something!

IRINA   Well, I'll bring you another sandwich. *(she brings him another sandwich)* You spent a huge amount of money.

REUTSKII   You never used to notice. Darling Irina plus four years... I wanted to come and see you straight afterwards... I didn't manage it.

IRINA   You're earning money?

REUTSKII   Is that a bad thing?

IRINA   Why should it be?

REUTSKII   It's very addictive!

IRINA   I believe you.

REUTSKII   When you've got money, you feel different.

IRINA   A real man.

REUTSKII   Yes.

IRINA   Funny, I've heard that before...

REUTSKII   We always had it drummed into us that people don't need a lot of money. And so when you've got a lot...

IRINA   Funny... A few years back you were perfectly happy with what you had.

REUTSKII   Did you like that in me?

IRINA   I've never thought about what I like in you.

REUTSKII   I like my work. *(pause)* Ira, why won't you call me Aleksandr? *(pause)* Well, say something... Say: 'It's funny...' *(pause)*. Was that your husband I saw this morning? Nice suit, briefcase? I heard you'd divorced.

IRINA   Do you want to see my passport?

REUTSKII   And the girl?

IRINA   That was my daughter. You must have been standing outside my door for quite a while. Any more questions?

REUTSKII   I know I don't have any right to ask.
(*A noise comes from the Old Man's room. Reutskii jumps and turns round*) What's that?

IRINA   I think he's inspecting a parade. He adores parades.

REUTSKII   Yes... it's appalling... (*pause*) To me, you were like a girl from another planet... But now you're – in this place... A few repairs wouldn't hurt... Your ex-husband, the old man...

IRINA   Don't get it all out of proportion. I loved my father very much. (*pause*) He was already over forty when I was born, but he was still an outstanding army officer. I remember going somewhere on a train... I was two or three... There were mirrors everywhere... I looked into them... I was so pleased with my reflection! What happened to those railway carriages? It's as if they've fallen into an abyss and vanished... I remember those mirrors... The mirrors, the smell of 'Krasnaya Moskva' eau de cologne, the smell of cognac and expensive cigarettes... I ate oranges and threw the peel onto the floor, onto the carpet, and my father drank cognac with his friends and smoked and played cards... It was all so – chic! (*pause*) Though, you know, really, he came from an ordinary family. They all came from ordinary families. But they had opportunities and they revelled in those opportunities like children. Like you, when you carted that heap of expensive food back here. What is there to say? Everyone fought for those opportunities. Or whatever you want to call them... Money, power, strength.

REUTSKII   You've always liked real men, since you were a child?

IRINA   I don't know. I haven't thought about it. (*pause*) Mother was wildly jealous of him. But deep down I was on his side. I used to think: 'What does he see in this woman, crawling round the flat all day, dusting?' It was a different world. It had railway carriages with mirrored walls, parades, marches... It's vanished somewhere. Like Atlantis... and everything that came after it has vanished too. Sometimes I think: 'Where has it vanished *to*? What is the past?' Things age... Is memory all we have left? And memory is so subjective! (*pause*) The heavens

opened...
(The Old Man's shouts are heard through the wall.)

REUTSKII   Do you love him as idealistically now?

IRINA   I feel sorry for him.

REUTSKII   You have to get away. You won't sort yourself out just by re-doing this place.

IRINA   Start a new life? Reutskii, don't fool yourself, fresh starts can't happen. Whatever your new life is, it's just a continuation of the old one. But even that doesn't upset me. I get on quite well with my life – the old and the new. I've got no choice. I've got no choice. Do you understand?

REUTSKII *(pause)* You're going through a bad patch... It was the same for me, there was a time when nothing mattered.

IRINA *(mockingly)* And now, naturally, things are different?

REUTSKII   Absolutely!

IRINA   Reutskii, you make me laugh! You really make me laugh! *(pause)* Whatever the situation, things always matter to you. Even when you think they don't, they always matter. *(she laughs.)*

(Olya comes into the hall.)

OLYA   Excuse me, I'm looking for the kitchen.

IRINA   Straight ahead... straight on! Wait, I'll put the light on. *(she puts on the entrance hall light.)*

OLYA   Thank you. *(she goes out.)*

IRINA   Don't mention it.

REUTSKII   What are you running here – a hostel?

(Olya returns.)

OLYA   I'm sorry, I'm lost again.

IRINA *(kindly)* It's the door nearest you.

(Olya disappears inside. After a pause, to Reutskii)
Are you shocked?

REUTSKII   I don't know. I haven't had time to think about it.

IRINA   Are you a hypocrite?

(Olya appears again.)

OLYA   Stanislav Sergeyevich is asking for some nitroglycerin.

IRINA   Just a minute... *(she takes a medicine capsule from the cupboard and gives it to Olya.)*

OLYA   Is it dangerous?

IRINA   No, he's used to it.

(Olya goes out.)

REUTSKII   Nice suit, briefcase, takes nitroglycerin...

IRINA   I should think you're ready for bed, aren't you?

REUTSKII   I see.

IRINA *(pause)* You're offended, aren't you? I'v disenchanted you, Reutskii. You wanted a special day, a celebration dinner... you only wanted to eat, after all.

REUTSKII   It doesn't matter, I'll find something.

IRINA   Make sure you do.

REUTSKII   I will. *(pause)* Goodnight.

IRINA   Goodnight.

Reutskii goes out. Slava enters.

SLAVA   Who's that?

IRINA   What business is it of yours?

SLAVA   None, but tell me anyway.

IRINA   I never ask you that kind of question.

SLAVA   I'm a man.

IRINA   Don't be ridiculous! *(Slava's face contorts mournfully)* Don't use emotional blackmail... Nastya was telling me about your blood pressure.

SLAVA   What does she know about it?

IRINA   Quite a lot, in fact.

SLAVA *(hanging around in the doorway)* Whose is that food? In the fridge?

IRINA   Have some. Not all of it, of course, just some of it.

SLAVA   Vanda took the clock to the mender's – but she hasn't brought it back. She'll take your whole house before long.

IRINA   She won't do that.

SLAVA   Are you having something to eat yourself?

IRINA   No, I'm not.

SLAVA   I – I'll take a bit. I haven't had time to go shopping... I'm absolutely starving.

IRINA   I've already told you. Have some.
(Vanda looks in. Slava goes out)
Aren't you staying? Vanda Petrovna, stay! I've had a really hard day today, for some reason. I'm exhausted. *(pause)* Why don't I give Nastya a ring? She'll come and give him an injection.

VANDA *(listening)* There... he's thrown something again.

IRINA   Stay, Vanda Petrovna, please!

VANDA   You know very well that I will.
(Vanda goes out. Olya appears – she has been waiting to catch Irina alone.)

OLYA   Can I have a word with you?

IRINA   Me? *(pause)* What on earth are we going to talk about?

OLYA   There's no need to be so stuck-up.

IRINA   I'm simply asking what we're going to talk about.

OLYA   You aren't making it any easier for me, are you?

IRINA   Well, come straight out with it then.

OLYA   Can't Stanislav Sergeyevich live here?

IRINA   He does live here...

OLYA   Yes, on his own.

IRINA   So what's the problem?

OLYA   There's such a lot of room here...

IRINA   It's my father's flat.

OLYA   It's home for Stanislav Sergeyevich, too. This address is on his papers...

IRINA   Listen, if all the men I've known made a claim to these living quarters, where would I be?

OLYA   He was your husband.

IRINA   I've had three husbands.

OLYA   Oh, you make things so difficult. It's true what people say about you.

IRINA *(suddenly angry)* Well, go on, tell me, what do people say about me? How funny!

OLYA   You don't remember me, of course.

IRINA   No, I don't.

OLYA   Well, I work at Poltoranin's.

IRINA   Poltoranin's? I don't recall.

OLYA   You never noticed me. It's not surprising you don't remember! You never noticed anyone but yourself. You were always so stuck up. No-one could stand you! Who were you? Somebody's daughter! But why are you so stuck up these days? What are you now? Back then, at least you were somebody's daughter. You're not a person, you haven't been for ages. You're a bit of debris – like something from a shipwreck! You're just clinging on to your junk, to all this space... it makes me laugh! It really makes me laugh!

IRINA   Why are you being so aggressive? God, I've never done you any harm! *(pause)* If you want to marry Stanislav Sergeyevich... go and talk to *him* about it.
(Slava looks in.)

SLAVA *(to Olya, harshly)* What are you doing here?

IRINA   Would you please choose your girlfriends with a little more care... someone's been making claims of a territorial nature.

SLAVA   What do you mean? What claims?

OLYA   You said yourself...

SLAVA   Oh my God!

OLYA   You *said* that you couldn't talk to her yourself.

SLAVA   You stupid little cow! *(he pushes Olya into his room)* Just get out! Move!
(Vanda appears.)

VANDA   I'm sorry, but I've just about had enough with him.

IRINA   I'll phone right now... *(she goes into the lobby and dials a number)* Nastya? Nastya darling, could you come over? Grandpa's restless again..

VANDA   He's been throwing everything about, chucking things. I pick them up, he throws them on the floor again, I pick them up, he does it again...
(Slava comes back.)

VANDA   ... have you put the glasses back where they belong, Stanislav Sergeyevich?

SLAVA   Yes, I have. (*Vanda goes out.*)
(*quietly*) Say something to her about the clock. (*pause*) Irina...

IRINA   Slava, go away. I can't stand any more from you.

SLAVA   I can explain...

IRINA   Go away, will you?

Reutskii arrives.

SLAVA (*seeing Reutskii*) Alright, I'm going. (*Slava goes out.*)

REUTSKII   Ah, the happy home! And happy faces here to greet me!

IRINA (*nastily*) Come and join us! (*after a pause, heart-felt*) Reutskii, I never promised you anything! We haven't seen each other for years! We met in a different world! It was a hundred, two hundred years ago! You turned up... stay or go, it's up to you, but don't ask me for anything. (*pause.*)

REUTSKII   You're right. You're absolutely right! I – it doesn't... (*he walks about the room and stops by the window*) How did you put it? 'The heavens opened'...

IRINA   My husband was a Komsomol member for many years... I did tell you before that he worked in the Komsomol. Working there was like being in a cage. Maybe that was what made me feel so deeply for him. But in the evenings, he opened up, softened. The more he bottled up in the day, the more he opened up in the evening. (*pause*) And do you know why he doesn't move out? He could have moved into some kind of separate accommodation years ago. But no, he loves this flat! He loves writing this address on his letters! He loves telling everyone he lives here. Just think, he was one of the *first* to tear up his Party card, but he'll crawl back here to die. It's as important to him as it is for some people to be buried within the walls of the Kremlin. What else would you expect, with his whole life spent in the Komsomol? With people who know nothing but power.

Nastya comes into the flat, dressed in a white nurse's uniform.

NASTYA   Hi, Mum. How are you?

IRINA   Alright.

NASTYA *(looks Reutskii over carefully)* Hello... Mum, I'll give him the jab and go straight back. I only just got permission to come away... the second my shift finishes, Valerka starts watching the clock... There'll be a row if I'm not back on time.
(Nastya disappears into her grandfather's room.)

IRINA   That's my daughter.

REUTSKII   I can see. *(pause)* I'll try and get away a bit earlier tomorrow. When do you finish? I'll come and pick you up and we'll go out somewhere for a while, somewhere different...
(Nastya comes out.)

NASTYA   Mum, I've got to run! The sound of his voice on the phone was so – oh, he's a terror! I'll call in tomorrow for dinner.

Nastya runs out of the flat. Pause.

IRINA   Reutskii, I don't have anywhere else. They sacked me a few months ago. There were staff cuts. It's a good word, isn't it? As if they performed some kind of surgery. Anyway, they threw me out. I haven't found any work yet. *(pause)* I wasn't that bad a worker. I didn't do anyone any harm. I don't know why they did it with such glee.

REUTSKII *(pause)* It happens. *(he is silent for a moment)* But I do often think back to the South. And you. I've been to the South since then. But it wasn't the same. The cypresses, the wine... darling Irina, my white trousers... You do remember my white trousers, don't you? *(Irina smiles)* I'm not a pessimist. When things are lousy, I think back to times when they were good! Islands in a stormy sea! For me, you were one of those islands!

IRINA *(pause)* Reutskii. *(pause)* Come to my room, Reutskii... come on... God, you're so stupid! You make me laugh! Stupid... It's so easy. Come in.

SCENE 3
The morning of the following day. Slava and Olya tiptoe out of Slava's room and through the lobby. Slava lets Olya out of the flat

and retraces his steps. The Old Man appears in a white undershirt. A small portable tape player dangles around his neck. He wanders through the flat, muttering quietly. Suddenly an old Soviet anthem shatters the silence. The Old Man has knocked the tape player. Vanda, woken by the noise, rushes out, switches off the tape player and drags the Old Man back to his room. Irina and Reutskii come out. They go into the kitchen.

IRINA   Coffee?

REUTSKII   I haven't got time. I still have to find out exactly where I'm going. *(he looks out of the kitchen window)* You've got so many pigeons here!

IRINA   Nastya encourages them! *(she raps on the window)* Shoo! Go away!

REUTSKII   When shall we meet up?

IRINA   You don't give up!

REUTSKII   Of course not! I want to see you somewhere... not here.

IRINA   It won't be the Black Sea coast, wherever it is.

REUTSKII   It doesn't matter.

IRINA   You're so stubborn. Well... let's say five o' clock.

REUTSKII   Fantastic! Where?

IRINA   By the Post Office.

REUTSKII   Fantastic! *(pause. Reutskii does not go.)*

IRINA   Well, are you going? Or are you staying for coffee?

REUTSKII   I'm going. *(pause)* Ira... I've had a sudden feeling you won't come...

IRINA   Why? I *promised.*

REUTSKII   Do you remember how I waited for you by the fountain?

IRINA   It couldn't be helped. *(she laughs)* Well, what are you looking at me like that for? For God's sake, you know I couldn't make it that time! You don't forgive and forget, do you?

REUTSKII *(grabs her and pulls her violently towards him)* Ira plus four years! You're different. It doesn't feel like you're really here. You're here, but you're not here.

IRINA　　　　Don't grind your teeth.

REUTSKII　　　It drives me mad. Why won't you call me Aleksandr? *(after a pause, as he lets her go, he pushes a business card
into her hand)* Look. I'll write it down. Central Post Office. Five
o' clock. Here, take it.

IRINA *(laughing)* I'll be there. When's your train?

REUTSKII　　　Eleven this evening.

IRINA　　　　I'll be there.

REUTSKII　　　So, five o clock, then?

*Irina sees Reutskii out, then goes back to the kitchen. Vanda arrives,
looking offended.*

IRINA *(cheerfully)* What is it, dear Vanda Petrovna?

VANDA *(severely)* I have to say, Irina Nikolayevna, that my
position in your house is open to misunderstanding. There's a
stranger in the house, while I'm spending the night in a man's
room.

IRINA　　　　Vanda Petrovna, what on earth do you mean?
Father's eighty three!

VANDA　　　　He's a man.

IRINA *(irritably)* What misunderstanding could there possibly be?
You're a friend of the family. You're practically a relation!

VANDA *(pause)* I've been meaning to go to my sister's for a long
while. I must write and tell my sister.

IRINA　　　　Is that the one in Byelostok?

VANDA　　　　That's her.

IRINA　　　　I don't understand you, Vanda Petrovna.

VANDA　　　　What is there to understand? A woman comes to a
man's home and – takes care of him.

IRINA *(pause)* You never thought of marrying him?

VANDA *(pause)* A friend of mine married a nice old man... they live
very happily. The children are pleased, they help out.

IRINA　　　　Father's eighty-three... And then, he's not at all
well.

VANDA   I know, I know, how are we to take care of him and
all that, Vanda Petrovna is absolutely... she's a gem, is Vanda
Petrovna... No, I'm going to my sister's. I haven't seen my sister
for sixteen years.

IRINA   Father's a sick man.

VANDA   A sick man needs a wife even more than a healthy
one.

IRINA *(pause)* Wait, Vanda Petrovna... let me think! You've given
me a bit of a shock.
(Slava comes in wearing a tracksuit.)

SLAVA   Good morning, Vanda Petrovna!

VANDA   Good morning, Stanislav Sergeyevich!
(Vanda leaves. Slava fusses around the stove.)

SLAVA   Good morning, my friend.

IRINA   Hello.

SLAVA   Well? And just how long is our guest intending to
stay?

IRINA   He's leaving today.

SLAVA   I see. *(he sings a few lines about the charms of the
Black Sea.)*

IRINA   Don't be facetious.
(Slava notices Reutskii's business card. He grabs it.)

SLAVA *(reading)* 'Orestes Associates... AP Reutskii'. He's rich, the
bastard. Central Post Office.

IRINA *(snatching the card from his hand)* That's mine.
(Slava turns back to the stove, singing) Are you going to let me
drink my coffee? Or shall I go?

SLAVA   It's alright. I didn't mean anything. He's rich... A
decisive character. A well-connected friend! Where am I going to
find myself a well-connected girlfriend? And stinking rich. A
decisive character. *(he shouts with laughter.)*

IRINA   You know... it's funny... Vanda wants to marry
father.

SLAVA *(pause)* Who? Vanda? *(he roars with laughter. After a
pause)* So what? She's got common sense!

IRINA   I came to the same conclusion. Then... I'll be free.

SLAVA   You've gone out of your mind, dearie. Sweet old Vanda needs your father! She'll just cart out of this place everything she hasn't carted out already.

IRINA   There's nothing left to take.

SLAVA   That woman will find something. *(pause)* Don't treat it so lightly. This is all you've got.

IRINA   She does get on well with father, I can see that.

SLAVA   How long is it since you paid her?

IRINA   We have a very good relationship. She's practically one of the family.

SLAVA   Well, she will be when she marries your father! Ugh, I've overcooked them again! It'll be like eating rubber! *(he laughs loudly)* Vanda's going to be your mother!

IRINA *(looking round at the door)* Shh!

SLAVA   Irina, you're a fairly intelligent woman, but you're an idiot.

IRINA   I know.

SLAVA   Keep that in mind. *(he moves away, taking his eggs and singing a tune)* The Central Post Office... the Central Post Office... AP Reutskii...

IRINA   The tears my mother cried over my father! Oh, no, it's all so horribly funny! There's no need for punishment or torture! Time passes and everything's turned on its head... that's who the chief torturer is – time! Vanda's going to be my mother! It's appalling! Appallingly funny!

SLAVA *(turning away)* Calm down! Having a good laugh is impossible with you. You always end up in hysterics.

SCENE 4

A few hours later. Vanda and the Old Man appear. They walk once around the flat. Slava comes in from the street.

SLAVA   What's Moscow, off to Moscow... *(soothingly)* Oh, so how are things up there in Moscow?

VANDA   It's cold in Moscow, everyone knows that.

SLAVA   Are you going to inspect a parade?

VANDA   What do you mean? Of course we are.

SLAVA   Then why the casual dress? Put some medals on, at least. A parade's a parade, after all!

VANDA   He's been asking for them himself for ages. I can't find them, I've looked and looked.

SLAVA *(pause)* Keep looking, keep looking. These days there's a market for little things like that. Foreigners will kill for them.

VANDA   What are you doing home so early?

SLAVA   Things to do, Vanda Petrovna, things to do. Life is in turmoil. *(pause)* Life is in turmoil. The apple trees are in bloom.
(Irina comes out of the bathroom, a towel wrapped around her head. Vanda and the Old Man go out.)
We have to talk.

IRINA   For some reason or other we've been talking a lot lately. Can you make it quick? I'm going to do my hair.

SLAVA   I've been making some enquiries about your A.P. Reutskii.

IRINA   You little bastard, Slava. I always knew you were a bastard.

SLAVA   Why are you being so rude? It's just that I don't take things as lightly as you do. And I'm not totally indifferent to what you do with your life.

IRINA   Mind your own business. Whatever it is I need to know, I'll be the one to find it out.

SLAVA   You haven't found out very much yet. *(pause)* A.P. Reutskii, deputy director of 'Orestes', a retail goods firm... deals in computers, electrical equipment... was under investigation... did some time in prison... *(pause. He watches Irina out of the corner of his eye)* That's all for now, my dearest. You'll get the rest in instalments.
(Vanda appears.)

VANDA   Irina Nikolayevna, where are our medals? We want to put our medals on.

IRINA *(soothingly)* I don't know, Vanda Petrovna ... I haven't seen them for ages. They must have got lost somewhere...

(Vanda goes out. Slava makes his way to his room. Irina follows him and stops at his door.)

IRINA   How long was he in for?

SLAVA   Three years.

IRINA *(pause)* What else did you find out?

SLAVA *(comes out of his room with a packet of soup and goes into the kitchen)* In instalments, as I said... you're keeping me from my dinner... (*he puts a pan onto the stove and pours the soup into it. Irina comes and stands behind him.*)

IRINA   Is this all because you're jealous? Who are you now, with your whole career behind you? You wagged your tail, you sat up and begged, you shut up when they told you to, you barked when they told you to, like a poodle.

SLAVA *(muttering bitterly as he stirs the pan)* You're wrong! I'm nobody's lapdog, I still count for something and in future I'll count for even more, just give me time! Who was it got you all this information in the space of two hours? Was it Santa Claus? No, it was poor old Slava, because poor old Slava's got friends. We worked our backsides off together in the Komsomol, we had a few drinks, we were all in it – together. It runs deep, all that, it binds you. And that's how it was, darling. How did you think it was?

(Slava starts the soup, but hunger gets the better of him and he starts to drink it greedily out of the pan)

Go and take off your head-dress. I don't like this natural look of yours. A woman ought to make a bit of effort when she's got company. Put a little bit of colour on. Dress up a bit. Be chic – and that includes when she's in bed!

IRINA   Oh god, I've singed my hair!

She runs out. Slava gulps his soup down carelessly. He burns his mouth. Nastya arrives.

NASTYA   Hi, Dad.

SLAVA   Hi.

(Irina runs out of the bathroom and past them.)

NASTYA   Mum! What's the matter with your hair?

(She follows Irina into her room.)

IRINA   I wanted to do myself up a bit, so I did my hair.

NASTYA   Oh Mum, what on earth are we going do to with it?

(She pulls out a brush and darts towards her mother.)

IRINA *(listlessly)* Don't bother.

NASTYA   Experimenting at the wrong time, as always.
(pause) I had a pretty good look at him… I'm no psychologist, of
course… but he's positive, you can see that and actually, he'll do
you good.

IRINA   You don't have any idea what does me good!

NASTYA   Don't you believe it! I've got a pretty good idea.

IRINA   Am I capable of attracting anyone?

NASTYA   *You* don't know what you're capable of. Before she
died, grandma was always saying: 'I haven't lived yet…' I really
hate what you've done to your hair. Of course you won't attract
anyone with that mess going on on your head! Why don't I just
trim the ends… *(she picks up the scissors and cuts Irina's hair)*
Oh mum, I really hate it!

IRINA   Did grandma talk to you like that?

NASTYA   Yes.

IRINA *(pause)* If you lived here, it would all be different! I wouldn't
have got myself tangled up with all this! I put up with Slava
because he keeps Vanda happy. I put up with Vanda because if
she goes life will be hell. I'm constantly putting up with things!
How much can I put up with?

NASTYA *(also raising her voice)* We're not going to talk about this!
You know I can't live here! Valerka will never say yes! Do you
want me to divorce him? Oh why do parents go on at their children? Grandpa goes on at you – you upset me…

IRINA   I won't upset you any more.

NASTYA   I didn't mean that. It's everything!

IRINA   I didn't mean to upset you!

NASTYA   Mum!

IRINA   Alright. Enough said.

NASTYA   Oh, now you're offended again! Mum, I can't stand
much more of this! I'll crack up. You and Valerka are screwing
me up, between you. I come back from seeing you and he's sulk-

ing. I come round here and you're sulking. It's a nightmare! Do you want me to divorce him? Do you think there are available men around every corner? You were the stunner in our family. Who needs me? I'm twenty-three years old!

IRINA Fine. Go on. I've no time for this, I've got things to do.

NASTYA What things?

IRINA Oh, so I can't have things to do?

NASTYA *(softening)* Oh mum, don't be offended. You know, now I've had time to get used to it, that hairstyle actually suits you. It makes you look younger! *(pause)* Mum, that's enough now, don't sulk. I've got to go... don't sulk now, will you?

Nastya goes out.

IRINA *(pause)* Vanda Petrovna! Vanda Petrovna! *(Vanda appears)* Vanda Petrovna, I've been thinking... you're right! *(she rummages feverishly in a chest of drawers)* We have to get things straight, sort things out, so that everyone's alright. Parents shouldn't make their children's lives a misery! I must find that dress for you... It's beautifully made, it's expensive wool! *(she throws the dress to Vanda and at the same time pulls out from the depths of the drawer a high quality, expensive handbag.)*

VANDA Are you off somewhere, Irina Nikolayevna?

IRINA Not for the moment, no... but later, who knows? There were years when my father forgot all about me! He just lived. He loved life! He was already getting on a bit, but he had lovers, my mother was jealous, her life was hell... I got married early, I had Nastya, I lived my own life... *(she gets changed quickly)* I'm popping out for a while.
(She goes into the lobby, puts on her shoes and grabs her handbag. Slava appears – he's been lying in wait for her in his room.)

SLAVA I haven't told you the whole story. Your Reutskii's married. He's got a young wife and two children.

Lights fade.

ACT TWO

Late evening. The flat is dark. The doorbell echoes around the flat.
Irina puts on the light in the entrance hall. She is wearing the same
man's dressing gown.

IRINA *(standing at the door)* Who – who is it? *(she listens)*
Reutskii, is that you?
(She opens the door. Reutskii comes in.)
You didn't leave?

REUTSKII I haven't tied everything up yet. *(pause)* Aren't you
glad to see me? Why aren't you glad to see me?

IRINA I am glad to see you.
(Reutskii walks a little way through the lobby and knocks his leg
clumsily against a chair.)
Sshh! I've only just got father to bed.

REUTSKII So where's the old dear with the perm?

IRINA She's gone home. *(pause)* Do you want something to
eat?

REUTSKII One of your classic sandwiches?

IRINA You can have something else.

REUTSKII No, thanks. I ate at a restaurant. *(pause)* You're
cross.

IRINA What about?

REUTSKII Because I didn't make it that time. *(pause)* And...
because my plane left earlier.

IRINA Fifty minutes earlier. *(pause.)*

REUTSKII You're too far away... Can I come closer?
(She does not answer. Reutskii comes closer and puts his arms
around her.)

IRINA Why didn't you come that time?

REUTSKII Did you really want me to?

IRINA I stood for days at the window like an idiot,
watching that archway. I thought you'd turn up at any second.

REUTSKII And I did, in spirit.

IRINA It was hot, as if it was still in the South. I stared at
the archway... the whole yard was sunlit, but the archway was in

shadow… something in it kept shimmering. *(pause)* Did they put you in prison straight away?

REUTSKII *(pause)* No, not straight away. *(pause)* The trouble started straight away. As soon as I got off the train. It wasn't what you think… Crime is when you steal or rob or kill someone… This wasn't like that. There were papers, red tape… and proving to imbeciles that you're not a thug. It's not easy keeping your hands clean when things get tough. They can always find something against you. *(he thinks for a while.)*

IRINA *(pause)* You poor thing… And – didn't you have any private life?

REUTSKII   It seems you know more about me than I do.

IRINA   I don't know anything, Reutskii!

REUTSKII   I had a private life, unfortunately.

IRINA   Why unfortunately?

REUTSKII   You're a devious woman! Don't play around with me! You did that four years ago, by the fountain! You did it today! Two hours I waited! At the Post Office… are you playing some kind of game now too?

IRINA   You're the one who's playing games.

REUTSKII   I can't stand this!

IRINA   No, you can't, can you? You're too weak.

REUTSKII *(pause)* She's done a lot for me… and for my mother… I can't be a bastard to her. So don't expect me to. It's a completely different thing!

IRINA   Is she 'different'?

REUTSKII   You're 'different'.

IRINA   …'an island in a stormy sea.' *(pause)* I'll never forget how you ate shashlik in Novii Afon… your eyes were bigger than your belly.

REUTSKII   I was starving!

IRINA   You weren't starving – you're just greedy. You want it all. Everything! And it's agony for you when you can't have it. I actually like that in you, there's something innocent about it. You're as innocent as a child.

REUTSKII   You don't believe me…

A key turns in the lock. Slava and Olya come in.

SLAVA *(pause then loudly)* Aren't you asleep?

IRINA   No... but be quiet. I've only just got father to bed.

SLAVA *(nudges Olya towards his room)* Get a move on.
    *(he suddenly notices the bag which Reutskii has left lying there.
    Even his voice changes; he cannot control his emotion. Irritably)*
    Have you got visitors again? *(he whistles)* We've got visitors...!
    (Irina goes out.)

IRINA *(quietly)* Slava, if you let anything slip... if you say one word
    to him, it'll be the last word you utter in this house!

SLAVA   You've really fallen for him, haven't you, my pet?

IRINA   Do you understand?

SLAVA   I won't say a word.

Lights fade.

SCENE 2

*A week later. Slava is standing by the kitchen window, throwing
breadcrumbs to the birds. When Nastya appears, he jumps away
from the window, as if he's been taken by surprise in some shameful
activity. Nastya is too preoccupied to pay any attention.*

NASTYA   Hi, Dad... is mum here?

SLAVA   No.

NASTYA   Well, where is she?

SLAVA   She doesn't keep me informed of her movements.

NASTYA   That's strange...

SLAVA   You're mum's *in lurve!*

NASTYA   At her age?

SLAVA   You're underestimating her. She's not old.

NASTYA *(pause)* Is it serious, do you think? *(Slava whistles)* She
    hasn't called me for a few days... it's strange...
    (Slava takes a pan and puts it onto the stove) Is that all you eat,
    boiled eggs?

SLAVA   It's the easiest thing.

NASTYA *(pause)* Let me make you something… *(she rummages in the fridge and starts to get something ready.)*

SLAVA The butter isn't mine… it's not mine.

NASTYA Don't fuss. How are things with you?

SLAVA Alright. That's something you haven't asked me for a while. I'm touched.

NASTYA Who on earth does that man think he is? She doesn't even know him!

SLAVA Music to my ears!

NASTYA And she hasn't phoned me at all. *(she puts a plate of food in front of Slava.)*

SLAVA That was quick! Thank you, Nastya darling! Fantastic. You know, your husband's a lucky chap.

NASTYA Yes, he thinks so, too.

SLAVA *(eats, moved)* Nastya, love, do you remember how we used to go to the park?

NASTYA Of course I remember! You always used to buy me ice cream… I loved ice cream. We'd run off, I'd eat my lovely ice cream! And I was never sick.

SLAVA Your mother would have killed me! *(pause)* And do you remember the mouse?

NASTYA What mouse?

SLAVA We used to go and visit her.

NASTYA No, I don't remember.

SLAVA *(rather offended)* How can you not remember? You were grown up by then. You know, the metal door on the first floor.

NASTYA I don't remember. *(pause.)*

SLAVA Has mum told you she wants to marry Vanda off to grandpa?

NASTYA Grandpa? What are you on about? You're mad!

SLAVA I can see her point of view.

NASTYA Whose? *(pause)* Dad, I'm not clear exactly…

SLAVA Your mum's, of course. She wants some freedom. She wants to live her own life for a while. She is still fairly young.

NASTYA But Dad, won't you say anything?

SLAVA   Say what, exactly? Say no to the marriage?

NASTYA Say no to Vanda, anyway!

SLAVA   Have we got a choice?

NASTYA It's ridiculous!

SLAVA   Let's laugh about it, then.

NASTYA Dad, you do realise I don't intend to live my whole life in a flat with my husband, don't you?

SLAVA   Yes.

NASTYA This is mad. *(pause)* Will she be here this evening some time?

SLAVA   I don't know. I can't guarantee it.

NASTYA *(pause)*.Alright. I'll call back later.

Nastya leaves. Slava wanders aimlessly around the flat. Vanda appears.

VANDA   Why are you always at home, Stanislav Sergeyevich? Aren't things going well at work?

SLAVA   Work's alright, Vanda Petrovna. It won't run off if I'm not there to look after it.

VANDA   If you're going to be here, I'll run out to the shops.

SLAVA   Go on, then.
(Vanda brings the Old Man out and sits him down in an armchair.)

VANDA   We're quiet today. We're having a little sit down.

SLAVA   You're very good with him... I do admire you!

VANDA   My husband was just the same.

SLAVA   The frontier guard?

VANDA   No, the other one. He was an engineer for the Post Office. His legs just gave out. And what was I supposed to do? I really got depressed... I'd get up in the morning and I'd say: 'Well, Vanda my girl, get a move on!'

SLAVA   Go to the shops, Vanda Petrovna, go on!

VANDA   I'm going.
(Vanda leaves.)

(Slava walks around the room and stops by the window, thinking. The Old Man stirs in his chair, reminding Slava that he is there.)

SLAVA *(turning)* What, Dad? *(pause)* Yes, you put me in some difficult positions, to put it mildly... some difficult positions... *(pause)* Poor little Slava negotiating the hearth-rug, knees trembling, mouth dry, breath catching in his throat... Kow-towing like in mediaeval China... There was no way of figuring it out in time, figuring out they were just normal human beings standing there... normal human beings, and pretty shabby ones, at that. Paper tigers, chinese walls...! *(pause)* And daddy's girl... Now if there's one thing little Slava did know about – it was women! Daddy's girl... the lads used to cry with envy. They sobbed, they went up the wall! 'Katyshev, you conned us', What could they do? You could hear the groan right through the Komsomol! That was the biggest kick little Slava ever got – the lucky bastard, the chosen one... And all the others were down there somewhere, crawling about, so far down there, they were invisible. *(pause)* Poor little Slava... *(the Old Man stirs)* What is it, Dad? What? *(The Old Man is becoming more and more restless; he is getting angry and raps the floor with his stick. Slava clowns around, clapping his hands as if he has a small child in front of him)* Well, Dad, eh?

(The Old Man is still restless. Slava takes some glasses from the cupboard and begins to play a tune from Carmen on them. He sings) Ladies and gentlemen, I give you – Stanislav Katyshev! The Soviet Union! *(he starts to sing again.)*

Vanda comes in. Slava falls silent.

VANDA *(pause)* Put the glasses away, Stanislav Sergeyevich! *(pause)* Have we been good?

SLAVA   We've been quiet. *(he turns to the window, takes a tablet out of his pocket and puts it into his mouth).*

VANDA   If you didn't worry so much you'd be healthier.

SLAVA   You're a wise woman, Vanda Petrovna, and you look stunning in that dress.

VANDA *(pleased)* It's my colour.

SLAVA   It's absolutely your colour.

Irina arrives.

IRINA *(brightly, to Slava)* You're at home.

SLAVA   Yes, I'm feeling a bit rough today.

IRINA   It's the magnetic storms. Everyone's ill. Vanda
  Petrovna, is everything alright with Father? Oh, excellent! I
  noticed it a while ago – when there are magnetic storms,
  everyone's sick, but father is fine.

SLAVA   He's a tough old bird. He'll outlive us all. *(pause)*
  No, I'll outlive you all! *(he goes into his room.)*

VANDA   He's always worrying… if he didn't he'd be healthier. *(she puts the glasses into the cupboard)* You've brought the
  dirt in, and all this dust. They don't lift a finger.

IRINA   I'll clean up somehow.

VANDA   It's always: *somehow* this, *somehow* that. You live
  your whole life *somehow*. *(she takes out a cloth and begins to rub
  over the crockery in the cupboard.)*

Nastya comes in.

NASTYA   Oh, found you at last!

IRINA   Hello! Where have you been?

NASTYA   I should be asking you that. I've called in almost
  every day. *(pause)* Vanda Petrovna, please, put them back, I'll do
  them myself somehow! They're antiques. We've hardly got anything left. When my grandmother was alive that cupboard was
  full. *(Vanda, taken by surprise, freezes, a glass in her hand.
  Pause)* Oh, for god's sake, Vanda Petrovna, I've come to see my
  mother! Can't I speak to my mother alone for a while without
  other people hanging around?
  (Vanda goes out slowly.)

IRINA *(pause)* Nastasya, that was rude. *(pause.)*

NASTYA   So what? *(pause)* I told you that hairstyle makes you
  look younger. You haven't asked me how things are.

IRINA   How are things?

NASTYA   Fine, thanks. *(pause)* Mum, is it serious?

IRINA   What do you mean?

NASTYA   You know exactly what I mean!

IRINA   I don't know. I hadn't thought about it.

NASTYA   You hadn't thought about it! You're not a teenager.

IRINA   Teenagers spend all their time thinking about it.

NASTYA *(pause)* You don't even know him... I've lived with Valerka for a year and I still can't say that I know him.

IRINA   You liked him.

NASTYA   I liked him?

IRINA   You said, he'd be good for me.

NASTYA   Well, that wasn't saying much, was it? I don't even know him! How could I? He's a stranger! *(pause)* I just don't like the colour of his socks.

IRINA   What have his socks got to do with it?

NASTYA   I don't like it when men wear such loud socks. He's got no taste. *(pause)* Mum... you aren't on your own, you know... you've got grandpa, you've got me...

IRINA   That's not the point.

NASTYA   It won't be long before I have a lovely little baby. We'll do this place up... we'll be fine here. And we'll talk Valerka round. Do you like the sound of that?

IRINA   Yes.

NASTYA   That's wonderful! *(she hugs her mother tight)* Wonderful!

IRINA   You'll smother me with all this passion! *(pause)* I've always known you were an egotist!

NASTYA *(laughing)* So what if I am? *(pause)* You know, mum, you'll have to do something about Vanda. She gets her hands on everything, she orders people about. It's not as if this is her house. I was shocked to see her in grandma's dress.

IRINA   Grandma never liked that dress.

NASTYA   Grandma may not have liked it, but we ought to keep it, for her sake. *(pause)* Well, I've got to go. This is the second time today I've left work. All because of you. Give everyone my love.

Nastya leaves. Irina is alone. Vanda appears.

VANDA *(trying to catch Irina's eye)* Is something wrong, Irina Nikolayevna?

IRINA   Everything's fine, Vanda Petrovna. It's just... now I look at you... I don't really like that dress on you... I'll find you something else.

VANDA *(harshly)* As you wish, Irina Nikolayevna. You know best.

Lights fade.

SCENE 3
Late evening. Irina and Reutskii come in.

IRINA   Oh, my heel's nearly come off! *(she laughs)* I've been laughing all day, it can't be a good sign. Reutskii, you know, I'm drunk! It's only happened to me a few times in my life and somehow or other it's always been with you.

REUTSKII   I'm an alcoholic.

IRINA *(changing her shoes)* Oh, I've put the wrong shoes on, these are father's old slippers! That can't be right! *(she shuffles into the room in the pair of man's slippers. Reutskii follows her.)*

REUTSKII   I drink at night. And in the mornings, too.

IRINA *(stumbles)* Give me your hand, can't you see I've fallen over?

REUTSKII *(holds out his hand to her gloomily; he has been gloomy all day)* When will you stop calling me Reutskii?

IRINA   That's better! Do you know how long you've been here? Almost a week. What's wrong with you?

REUTSKII   I told you. I'm an alcoholic. I do everything in binges. *(pause)* The worst thing is that I've got a wonderful wife. She's beautiful, kind-hearted...

IRINA   Oh, how awful.

REUTSKII   She's a decent, devoted woman...

IRINA   Reutskii, don't do this! Don't make me out to be the criminal in all this! You're so selfish! I'm surrounded by selfish people!

REUTSKII   You have to love me. You've always loved winners, clearly. And I'm a winner! I got out. I've made something of myself.

IRINA   I respect you, Reutskii. I respect you. But you're selfish. You're barbaric, you're full of the most barbaric instincts.

REUTSKII   That's life. What do you know about it, love?

IRINA   I know more than you think. You're the barbaric one – not life. Life's full of order and meaning. You've just never thought about it. Look around you at the way everything's made. The smallest flower or bug or blade of grass. They're perfect.

REUTSKII   Yes, there's someone behind it all, there's someone up there.

IRINA   It seems to me we just have to do what we're made for... people do have some kind of overriding task... like ants or bees...

REUTSKII   You're idealising nature. It's really very cruel.

IRINA   It's cruel, but it isn't senseless.

REUTSKII   But look at how they eat each other! From the microbes right up through the food chain. They *eat* each other!

IRINA   Because they're supposed to. Reutskii, do you know what I love, right at this moment? I love the garden in autumn. All that – gardens, forests, fields... I'm a part of them, a tiny part, I'm an ant out there in the garden... I can see it so clearly... I'm happy now just because I can see it so clearly as if it were a picture... the whole of creation... it's breathtaking... the whole divine plan... Reutskii, let them eat each other... There's no need to be cynical about it... it was meant to be that way. One thing merges with another and together they make a whole. Both the hunters and the hunted together. It's clear to me. Reutskii, I'm happy and at peace... But oh god, I can't hold on to that feeling and I start hurting again, I start worrying...

REUTSKII   You're not here, you've gone wandering off somewhere.*(pause)* You have to love me!

IRINA   No, you must be out of your mind!

REUTSKII   When my plane took off and left you and the earth behind, I thought: 'She has to love me, or I'm nothing.'

IRINA   Reutskii, calm down... I love you. I like the fact that you're so barbaric, that you're a selfish bastard in loud socks. Nature made you that way. So what now? Have you got a confession? Are you happy? *(pause)* But I don't like this state of inebriation. It makes me dizzy. Reutskii, get me some water.
(Reutskii fetches some water from the kitchen and then notices that Irina is dozing off. He watches her for a while. Then he picks up his bag and goes quietly into the lobby. Slava comes to meet him.)

SLAVA *(pause)* Are you off, old chap? *(pause)* Listen, there's been a delay with the pay cheques... you couldn't lend me a bit, could you? Until next time? I can post it back to you if you like?
(Reutskii slips his hand into his pocket, pulls out some money and, without counting it, pushes it towards Slava) Thanks, I'll pay you back next time. Thanks, old chap... I'll pay you back.
(Slava sees Reutskii out.)

SLAVA   Thank you!

REUTSKII   Take care of yourself!

Reutskii leaves. Slava closes the door behind him and quickly counts the money. He glances into the room and looks at Irina asleep. Then he goes to the telephone and dials a number.

SLAVA *(actually trembling with emotion)* Olya? Can you come over? I feel like celebrating... I really do...
(Irina comes out into the lobby.)

IRINA   God, I fell asleep... it's never happened to me before... *(she walks around the flat. Slava watches her.)*

Lights fade.

SCENE 4
Next morning. Slava and Olya are having breakfast in the kitchen. Irina comes in. It is clear from her pale, drawn face that she has had

a sleepless night. Olya makes a frightened movement when she sees her.

SLAVA *(banteringly)* Olya, sweetheart! Why aren't you looking after me? *(to Irina)* Good morning, madam. Would madam like coffee?

IRINA   I can wait.

SLAVA   Why? We'll squeeze up a bit. The more the merrier. Olya darling, do me a favour and move up a fraction. *(pause)* How is madam?

IRINA   Well, thank you.

SLAVA   You must have put too much salt in this, love... or else I'm just not hungry. *(pause)* I've been thinking, madam... the single life's not ideal for men of my age. Empty stomach in the mornings, trousers all creased, shoes in a state... *(pause)* The thing is, this address is on my papers, madam. I've got every right to move my wife in with me. *(pause.)*

IRINA   Do what you want.

SLAVA   You don't object?

IRINA   Whatever you want.

SLAVA   There'll be kids running around! You know how much I love kids. I've always wanted kids. You'll be in the kitchen with Olga, quarrelling over how much salt to put in the soup. *(he bursts into song)* There'll be nappies hanging everywhere – it'll smell like a maternity ward!
(Irina gets herself some coffee and goes out of the kitchen.)
Where are you off to, madam? I haven't finished yet! Let me finish telling you about our wonderful future together!
(Vanda comes out into the lobby carrying a bag. She puts on a raincoat and knots her headscarf.)

IRINA   Hello, Vanda Petrovna.

VANDA   Good morning, Irina Nikolayevna

IRINA   How's father?

VANDA   He hardly slept last night. He kept worrying about something. Goodness, how he tossed and turned! He only got to sleep towards morning, so don't wake him up. Have breakfast

yourself. *(pause)* I've put your dress on the settee. The clock and
the curtains are in the kitchen...

IRINA *(pause)* Will you be out for long, Vanda Petrovna?

VANDA   Yes, Irina Nikolayevna, I will. No, Irina
Nikolayevna, I won't be back.

IRINA   You're offended.

VANDA   I don't get offended with people. Live and let live.
(pause) I've been coming here for three years now...

IRINA   Is it that long?

VANDA   I need a bit of time to myself... *(pause)* Put an
advert in the paper... make sure you ask a lot of questions, check
their references... letting a stranger into the house! I know you
don't take these things seriously! You might find someone
suitable... *(pause)* Here's the key... *(she leaves the key)* I've left
the key...

IRINA   I can see that.

VANDA   Goodbye.

*Vanda leaves. Irina stands without speaking, lost in thought. Slava
looks in.*

SLAVA   Where's she off to?

IRINA   She's gone. *(pause)* For good.

SLAVA   For good? What on earth do you mean? *(pause)* The
crafty old biddy! She's found something better! You'll see!
Aren't you going to go after her?

IRINA   There's no point.

SLAVA   You're useless. *(pause)* Useless.
*(Irina goes into her room. Slava goes back to the kitchen. After a
pause, maliciously)* Well, Olya dear, this is going to be fun. What
are your plans for the future? Washing? Cleaning? Ironing?

OLYA *(pause)* Could we go out somewhere? Couldn't we go
somewhere on Saturday?

SLAVA   A family outing? No-o, I'd better get some sleep on
Saturday. You need to sleep at my age. Alone, that is! Women
take it out of you, darling.

OLYA   So you were joking, then?

SLAVA   What about, my little one?

OLYA *(pause)* About wanting to get married.

SLAVA   What, you mean joking's not allowed?

OLYA   Were you joking? Were you? *(she starts to throw any object she can lay her hands on at Slava. He ducks)* Were you joking? Well?

SLAVA   Olya, you're a big girl now. You've got a son at school. You don't really take jokes seriously, do you? What's Uncle Slava got to do with it?

OLYA   What have you got to do with it? Are you saying you've got nothing to do with it? You sod! *(she throws herself at Slava and starts to beat him).*

SLAVA *(holding her at a safe distance)* Hey! Hey! You know what, Olya, you're nothing like Irina. You're worlds apart. You're badly brought up. And you've got no manners... You're a factory tart!

OLYA   I must be out of my mind to come back here! I'd calmed down, I'd got it all sorted out. You're a complete bastard. *(The door slams. The Old Man comes out, half-dressed.)*

OLD MAN *(angrily rapping his stick)* Who's there? Who's there? *(He raises his stick and shoots at Olya excitedly)* Bang!

OLYA *(terrified)* Oh my God!

OLD MAN   Bang! Bang!

SLAVA *(composedly)* There you are... you've woken Dad up!

OLYA   Oh!

She rushes into the entrance hall, grabs her raincoat and runs out into the street.

OLD MAN *(in her wake)* Bang! Bang!

SLAVA *(after a pause, taking the stick from him)* That's enough Dad, let's go into the kitchen... you were a good mate there... you helped me out, and now I'll help you out. I'll do you a couple of eggs. It's good food, real peasant food. And then we'll take a trip out somewhere. Not to a parade though, you've had enough parades. We'll take a look at a funeral, maybe...

He pulls the Old Man's fur hat over his eyes, shoves the first news-
paper he can find into his hands and goes into the kitchen, humming
a funeral march. The Old Man follows him, holding the newspaper in
his outstretched hands.

Lights down.

SCENE 5

Some time later. Nastya comes out of her grandfather's room wear-
ing a white uniform. In the kitchen, Slava is cooking his usual meal.

NASTYA   Hi, dad.

SLAVA   Hi.

NASTYA   You know, mum's at the end of her tether.

SLAVA   I know.

NASTYA   She can't cope on her own. Grandpa's an awful lot
to put up with.

SLAVA   Yes, we still haven't found another Vanda.

NASTYA   Some of those places aren't bad. The care's alright, I
went and found out…

SLAVA   You mean a home?

NASTYA   There are lots of places like that. I've been in one.
The care's alright, honestly. Mum's just being stubborn.

SLAVA   What about you – you've been a long time deciding
about the flat.

NASTYA   You know what Valerka's like. He can't stand being
dependent.

SLAVA   I understand that. These walls put him in a difficult
position. And your grandfather's not exactly good company. He's
extremely trying company, to be honest with you.

NASTYA   That's not the point. Its's just that you're a different
generation. You see things in a different way. *(pause)* You don't
even know what it is to be free.

SLAVA   Of course we don't. What is there left to say of us? We're the last of the slaves... we're dying out and we're leaving the way clear for you – and you're free!

NASTYA   But why? Don't die out!

SLAVA   Well, we will anyway. *(pause)* But I do wonder how a free man like your young husband can live off the proceeds of selling your grandfather's medals. I wonder how he squares it with his conscience.

NASTYA *(pause)* Well, he does. It's my inheritance.

SLAVA   Has your mother told you that?

NASTYA   I'm the only heir, don't you know that?

SLAVA   I see.

NASTYA *(pause)* Dad, you know, we don't get on too badly, do we? I love mum a lot, but she's different.

SLAVA   Yes, you take after your grandfather.

NASTYA   How are things with you?

SLAVA   Fantastic! We've been after some machinery from Kazakhstan. They've lost half of it and the other half's been nicked. We probably won't even make enough to cover the petrol.

NASTYA   What are you cooking there? Something exotic?

SLAVA   Chicken.

NASTYA   You could've fooled me. You're still good-looking, dad. Why did you and mum get divorced?

SLAVA   She divorced me. When things started to go downhill, she divorced me. That's how it is with women.

NASTYA   You're not being fair.

SLAVA   Possibly not. *(pause)* When a healthy sort of bloke starts to get in over his head, it's not a pretty sight. He struggles, chokes, curses...

NASTYA   You're right, not a pretty sight.

SLAVA   Then he drags himself onto dry land and starts throwing up.

NASTYA   What a nightmare. But back then, things weren't too good anyway.

SLAVA   They weren't that bad either.

NASTYA *(pause)* Are you at rock bottom now?

SLAVA   No, I'm on dry land. I'm throwing up.
(pause. He tries his stew) What's up, Nastya? Is it hard being free?
(Irina comes out of her room.)

NASTYA   I'm going. Give him three tablets before bed.

IRINA   Why so many?

NASTYA   Do as I say. I've checked. Otherwise you'll have another sleepless night.
(Irina sees Nastya into the lobby)
By the way, Dad's eating the pigeons. His firm's crashing.
(pause) I can see from your face that's made absolutely no impression on you.
(The Old Man comes out of his room, goes to the coat rack and puts on his overcoat. Nastya looks at her grandfather.)
I'll call in tomorrow. See you soon. *(Nastya disappears.)*

OLD MAN   I'm off. Did I tell you? She doesn't understand anything! But *I* know... I'm off.

IRINA *(apathetically)* Yes, Dad, you said. Slava, stay with him for a while, please, I'll air his room. *(Slava appears.)*

SLAVA   So, Dad, off to Moscow?

At this point, the Old Man turns on the tape player. It is a recording of a parade in Red Square. We hear the voice of Levitan. The crowd is shouting. We feel the pathos of a great country, in which both Slava and the Old Man occupied until so recently a recognised place. The myth of that land. Slava's face is surprised out of its cynical mask. He stands to attention, an unshaven, empty man in his pitiable trousers. From somewhere in his chest comes a sound which is part wheeze, part suppressed sob. He is transfixed by the sound. He is there, in that grandiose parade of his youth. Beside him, the Old Man has fallen silent. Irina stands frozen, in the doorway.

Lights fade.
The end.

Elena Popova

I was born on the 12th October 1947 in Legnitsa in Silesia, in the part of Germany that was ceded to Poland after the war. My father was a war correspondent. I was three when he was transferred to Minsk. I have lived there all my life, except for my time at university.

After high school I got involved with theatre, amateur drama and dancing. I started to write short stories early on but the theatre influenced me very strongly and I began to write plays; I did a play-writing course at the Gorky Institute of Literature and graduated in 1973. I went through various changes of job and career, but continued to write; writing has always been at the centre of my life.

In 1975 my play *Victory Square* came first in Belorussia and third in the Soviet Union in a competition for plays about contemporary youth. However, censorship meant that performance of the play was banned; it was only published ten years later in *Teatr*, the theatre magazine. My theatrical debut was in 1978, with a production of the play *Early Trains* by the National Academy Theatre of Vitebsk. *A Quiet Place* was performed in St. Petersburg in the same year. I was admitted to the Writers' Union. But life in the theatre was not simple. Few of my plays were performed, some were performed once, others closed or met with official disapproval. There were some successes, however, including *Announcement in the Evening Paper* at the Minsk Russian Theatre and *Korytsin's Life* at the Yanki Kupali Belorussian Academy Theatre. With the advent of perestroika, my life as a playwright opened up.

Belgrade Trilogy

The play was written in 1996, the year after a big emigration wave in Serbia, when young people (around 200,000) were leaving the country, trying to find a better, or at least different life. Most of all, young intellectual people from Belgrade were leaving because they were against the war, they couldn't live any more in economic crisis, without jobs and with no hope that things would get better. They went to different continents, working at different things, usually below their educational level. In a way, this is a story about real existing people, author's friends that went away, but also about others who stayed, wondering every day, was it a good decision or not?

It is also a play about the author's life – the life of a young Serbian woman in the middle of an era that nobody wants to live in.

The play opened in April 1997 in one of the two biggest theatres in Belgrade – Jugoslovensko Dramsko Pozoriste, under Goran Markovic's direction. The play was well received, especially by young audiences and the non-regime media. It is still on the repertoire and very popular, as the question of whether to leave or not, still remains.

It has been translated into German and published in *Theater der Zeit* (May 1998), produced as part of the Bonner Biennale in 1998 and at the Essen Schauspiel Theatre, Germany in 1999.

Biljana Srbljanovic

Belgrade Trilogy

by Biljana Srbljanovic
translated by Ellis

First performed at the Jugoslovensko Dramsko Pozoriste, Belgrade
in April 1997. Directed by Goran Markovic.

CHARACTERS:
PRAGUE – **Kica Jovic, Mica Jovic, Alena**
SYDNEY – **Sanja, Milos, Kaca, Dule**
LOS ANGELES – **Jovan, Mara, Daca**
BELGRADE – **Ana Simovic, Men's voices.**

SCENE I, PRAGUE
*Flat belonging to the brothers Kica and Mica Jovic, both in their
twenties. One room, two beds, three lamps and lots of photographs,
all with the same themes: Belgrade, a girl, friends. A table, chairs, a
ring cooker, lots of dirty dishes constitute a 'kitchen area' in the
right corner. Kica stands between the mirror and an open wardrobe,
considering what he's going to wear. The only choice is a Latin-
American dance costume, his work gear. We hear quiet Latin American mambo dance music [instrumental]. Kica hums along and does
small dance steps as he dresses. The music fades slowly. Mica enters
carrying pine branches and a supermarket shopping bag. He is in a
bad mood.*

KICA   Where have you been? For God's sake, do you know
how late it is?
MICA (*looks at his watch, gives up*) No.
KICA   O, Mica you are so stupid. (*walks energetically
towards him*) It's exactly… (*looks at his own watch for a long
moment, gives up*). We have to hurry. (*he mutters to himself
something we don't catch*) If it goes well this evening I swear I'm

going to buy a digital watch. (*he mutters again while Mica sadly hangs the branches on the wall and drapes round them some tree lights he takes out of the bag.*) They're not going to make a fool of me again with these stupid things with hands. Go on. Hurry up, get dressed, we've not got much time... What are you doing?

MICA   Brighten the place up a bit, it's New Year after all. And anyway it was reduced for a quick sale.

KICA   Of course it was. Those are the branches they put on graves. Who would bring something like that into the house?

MICA   No, Kica, the man selling them said to me, 'Here in the Czech Republic, *pane,* we use that for indoor decoration'.

KICA   He said that?

MICA   Yes.

KICA   Tell me what he said exactly, please. In his own words.

MICA   How do you mean?

KICA   I mean, in Czech. How do you say that in Czech?

MICA (*thinks very hard*) I don't know.

KICA   I know you don't know. It has taken you two years to learn: 'Hey, how much cost?' and now you're trying to tell me you've been discussing aesthetics with Czech foresters.

MICA (*says nothing. Then remembers*) No Kica, he wasn't a Czech.

KICA   What was he then?

MICA   One of ours. I mean, a Croat... One of us... I think he spoke Serbian. I mean Croatian. Whatever. The main thing is, I could understand him. Look, he gave me a discount. Really it cost me nothing!

KICA   Mica...

MICA   Yes?

KICA   You're telling lies.

MICA   No, Kica, I swear by my mother...

KICA (*hits him in the face*). Don't swear by our mother, you idiot!

MICA (*holding his cheek*) I bought the branches on the market from a Czech guy. I paid the full price, and I think he cheated me out of my change.

KICA   Well, there you are then. And you tried to give me all that emotional stuff, fraternity and unity and that... OK, never mind. Only don't lie to me.

MICA   No.

KICA   Does it hurt?

MICA (*holding his cheek*) Not at all.

KICA   I'm sorry. You know I'm sensitive where Mother is concerned.

MICA   I know. I'm sorry too.

KICA (*throws him a shirt with ruffles like the one he's wearing himself*) Go on, get dressed.

MICA (*starts dressing reluctantly*) You'll be the end of me, mamma mia...

KICA   What's that?

MICA   Nothing. I'm thinking of Mama...

KICA   Do you have to think right now? We have to practise our number.

MICA   What is there to practise? We've done the same thing for two years.

KICA   What? Do you want another one in the mouth?

MICA (*quickly puts his hands up to his cheeks. Sadly*) No.

KICA (*sighs, goes up to Mica, they are clearly starting an old argument*) Sit down, Mica. (*Mica does what he is told*). So Mica, tell me who brought you here.

MICA   The army.

KICA   No Mica, the army drove you out of the house, but they didn't bring you here, did they?

MICA   No, that's right.

KICA   So who brought you here?

MICA   Who, Kica?

KICA   What do you mean, who? Who grabbed you when they were going to get you, and who sorted the whole thing with Prague out overnight? Who?

MICA   You did, Kica.

KICA   I did, Mica. And who promised Mama to look after
you, and see you didn't land in the shit and get cheated by God
knows who... who was that, then?

MICA   You, Kica.

KICA   Me, Mica. So who's responsible for you then, tell
me that?

MICA   Me, Kica.

KICA   You, Mica... Hang on, what do you mean, you?

MICA   Everyone is responsible for himself and his own
fate.

KICA   Who told you that?

MICA   The man who sold me the branches.

KICA   That Croat?

MICA   So you know him as well! What did you hit me for
then?

KICA (*embarrassed*) Hang on, there's something here I don't quite
get...

MICA (*throws him his coat*) Hurry up, get dressed.

KICA (*dresses himself thoughtfully. Mutters to himself*) He'll be the
end of me, mamma mia...

MICA   What did you say?

KICA   Nothing I'm just wondering...

MICA   What for? We haven't got time to start wondering
now, we've got our number to practise.

KICA (*confused, but obeys instantly*) Yes. At once. (*takes up his
position, still lost in thought. Mica stands opposite him.*) Hey,
Mica.

MICA Yes, Kica.

KICA (*suddenly boxes him hard on the ear*) You want to finish me
off, hey? Where's the sense in that?

MICA (*sadly, rebelliously*) That's just what I ask myself Kica.
What's the point of it all?

KICA   What the devil's the matter with you this evening?
Are you drunk or high or something?

MICA   You know I don't drink.

KICA   I do know and that's why I'm wondering.

MICA   What's so remarkable, Kica, after two years of demeaning work in the same town, in the same bar and for the same bloody miserable wages, if I ask myself what is the point of it all!

KICA   No work is demeaning.

MICA   Yes. This is.

KICA   Listen, if you've got anything better, just go... (*Mica hesitates*) Go! What are you waiting for? (*Mica takes a step towards the door*) Just so as you know, I'd be happy if someone gave me what I give you, but you don't need to think about that. You're free, go. (*Mica takes another step*) No, I'd snap at the chance – easy money, four hours work, in the evening at a disco. A bit of a dance, a bit of a drink, the girlies falling over each other...

MICA   That's the alcohol.

KICA   No! It's 'cos they got the hots. They admire us, they want us. We just have to take our pick. If we want to, OK. If we don't want to, we don't have to, get it?

MICA   I made my choice long ago. The address for me is 44 Grocanska Street.

KICA   There you go again! I offer you a life on the stage, show business on an international scale, a future others only dream of – gelt, girls, not much work, and you can only come up with that old camel from the Zvezdara District! What kind of thing is that? (*Mica is silent*) Or is his lordship cross perhaps, because I didn't leave him in the shit, I didn't allow him to be called up, to play at being a totally unarmed nation, to defend our wonderful Serbian identity, whose limits are known only to God, for all of five minutes before the first bullet came along to send him to St Peter and his blessed duty free! (*Mica is silent, hanging his head*) That's the thanks I get for voluntarily giving up my well-paid job as a ticket tout outside cinemas, and emigrating, quite unnecessarily because the army wasn't after me. That's the thanks I get. No, just go. I'm not cross with you.

MICA (*indecisive, takes a few steps, stops, turns. Puts his hand to his heart.*) Where, Kica?

KICA   What does that mean?

MICA   I mean, where should I go? You keep saying: 'Go, go' – but you don't say where.

KICA   I'm supposed to tell you... Well, where did you want to go to?

MICA   Nowhere. I thought you had somewhere definite in mind you wanted to send me. (*Kica looks him up and down as if he were an idiot, which he probably is)* He says: 'Go, go' and I'm waiting for him to say, where to. (*they look at each other.*)

KICA   Mica...

MICA (*automatically puts his hand to his cheek*) Yes, Kica?

KICA   You are very stupid.

MICA   I know, Kica. Everyone says that. (*he says nothing for a few moments, then reaches for his shoes and puts them on*) OK then, let's do some practise now. You can see how late it is.

KICA *(pulls on his jacket as if nothing had happened)* Whatever you say. (*grabs Mica's other hand, looks at his watch, gives up.*) Bloody hell, I've gotta buy a digital watch.
(Kica and Mica are both now dressed. They look very comical: buttoned-up shirts with ruffles, gold chains, shoes with high heels.)

MICA   OK let's go.
(*turns the music on. A quick 'mambo' (South American dance). Both pick up the rhythm. They clearly have a practised routine. Crescendo. Then the telephone rings. Mica rushes to answer it)* Hello! Hello! (*To Kica*) Turn it down, it's Belgrade (*into the telephone*) Hello... Mama... It's you. Hi, Mama, it's me Mica Jovic... No, I know you know that... Never mind, how are you Mama? We're fine, Kica too. I'm doing what he says, Mama, always... We've got money, don't worry... what's it like there? So-so?... Has... (*interrupts suddenly, turns his back on Kica, speaks softly*) Mama, did Ana ring? (*repeats louder*) I said, did Ana ring?... I'm not shouting, but you're not understanding me. No of course she's not more important than... I'm only asking...

KICA (*takes the receiver out of Mica's hand*) Give it to me!... Hello, Mama, Kica Jovic here... No, I know you know that. But tell me, how are you?... We're very well. We're both working in that firm I told you about. Yes. Export. It's going great. And we're speaking Czech as well as Serbian already. Mica too... And how are things there? What's the gang doing… You know, the ones from the red light district. You haven't heard from them… Good, Mama…

MICA (*calls to him*) Ask about Ana.

KICA … where are you going this evening?… Power cut? How come, a power cut? Why hasn't it been sorted? Oh yeh, New Year's Eve, no-one on duty. That figures. No, everything super here. We've got dough, we've got an office party this evening… of course there'll be girls…

MICA (*shoves him*) Don't talk rubbish, Kica, what girls?

KICA No, Mama, not Czech girls, ours…

MICA Stop that, you idiot. She'll tell Ana when she rings.

KICA OK, Mama, we send you a kiss too. And Happy New Year to you too.

MICA (*shouts*) Tell her, Kica, d'you hear?

KICA Mica sends his love too. Bye, Mama, bye. (*hangs up*) What are you shouting for, you fool? D'you want to get Mama all upset?

MICA And what sort of nonsense are you talking? What girls? If Ana rings, Mama might tell her…

KICA She won't tell her anything. Mama can keep secrets.

MICA What secrets? I haven't got any secrets. I love Ana.

KICA Because you're stupid.

MICA Because I have feelings.

KICA Same thing.

MICA I don't care what you think. Give me the telephone.

KICA Who are you going to ring?

MICA None of your business. Give it me!

KICA You can't ring Belgrade. We can't afford that.

MICA I've got money. I saved some.

KICA Oh really! Show us then.

MICA (*takes money from his pocket*) Here.

KICA (*takes the money out of his hand*) Great. That's just what we need to make up the rent.

MICA Give me that money back. It's mine, I saved it.

KICA   ...and wasn't that kind of you, 'cos you know what debts we have.

MICA   Oh man, come on, please, I haven't spoken to her for three months.

KICA   So why hasn't she phoned?

MICA   She can't afford it.

KICA   And you can?

MICA   Yes, if you give me that back. Listen, you can't tell me what to spend my money on!

KICA (*grabs Mica by the throat in a rage and starts to throttle him*) Listen, little boy, there's no mine and yours any more. Everything in common! When we get on our feet, when we've paid off our debts, you can ring, if you want and you can spend your dosh on whatever you like. But 'til then – shared kitty, shared earnings, shared debts. Nothing separate, get it?

MICA (*choking*) OK (*Kica holds him a moment longer, then lets him go. Mica coughs*) But shit, that's Karl Marx stuff. Dictatorship of the proletariat. (*Kica is really angry. He sits down, Mica sits down too*) What time is it?

KICA   Arsehole. (*silence from both, then the door bell rings*) There they are. (*he goes to open the door. Mica makes immediately for the telephone. Simultaneously Kica turns, takes the cordless phone out of his hand and takes it with him*) Just in case. (*goes out into the hall.*)

MICA (*calls after him*) I wasn't going to phone, anyway!

KICA (*comes back closing the door behind him*) Of course you were, don't lie. Listen, we've got guests.

MICA   Guests? (*starts laughing*)

KICA   Mica, be serious, please. We really do have guests.

MICA (*seriously, even surprised*) You're crazy. What kind of guests? Who'd want to visit us?

KICA   Don't say things like that. It's New Year's Eve.

MICA   That's why I'm surprised!

KICA   Please, Mica, these are nice girls.

MICA (*thinking aloud*) If this is the most fun anyone could have, what must it be like elsewhere... Girls? Did you say girls?

KICA   Nice girls, so stop shouting. They'll start to think there's something wrong. *(goes to open the door)*

MICA *(stops him)* Wait, Kica, something *is* wrong, really. Imagine if some girls in Belgrade went to a party with two Russians. What would you say?

KICA   It's not the same.

MICA   No. Here we haven't even got a party.

KICA   And we're not Russians.

MICA   That's what I'm saying. We're Serbs, for heaven's sake! It could get nasty! I mean, what mother would let her daughters come to us?

KICA   That's not your problem. I've got to let them in now. You can't have them standing around on the staircase.

MICA   No wait! What are we going to do with them? I mean, what do they want?

KICA *(ironically)* Books?

MICA   We haven't got any, Kica.

KICA   Right? So?

MICA   Haven't a clue.

KICA   We'll have to entertain them. *(turns energetically towards the door.)*

MICA   Hang on a minute Kica. How are we going to entertain them?

KICA   Don't worry. We'll chat for a bit, have a drink and then go to the disco.

MICA   Ah. *(thinks)* How come?

KICA   How come what?

MICA   How come we're going to have drinks and that?

KICA   Because they're high-class girls. You can't just go ahead and fuck them, just like that.

MICA *(highly excited)* I knew it! You want me to be unfaithful to Ana!

KICA   First of all, stop yelling. I told you they were high-class bits. And secondly. I don't give a damn about Ana.

MICA   Well I do, Kica. I love her and she loves me and I
don't know what bothers you about the fact that we love each
other.

KICA   What are you talking about love for, you stupid ass?
Love –when you're so far apart, who does that any more? You're
here, she's there and where's your love?

MICA   When I've made it, I'm going to ask her to join
me...

KICA   You'll miss the train long before that, mate... Were
you in the army?

MICA *(sadly)* No I ran away. That's why I'm here.

KICA   Oh yeh. I was, little brother. In Valjevo, not so far
away, and you know how mine cried when I was called up.

MICA   She cried because she was drunk.

KICA   She got drunk from sheer misery.

MICA   No, from whisky. A whole bottle it took... I
remember it exactly.

KICA   Good that you remember so precisely. Because
you'll also remember what a love that was. I wanted to marry her.

MICA   Yeh, if Mama had agreed.

KICA   Mama isn't important now. It was a question of the
desire, the idea. It was a strong love.

MICA   The strongest. And?

KICA   What d'you mean, and? She loved me and in spite of
that, she gave me the push. Right after I'd been sworn in. What
does that tell you?

MICA   That she was a slag.

KICA   True, but not important in terms of my present
theory. For the last two years I have been trying to explain to you
that love at a distance is absolutely impossible and that you will
just have to get used to that once and for all! *(Mica is silent, head
bowed)* And so I have invited these pussycats – they're nice girls
from nice homes, very out-going, very chatty. They like getting to
know foreigners.

MICA   I'm sure.

(There is a knock at the door.)

KICA (*calls*) Just a minute! Come on, Mica, don't make me look a fool.

MICA (*unusually serious*) Listen Kica, do you really think Ana's been unfaithful to me?

KICA   Absolutely. (*looks at Mica, doesn't know what to say*) I mean, she's absolutely faithful. Ana is a fine girl, she worships you. She wouldn't... I only told you all that to fill in time. What's the matter with you, Mica?

MICA (*cold and absolutely determined*) Because if she has betrayed me, I'm a dead man. I'll kill myself, Kica.

KICA (*shocked*) Don't talk rubbish!

MICA   I've said what I want to say. Let those cows in. (*Kica hesitates*) What are you waiting for?

KICA   Thanks, Mica. You'll see, they're not cows... well, they're not exactly what you'd call good-looking. (*he opens the door, looks right and left, shuts the door and looks at Mica*) There's only one left.

MICA   That's fine, that'll do you...

KICA   But it's yours.

MICA   No problem. We're brothers. Help yourself.

KICA   I would, but she's not having it. She says you're the one who interests her. Please, Mica. I promised the girl...

MICA (*sighs*) OK, a promise is a promise...

KICA   That's great, Mica, you're a real brother...

MICA   ... and you've got to let me phone Ana.

KICA   ... Idiot.

MICA   I thought you were a sensible chap and we'd settled it all.

KICA   I can't work to pay the telephone company. The bills we've had to pay, we could have bought a duck for the New Year.

MICA   Go put your head up a duck's arse.

KICA   What did you say?

MICA   Nothing.

KICA (*insulted*) That's the thanks I get. You should be ashamed.

MICA Sorry, Kica. I didn't mean it like that. *(there is another hesitant knock at the door)* Oh bring the girl in. Don't let her hang about there for no reason.

KICA *(takes a step towards the door)* OK, but only if you insist.

MICA *(sadly)* I insist.

KICA *(opens the door to reveal a rather plain, not very striking girl with a small hat on her head. She looks sad and pitiable)* Dobry den. *(the Czech girl nods shyly)* Where's the other one? *(he uses his hands a lot when he speaks Czech, or thinks he is speaking Czech)* Kde je...druha?

ALENA Gone.

KICA Yeh? Gone where?

ALENA Domu

KICA What? *(Alena shrugs her shoulders. She stares at Mica the whole time as if she can't believe she is so close to him at last)* This is my brother... bratr.

ALENA *(stretches out her hand without ceasing to stare)* Alena.

MICA *(takes her hand)* Mica.

ALENA I know.

MICA You speak Serbian?

ALENA No.

MICA English? Anglicky?

ALENA No.

MICA Great. Nor do I. *(she looks at him, he looks at the floor. Kica waits. Suddenly Mica points to the clock)* Oh, I almost forgot... excuse me, there's something important I have to do. *(turns towards the door, smiles in a friendly way at Alena. She looks at him sadly but with complete understanding)* OK, bye then. It was a pleasure.

ALENA *(waves at him in a placatory fashion)* Bye. *(On the way to the door Mica grabs the telephone.)*

KICA *(heads him off at the door)* Mica...

MICA Yes, Kica?

KICA *(holds out his hand. Mica gives him the phone)* Sit down, Mica. *(Mica obeys. Kica points Alena to the chair beside Mica. Alena sits. Kica to Mica)* Make conversation.

MICA (*doesn't know quite how*) Dobry den.

ALENA   Dobry den.
(Both are silent.)

KICA   Mica!

MICA *(has great difficulty with the Czech)* Ah, ah... Kak se
imenuete? Your name...?

ALENA   Alena

MICA   Oh right, Alena. I know that. *(says nothing for a
moment, then remembers something)* Kava?

ALENA   Ne.

MICA   Whisky?

ALENA   Ne.

MICA   That's good, 'cos we haven't any.

ALENA   Pardon?

MICA   Nothing, nothing. *(Alena shrugs again. Mica is
silent for a long time, then)* Svetr lezi na stole.

ALENA (*looks. There is nothing on the table*) Kde?

MICA   Pardon?

ALENA   Pardon?

KICA   What did you say?

MICA   Svetr lezi na stole. The pullover is on the table...

KICA   What pullover?

MICA   How do I know? It's in the lesson. The first one.
Czech for beginners, page one... on page two there's that about
the pullover.

KICA   Mica! That's a load of rubbish. What's the girl going
to think of that? Surely you can say something to her?

MICA *(jumps up and yells)* Sure. Je Jana prodavacka? Je Petr dobry
student? Je svetr na stole? (*climbs onto the table and shouts*) Jana
is a shop assistant. Peter is a good student. Helena is on the table.
Mam rad cestinu, mam rad manzela, mam rad tramvaj.

KICA   What's the matter with you, Mica?

MICA *(goes on shouting, jumps around on the furniture)* Chodi mi
se, chodi mi se, chodi mi se, chodi, ne chodi, chodi, ne chodi,
chodi!!!

KICA   Come down, Mica, please...

MICA   Vis? Vim? Vite? Vime! Vime? Vite! Vis? Vim!
Dozadu, dopredu, nahoru, nadolu, doprostred, doleva, doprava...
stoii, sedi, lezi.
*(lies down exhausted on the floor. Kica looks at him aghast,
doesn't know what he should do. Mica begins to sing a Czech
children's song very softly. Alena goes up to Kica and whispers
something into his ear. Kica looks at her, she nods. Kica turns
towards the door uncertainly. Mica carries on singing.)*

KICA   Mica...

ALENA *(interrupts him firmly)* Go. *(Kica does so reluctantly. Mica
goes on singing. Alena sits down beside him on the floor. He
doesn't look at her.)*

ALENA   Love? *(Mica looks at her but goes on singing)* Does
it hurt?

MICA   Yes.

ALENA   I know. *(Mica sits up, looks at her properly for the
first time)* Jak se jmenuje?

MICA   Ana.

ALENA   Je krasna?

MICA   Yes.

ALENA   Proc ne telefonujes?

MICA   No money.

ALENA *(takes a mobile phone out of her pocket and gives it to
Mica)* It's a mobile phone. Ring her.

MICA *(reaches hesitantly for the phone)* Are you sure?

ALENA *(nodding energetically)* Ano, Ano!

MICA *(hastily dials a number and gets through)* Hello, hello...
Evening, Auntie Nada, Mica here... Mica Jovic... in Prague,
yes... thanks, I'm well, and you? Are you keeping well?
*(He is polite but impatient. 'Auntie Nada' on the other end is
obviously going into as much medical history as the doctor when
he visits. Mica can't get a word in.)*

*Kica has come back noiselessly. Full of anxiety he follows Mica's
conversation behind his back. Alena is in the kitchen area and can't
see Mica, but listens.*

MICA   Aha... Aha... Aha... that's that again... aha, a kidney, I see... not so bad then, you've still got one... uh-huh... the other one, too, I see, aha...

KICA *(softly to Alena)* How could you give him the phone? *(Alena interrupts him with an energetic wave of her hand)*

MICA *(carrying on)* ... fine, Auntie Nada, great, I mean... I'm sorry, tell me, is Ana there?... No?... She's gone already... Since when?... Last week, uh-huh... *(he does a double take)* What do you mean last week?... No, Kica didn't tell me anything, what was the message? *(Kica is anxious, Alena just stands there)* Aha... Aha... Uh-huh... a businessman, I understand... these things happen, I understand... yes, yes, yes... a baby, lovely... yes, yes... a wonderful wedding... and a sit-down reception... I'm really sorry I couldn't be there... no. I'm not angry, not at all... I'm not disappointed *(tears roll down his face)* ...young, yes, that's something else... if I hadn't gone away... but I had to... *(can't hold back his tears any more, tries to speak with a firm voice)* OK, Auntie Nada, I have to hang up now... yes, I'm fine... he is too, thanks for asking... no problem, everything's OK... you look after yourself, now... and to you too...
(Breaks the connection, grasps the phone, as if trying to stop his tears. Alena at once starts to busy herself in the kitchen area like a housewife.)

KICA   Mica... I didn't know how to tell you, Mam told me... *(Mica is silent. Alena busier and busier in the kitchen)* Mica... *(Mica cries silently. Heartbroken)* I didn't know how to... *(tries to put his arm round his brother.)*

MICA *(tears himself away, wipes away his tears, laughs bitterly)* Leave me alone, arsehole!

KICA   I thought...

MICA   What?

KICA   Nothing... I thought nothing.

MICA *(determined but not happy. He won't ever overcome the pain of these events. His laughter becomes forced, his determination too severe)* Very sensible. Thinking never helped anyone. Besides, we haven't much time. Do you know how late it is?

KICA *(automatically looks at his watch, gives up immediately)* No.

MICA   Very late. Alena, come here!

ALENA *(comes obediently, but with determination. Mica grabs her and kisses her. She returns the kiss. They let each other go. Alena is a little unsteady on her legs)* Kava?

MICA Two.

ALENA *(rushes to the kitchen, Mica gives her a smack on the rump)* Ano, brzo!

MICA *(to Kica)* She's good, the little woman, isn't she? After the coffee we'll go. It's going to be good this evening, I have a feeling.

KICA If it's good, I'll buy a digital watch... I swear I will!

Lights fade.

SCENE 2, SYDNEY.

A flat not much different from that in the first scene. Somewhat tidier or rather, untidy in a different way. Toys, bottles and other evidence of a baby in the house. A decorated Christmas tree, the table decorated for the New Year's Eve meal. From off-stage we hear a baby crying: incessantly, insistently, unbearably. Sanja enters with the baby in her arms, followed by Milos.

SANJA Will this child ever stop crying? Come on, Johnny, be a good baby when Mummy asks you. Stop crying, sweetie pie. *(She rocks the baby a little bit harder than necessary.)*

MILOS I think you're holding him too tight. Maybe that's why he's crying.

SANJA Oh, hark at him, the great consultant pediatrician. Why don't you take him, if you know it all?

MILOS You know he cries when I take him.

SANJA And he doesn't with me? Please, Johnny, be a good boy, so that your Mummy doesn't commit suicide, on New Year's Eve and all! *(the baby cries with undiminished intensity so that Sanja and Milos have to shout to hear each other above it.)*

MILOS Did you take the meat out of the oven?

SANJA What meat? Oh right, the meat, no! I can't think of everything... you could help!

MILOS (*goes to the kitchen area stage right, opens the oven door*) When did you put the meat in?

SANJA   No idea, half an hour ago? Something like that.

MILOS   Nothing's happening. (*the baby stops crying.*)

SANJA   It looks as if he's fallen asleep. (*Milos shuts the oven door a little too loudly. The baby starts screaming again*) What are you doing for God's sake, he'd just settled down!

MILOS   I didn't mean to... The handle's covered in fat. And the meat's raw.

SANJA   Impossible. Johnny, please be quiet! I can't take any more. It's got to be ready soon. What time is it?

MILOS (*looks at his watch, holds it to his ear*) No idea. My watch has stopped.

SANJA   It would happen to you! Didn't I tell you, you needed to buy a new battery? Please, Johnny... This child is unbearable! (*it really is unbearable. It is screaming at full volume*) Please, Milos, do something, I can't take any more!

MILOS (*looking at the meat in the oven*) What am I supposed to do? Oh right... you didn't turn the oven on.

SANJA   Why didn't you turn it on? And why didn't you do the supper? It was your idea anyway to have the party here. Johnny, be quiet!

MILOS   No problem. I've turned it on. It won't be long.

SANJA   It's too late now. They'll be here any minute.

MILOS   There's time enough...

SANJA   How do you know how much time there is? You're not even capable of getting your watch mended. This doesn't happen to Australians. If we were still in Belgrade where there aren't any Swatch repair shops...

MILOS   On the contrary.

SANJA   What did you say?

MILOS   Nothing. Gone already. Not important. Just don't get hysterical, Sanja.

SANJA   And why not? I'll throttle this child, I swear!

MILOS (*takes the child from her*) Come to Daddy, Nikolas. Doesn't matter if they come now. They'll just have to wait. We don't have to eat straight away.

SANJA   We don't have to do anything! Nothing at all! It was your idea to invite guests, nothing to do with me. So you tell them you're the idiot who can't even get a shitty watch mended... let alone help his wife, who hasn't slept since God knows when, because for months on end she's been tortured by this bloody screaming!
(The baby screams louder than ever.)

MILOS   I think he's wet.

SANJA   So?

MILOS *(changes the baby's nappy)* Just imagine you were in Belgrade and couldn't get Pampers. You'd have to wash and iron nappies.

SANJA   So? My mother washed and ironed nappies and can you see anything wrong with me?

MILOS *(looks at her)* No.

SANJA   Are we being a little cynical or is it just my imagination?

MILOS   It's your imagination. *(finishes changing the nappy. The baby is quiet for a moment.)*

SANJA *(starts to yell and cry at the same time)* Kiss my arse, Christ almighty! *(at this moment the baby begins to roar and Sanja yells over its noise)* Why didn't you go and find someone better if I'm not good enough for you? After all you had a lot to offer – a big sunny two-roomed flat, grandmother thrown in for free. In the bigger room, of course. And for transport the city bus company's red Mercedes bus. Every day someone new to meet, to talk to, pure adventure...

MILOS *(can't contain himself)* And how come you had nothing to offer?

SANJA   Me? Who's father paid for the flight here? Yours by any chance?

MILOS   No.

SANJA   And who gave us money to help us get started? You?

MILOS   No. Your old man paid for everything.

SANJA   Exactly. He paid for everything!

MILOS   Is that OK now?

SANJA   No! … And don't you call him the old man. Call him my father. *(takes the child, which is temporarily quiet.)*

MILOS   Come on, Sanja honey, don't get so uptight. It's our first New Year's Eve in Sydney. It's nice and warm… the sun's shining. Just think what it'll be like in Belgrade, right now. Cold flats, guaranteed there won't be any hot water in my old one. There's never any hot water on New Year's Eve. Everyone wants to wash themselves specially, and because the demand's so high, there's not enough for everyone…

SANJA   That's just your district. In the centre we've got boilers.

MILOS   Hey, I never thought about that before. The phenomenon of bathing before New Year's Day. The desire for change, the desire to wash away all the nastiness, hope for the future…

SANJA   The hope of getting your leg over at the parties because everyone's drunk.

MILOS   You're so crude.

SANJA   And you're so very educated. His Lordship studied sociology and thinks he's a genius! He has to see something extraordinary in everything, something phenomenal. People wash themselves because they want to have a fuck and that's all there is to it!

MILOS   You really are crude.

SANJA   Piss off!

(They are silent for a while. Sanja rocks the baby, who appears to have gone to sleep at last. Milos puts plates on the table, one goes down a little too hard.)

Do you have to bang the plates down like that? If you don't want to do it, let me.

MILOS   I didn't mean to.

SANJA   And they're your guests anyway.

MILOS   I thought Kaca was your friend.

SANJA   Kaca? What makes you think that? We weren't friends in Belgrade. We couldn't stand each other!

MILOS   I thought things had ironed themselves out.

SANJA   When you thought that, were you hanging something on me? *(laughs maliciously)*

MILOS *(resigned)* That's vulgar and anyway illogical. How could I hang anything on you?

SANJA   However you like. Let's say, on my cock? *(laughs again.)*

MILOS   But you haven't got one.

SANJA   What haven't I got?

MILOS   Well, that.

SANJA   You mean, a cock?

MILOS   Sanja, please...

SANJA   ... prick, willy, tool...

MILOS   Really, Sanja...

SANJA   ... dick, member, weapon...

MILOS   I'm not listening.

SANJA   Oh yes you are, you can hear perfectly well.

MILOS   No.

SANJA   Yes!

MILOS *(enraged)* No! *(the baby wakes and starts to scream.)*

SANJA *(somewhat pacified, defensively)* Don't shout like that, you woke him up again...

The door bell rings. Milos goes to open it. Kaca and Dule enter.

KACA   Are we too early? Dules' watch stopped, we didn't know... *(Sanja stands up and goes towards the guests.)*

MILOS   You're bang on time.

SANJA   Milos is just as clever. His watch doesn't work either. Welcome... *(she makes to kiss Kaca three times, Kaca only accepts twice, so Sanja is left 'in mid air'.)*

KACA   Oh sorry, I'm not used to this stupid kissing three times anymore.

SANJA *(looking insulted)* My most intimate friends I only kiss once. *(kisses Dule once)* How are you, Dule?

DULE   Fine...

KACA *(bending, obviously indignant, over the baby)* How's my little one, then? Look what Auntie Kaca brought for you.

(She pulls a musical toy out of her bag) See, Nija, that's from your Auntie Kaca.

(The baby of course starts to scream.)

SANJA *(taking the present)* Thanks, you shouldn't have... and please, don't call him Nija. His name is Johnny.

KACA   I thought it sounded good, kind of cool: Nija-Johnny.

MILOS   He's called Nikolas, not Johnny.

SANJA   Well, that's not Nija either!

MILOS   Let's drop it.

SANJA   Piss off!

(The situation is unpleasant. They are all silent.)

DULE *(is the first to break the silence)* Listen, mine host, anything to drink in this house?

MILOS   Oh sure. *(brings a bottle of whisky)* Who wants ice, who doesn't?

DULE   What is it? Johnny... *(he means 'Johnny Walker')*

KACA   You see how daft it is to call him Johnny? In Belgrade you could have christened him Smirnoff or Slivovitz. *(She laughs. Sanja is cross.)*

DULE   Hey, where's that stuff we had last time?

MILOS   The apricot brandy?

DULE   Yes, the one from back home.

MILOS   None left. Sanja drank it all.

KACA   Oho! I didn't know you were keen on those peasant things.

SANJA   I didn't drink it, I made compresses with it. I had toothache.

KACA   My God, Sanja, if there's one thing there's loads of in this country, it's painkillers. Capitalism has no time for toothache, headaches, stomach-aches. You just go down to the drugstore and buy whatever you want.

SANJA   I don't know whether you've noticed, Kaca, but I am the mother of a small child, a so-called baby, which I am still breast feeding. I don't want all sorts of chemicals in my milk so that he gets addicted to analgesics from an early age.

KACA   And so you decide to use another poison. Sixty percent alcohol, just right for a child!

DULE   Really, Sanja, it was sheer waste!

KACA   Hey, Dule, since when do you go for these peasant brews? In Belgrade you always drank whisky, you couldn't stand the smell of Slivovitz, but now you can't get enough of this rot-gut!

MILOS   It's not rot-gut. It's real home-distilled fruit brandy. My old man makes it himself on our bit of land.

KACA   Thank God, in this civilised country it's against the law to poison people like that. I'd like a whisky with lots of ice and a glass of water as well, if it's not too much to ask.

DULE   Same for me. Without the ice and the water.

KACA   Why don't you just take the bottle and have it put in intravenously? Why waste time?

MILOS   Please, Kaca, let him have his glassful. It's not New Year's Eve every day.

KACA   Let him drink, not my problem.

MILOS (*pours everyone a drink*) OK, then. Cheers.

DULE   Cheers!

KACA   Chin-chin! (*Sanja says nothing. All chink glasses together*) Well, Milos, how's the office?

MILOS   Quite good. From the New Year, I'll have every Sunday off.

DULE   Really? And your pay?

MILOS   Stays the same. It's like a rise really. Instead of working seven days, I work six and get the same dosh as before.

SANJA   It'd be better if you carried on working Sundays for more money.

KACA   Exactly.

MILOS   They didn't offer me that.

SANJA   Don't lie. You just can't stand working.

MILOS   What do you mean? Me not like working? For the last year I've worked every day without a break.

SANJA   You had a holiday.

MILOS   One week. You think that's enough?

SANJA   Start a trade union then. Complain about the capitalists, only stop getting on my nerves. (*to Dule*) How's it going in the shop?

DULE   Quite well...

KACA (*interrupts him*) Please, Sanja, it's not a shop, it's an antique gallery!

DULE   It's all the same thing.

KACA   No, Dule, it is not! You're not a shop assistant!

DULE   What am I then?

KACA   An art dealer.

DULE   Don't be silly, Kaca... art dealer... (*to Milos*) Me too, please.

KACA   Excuse me, Dule – you studied Art History and you work in a gallery, therefore you are an art dealer. That's what it's called. Look in the dictionary.

SANJA (*holds her glass out while Milos is pouring*) Me too.

MILOS   You can't. Because of Nikolas.

SANJA   Rubbish. Makes no difference to him.

MILOS (*resolutely*) You're not having any.

SANJA   Go and eat shit.

KACA   We could buy two intravenous kits and connect up Dule and the baby. Then they can keep each other company in intensive care. (*laughs.*)

SANJA (*stands up*) Fuck off.

KACA   Ooh, aren't we sensitive?

SANJA   I'm going to put him down to sleep now.
              (*She takes the child out.*)

MILOS   It's post-natal depression.

DULE   Yes, I know, I've read about it.

KACA   You've read about it! Where, for God's sake? Since we came here you haven't picked up anything without a ball on the front cover. Well, perhaps a tennis racket or skis. You're not interested in anything else.

DULE   Yes I am. I read the Australian Lottery Weekly.

MILOS   What's that?

DULE   The forecast of the sports' results *(laughs)* Pour me
another.

MILOS   Never heard of it.

KACA   You didn't consult the expert.

MILOS *(stands up)* Sorry. I'll just go and see if she needs any help.

KACA   No problem. Dule's only on the first bottle. The
night's still young.
(Milos goes to see Sanja. Dule helps himself to more whisky)
Try to go a bit slow. We've got to spend at least another five
hours here.

DULE   Nobody forced you to come.

KACA   Oh no? And whose idea was it to celebrate New
Year with them?

DULE   I thought you'd enjoy it. We are their friends after
all…

KACA   Only because we're here. In Belgrade I wouldn't
have set foot inside their house. Red-necks…

DULE *(pours himself some more)* The old woman rang this
morning. Did I tell you?

KACA   No. Yours or mine?

DULE   Mine. She said, that young girl from your block, that
Ana, you know…

KACA   Ana Simovic, she's not from my block, she's from
the one next door, number 44, I know…

DULE   That's her. She's got a job on TV.

KACA   That little kid? She lisps and she's got a squint.

DULE   I don't know about a squint. But it's her all right.
She's a newsreader and presents the chart show.

KACA   See. If she's got into television, then, really… That
kid. She's got no qualifications!

DULE   She studied Geography.

KACA   Geography? So as a graduate journalist I should start
drawing maps or what?

DULE   Don't upset yourself. I was only telling you. Mama
said the whole neighbourhood is so proud.

KACA   That kid, the bitch! You know what she's done? She's taken *my* job, get it? *Mine*!

DULE   Hang on a minute, Kaca, how do you make that out? What's it got to do with you? You never worked in television...

KACA   No. Because those kind of people stopped me getting anywhere. I took the exams bang on time in June and in September. I was never seen in a pub, and in the whole four years I was at Uni', only once did I go skiing up at Kopaonik.

DULE   That's true. You always went to Breza in Macedonia.

KACA   That was to recover from all that hard work! But this little thing wags her backside a bit and before you know – she's in television!

DULE   Hang on, Kaca, how do you know that's how she got the job? Perhaps there was a test.

KACA   I know those sort of tests. Bust size and telephone number, that's all they want to know.

DULE   But her tits weren't very special.

KACA   How do you know what her tits are like? Did your mother ring you to tell you? Are we sending her money just so as she can give us information on Ana Simovic's tits?

DULE   Kaca, please, you don't know what you're talking about...

KACA   Your mother never liked me. Never!

DULE *(trying to calm her)* What's my mother got to do with it?

KACA   Quite a lot! It's all their fault. It's their fault that I'm sitting here and not at home, where I've got friends and where I could do the work I'm trained for and could earn a decent living and be independent! Your father and your mother and all those millions of others who in between distilling brandy and killing pigs found time to vote for those thieves and criminals! It's down to them that I couldn't stay in my own country, in my own town … because of those savages from the sticks who forced themselves into power and made decisions about my life and my future!

DULE   They did vote, that's true. But I can't kill them just for that.

KACA	You could have changed them.
DULE	How?

(Silence. Dule fills up both glasses. Sounds from the room off, as if, for example a plastic bath had fallen over on top of toys. Then baby Nikolas crying.)

KACA	Here we go again... *(calls)* Need any help?
SANJA *(off)*	Yes, if you don't mind!
KACA	Coming! *(to Dule)* Go and see what she wants.

Dule goes obediently into the other room. In the doorway he meets Milos who is carrying a baby's bottle.

KACA   What's the matter?

MILOS   Nothing. I just have to boil some water. He'll settle down OK now. *(goes to the ring, puts a pot on with water.)*

KACA *(without looking at him)* Why didn't you come yesterday evening?

MILOS   When?

KACA   Yesterday evening after work. We had a date.

MILOS   Yesterday evening... I couldn't.

KACA *(rises, goes towards Milos)* Why not?

MILOS   Because of Nikolas.

KACA   What was the matter?

MILOS   He had a temperature.

KACA *(presses up against Milos' back, puts her arms around him)* I waited for you...

MILOS   Please, Kaca, they could come in.

KACA   I had a temperature too. Saturday night fever. You know I hate being alone on Saturdays. *(deftly unbuttons Milos' trousers, while he tries to defend himself.)*

MILOS   Looks like you've still got a temperature.

KACA   Yes. Especially now.

MILOS   Please, Kaca – your husband's here, and Sanja isn't well. She's been crying...

KACA   If I had a bum like hers I'd cry too! *(she has already lifted up her skirt and manoeuvred herself and Milos into a position doggy style)* Come, just a little. See what it's like.

MILOS *(trying to resist)* We know that, Kaca...

KACA *(overcoming his resistance. Intercourse begins)* Do we?

MILOS   Yes. *(both are sexually aroused. Milos looks comical, while Kaca has the situation under control.)*

KACA   How's that, Milos?

MILOS   Good...

KACA   How good?

MILOS *(obviously at his climax)* Won-der-ful!

KACA *(smoothes her skirt down)* I didn't notice anything.

MILOS *(buttons up his trousers. Kaca goes towards the bathroom)* Where are you going?

KACA   To tell Sanja everything.

MILOS *(really shocked)* Are you mad?

KACA *(laughs)* Don't crap your pants. I'm going to the bathroom.

MILOS   Please, Kaca, this swearing doesn't suit you.

KACA   Tell that to your little wifey. She's so neurotic she might listen to you. *(she's almost out of the door.)*

MILOS   Kaca! *(Kaca turns round)* You didn't come again, did you?

KACA   What's it got to do with you? *(she goes into the bathroom, the bedroom door opens and Dule appears.)*

DULE   Sanja says: 'Where's the water got to?'

MILOS   Ah, the water? Coming at once. *(picks up the bottle, throws it to Dule)* Can you give it her, please?
(Dule opens the door, hands in the bottle, shuts the door. He comes to the table, sits down.)

MILOS   Another whisky? *(Dule is already pouring himself another)* You're drinking a lot.

DULE   Yes, but I never get drunk.

MILOS *(looks at him)* You don't look at all drunk. Haven't you been getting them down you? *(Dule shows him the bottle, the bottom of which is barely covered)* You have been laying into it. How come you're not pissed?

DULE   Just because I'm not.

MILOS   That's impossible.

DULE   Oh what the hell. I'm a phenomenon.

MILOS   I remember, mate, when we were giving Kica his send-off, you threw so much down you, I had to take you to Casualty. They pumped half a litre of vodka out of your stomach.

DULE   It was different then.

MILOS   If you say so. *(silence. Dule drinks.)*

DULE   Where's Kaca?

MILOS *(embarrassed)* In the bathroom... she's got a stomach pain.

DULE   Women. Whoever invented them should hang himself.

MILOS   Don't talk like that, Dule.

DULE   Sorry. It's different for you. You've got a wife and child, everything according to the rules. *(pause)* Tell me, did you ever think it would work out like this? Until recently you were the biggest son-of-a-bitch in town, a sociologist with a future and intellectual clout. Doesn't swear, doesn't drink, knows what's what, the women flocking round...

MILOS   Leave it out, Dule, that's all in the past now...

DULE   That's what I mean. Did you think it would all happen so quickly? Within a year you'd be married, a father, family provider, employee in a reputable travel agency in Sydney?

MILOS   I never imagined the travel agency bit...

DULE   ... that you'd be grateful for every free Sunday you get? Not many in the beginning, true, but it's better like that because when you're working non-stop, there's not so much time for spending your dosh...

MILOS   Sanja's got lots of time for that.

DULE   Yeh, but she had that in Belgrade too. Only you didn't have as much to offer her there.

MILOS   She wanted a flat. And a car. You know Dule, I didn't want it like this... all at once – marriage, baby... I wanted us to live a bit, try it all out. *(pause while he thinks)* Her folks insisted. Her old man didn't want us to live together without a marriage certificate.

DULE *(laughs)* Cohabitation and all that...

MILOS   Sure. So I got married. When she started on about a baby, I didn't mind... At least now we have a flat and some cash.

DULE   In Belgrade I had my grandmother's flat, but I had Grandma too. Kaca says that's crippled her sexually, that Grandma destroyed her libido...

MILOS   Oh come on, how could she do that?

DULE   She says, she listened to us. She knew exactly when we were at it, and then...

MILOS   Why should your grandmother listen to you?

DULE   I don't know. Kaca says, to get off on it.

MILOS *(appalled)* That's disgusting... *(thinks)* How could your granny?... I mean, she's old.

DULE   That's what I said. Then Kaca said I had an Oedipus complex. I ask you, how can you have an Oedipus complex about your granny?

MILOS   Mmm... I don't know. We didn't do that.

DULE   Anyway, Kaca was determined we should get married and emigrate to Australia. There's prospects here, she says. So I marry her, sell the Wartburg, the records and the speakers and go for it. We'd hardly got onto the plane, when granny goes and dies. Mama said, out of sheer grief.

MILOS   You know, if she died of grief... maybe she really was perverted.

DULE   Shit. Maybe she was... Where did you say, Kaca was?

MILOS   In the bathroom. She's got a headache.

DULE   I thought it was her stomach?

MILOS *(very embarrassed)* Maybe... I don't know, she's got something.

DULE   Ah... Tell me, Milos – are we friends?

MILOS   Yes, Dule, we are.

DULE   Are we best friends?

MILOS *(stands up, it's become uncomfortable for him)* What are you asking me that for all of a sudden?

DULE   Tell me – are we best friends?

MILOS *(hesitantly)* Yes.

DULE   Does that mean there are no secrets between us?

MILOS   What's the matter with you, Dule? You're drunk!

DULE *(stands up, puts an arm round Milos. He's quite in control. Completely sober)* I can't get drunk, Milos. Since I arrived here, since that first night, when I lay staring at the slats of the radiator, the marching columns of cockroaches... since I lay counting them and the sheep and the herds of kangaroos, trying to get just a little sleep... since then I can't get pissed any more, Milos. I just don't feel anything, no sensations, no emotions, nothing...
(Kaca comes out of the bathroom, stands behind the two men. Dule continues)
You know why? Because in the night, in that filthy hotel, while my wife, stupefied by the long flight and the jet lag, lay beside me sleeping peacefully, I shit myself. Fear of what was in front of me. Of life in a strange land. Of life with my wife. Of life, Milos.
(He is exhausted, Milos looks at him.)

KACA *(goes up to Dule, tries to smile)* You really know how to create a good atmosphere, Dule... a really good New Year's Eve atmosphere...

DULE *(carries on)* And that's not the only thing I can't do, Milos.

KACA   That's enough, Dule...

DULE   There's something worse, Milos.

KACA   I said, that's enough, Dule!

DULE   I'm thirty-two, I have a wife, a friend, the status of an emigrant in a rich country, but I can't get it up any more...

KACA *(shouts)* Shut your mouth, you idiot!

DULE   I can't get it up any more, little brother, so scared I can't fuck! I shit myself that first night, and since then nothing!

KACA *(shouting, tries to put her hand over his mouth)* You dirty liar! Please shut up! Right now!

DULE   So you just go right ahead and fuck her. Better you than someone else. Better a friend, if I can't!

Begins to laugh. Unnoticed, Sanja has entered. Kaca is crying. Milos hangs his head. Then he catches sight of Sanja, who is just standing there looking quietly at the others.

SANJA *(quietly)* He's gone to sleep.
(Everyone looks at her)
The meat will be cold.

DULE *(laughs)* I'll cut it up.
(He goes to the kitchen area, Sanja and Kaca follow him.)

SANJA   Kaca, would you help me make the salad?

KACA   No problem.
(They all get busy.)

MILOS *(alone for a moment, thoughtfully)* Shit.

(We hear the baby crying.)

SCENE 3, LOS ANGELES

The same flat, augmented by a palm in a pot. The New Year's Eve party is taking place in the garden. From outside the sound of loud hard core folk music and the sound of guests' voices. Lights are reflected in the pool. Even for California it's unusually warm.

Mara enters and closes the door behind her, which muffles the music somewhat. Without turning on the lights she sits down at the table. She brings out a small pipe, which she fills with cannabis and lights. The flame of the lighter lights up her face, but also that of Jovan who is sitting in an armchair behind her.

JOVAN   Hi. *(Mara starts)* Sorry. I didn't mean to frighten you...

MARA   It's OK. I was just surprised. *(looks at Jovan, as if sizing him up. Offers him the pipe)* Want some?

JOVAN   California grass?

MARA *(laughs)* Of course. My name is Mara. *(holds out her hand.)*

JOVAN   Hi Mara, I'm Jovan.

MARA   Jovan? You're one of us?

JOVAN   Looks like it. Where are you from?

MARA   New York. From Belgrade really. But I live here now. And you?

JOVAN   I'm from here. I mean, I come from Belgrade, but I live here now. In Hollywood.

MARA   That sounds good. A man from Hollywood.

JOVAN   Sounds good, but it's not a good area. My neighbours are all Latinos *(they take turns smoking the pipe.)*

MARA   Really? I always thought, Hollywood must be absolutely fabulous. Films, actors, showbiz and that. But – it's nothing really.

JOVAN   It's not nothing. But it isn't wonderful either. What do I know. It's normal. Quite normal.
(The door opens for a moment, the sounds of Turbo-folk, new folk music with primitive kind of lyrics, can be heard. A song about guns, war and money. Or something similar. The songs of those listening, join in with the soloist on the record. One voice, Daca's rises above the rest.)

DACA *(off)* Give me hope!
(The door slams shut again. Jovan and Mara look at each other, begin to laugh.)

JOVAN   He's got carried away. *(both laugh like idiots.)*

MARA   Do you know that they have all these folk songs on CD. The new technology...

JOVAN   Someone brought them with them.

MARA   That's what I mean. Someone packed up this rubbish and dragged it along... I'd like to inspect their brain... *(she fills and lights the pipe again.)*

JOVAN   That's good grass.

MARA   Californian! Do you know that song: 'Jo-Jo left his home, from Tucson, Arizona, for some California grass...?'
(They both sing the Beatles song.)

JOVAN/ MARA 'Get back, get back to where you once belonged.'
(They laugh)

JOVAN   But d'you know, on holiday on Vis I grew better grass in a flower pot than this stuff, believe me.

MARA   Did you really?

JOVAN   I'm telling you. It wasn't stronger, but better. Funnier. How did you come to be here?

MARA   I'm visiting my friend for the Christmas break.
(For a moment we can hear the dreadful music from the garden.)

JOVAN   Great. One wouldn't want to miss such a wonderful party. *(Mara laughs. Both take turns in puffing.)*

MARA   Do you know, when I close my eyes, I can imagine that I'm on the Floss. In block 45. Not that I've ever been there, but it's one hundred percent accurate.

JOVAN   I know these people. I just don't know how they got to be so ghastly. You're from New York then?

MARA   Yes. I've been there six months.

JOVAN   That's not long. I've been here three years.

MARA   And – do you like it?

JOVAN   Do you like it?

MARA   No idea.

JOVAN   What are you here for then?

MARA   I told you, a friend invited me...

JOVAN   'Scuse me?

MARA   She said, New Year's Eve on the beach...

JOVAN   I don't get it.

MARA   What? *(Mara and Jovan look at each other for a brief moment. Then Jovan gets it.)*

JOVAN   Ah, you mean the party. And I thought...
(He laughs, a bit high.)

MARA *(still doesn't understand)* What's so funny, tell me. *(Jovan is killing himself with laughter. Mara too, though she doesn't know why)* Go on, tell me. *(both laugh.)*

JOVAN *(calms down, wipes tears from his eyes)* Just a joke...

MARA   Bad grass, eh?

JOVAN   I didn't say it was bad, just that I've had better.

MARA   You know something... normally I don't smoke it.

JOVAN *(truly astonished)* You don't say! Why not?

MARA *(softly, a bit ashamed)* It gives me spots.

JOVAN *(laughs again)* What?

MARA *(somewhat insulted)* Don't laugh. It's true.

JOVAN *(with mock concern)* Really? Where then?

MARA *(pointing to her face)* Here, and here... everywhere!

JOVAN *(looking intently)* I never heard of that before. And I can't see anything. Your skin is superb. *(they look at each other in silence for a while)* Is your boyfriend here?

MARA *(starts and looks around)* Where?

JOVAN *(pretending to be 'cool')* No idea, just asking.

MARA　　　　　　Oh, right. No, I'm alone. I don't have a boyfriend anyway.

JOVAN *(opens his eyes wide at her)* What did you look round for then?

MARA　　　　　　No idea… I was totally confused. *(Jovan starts laughing again. Mara looks at him seriously)* You're really going to think I'm a silly cow.

JOVAN　　　　　Not at all.

MARA　　　　　　I'm not stupid you know.
(Jovan finds that funnier than ever, even Mara laughs. This 'attack' doesn't last long. Mara sighs. Jovan is silent. The situation is a bit embarrassing.)

JOVAN　　　　　So you don't have a boyfriend?

MARA *(indicates negative)* Ph.

JOVAN　　　　　How come? I mean, you're a great girlie… *(Mara looks at him reproachfully. Jovan tries to correct himself)* I mean, you're interesting…

MARA　　　　　　Don't talk rubbish.

JOVAN　　　　　Sorry.

MARA　　　　　　It's OK.

JOVAN　　　　　So?

MARA　　　　　　What?

JOVAN　　　　　So, why haven't you got a boyfriend?

MARA *(forcefully)* What business is it of yours?

JOVAN *(insulted)* I beg your pardon.

MARA　　　　　　It's OK. *(softly)* He kicked me out. When I left, we separated. He says, he's not interested in America. He's got his reputation in Belgrade, his job, his friends…

JOVAN　　　　　Does he?

MARA　　　　　　I think so.

JOVAN　　　　　And you? What do you do?

MARA   I'm a pianist!

JOVAN   You're kidding!

MARA *(laughs amusedly)* Seriously. And you?

JOVAN   I'm an actor. Seriously, I'm not joking. I did my diploma at the theatre school. And you? At the Academy?

MARA   Yes. I took my diploma in June. You're an actor, then. Maybe I've seen you somewhere?

JOVAN   Hardly. Oh yes, maybe. You know this ad, these tablets, something for the heart, based on garlic...

MARA *(has no idea)* For the heart? *(tries to remember.)*

JOVAN   You know, this advertising slot... I come in, and this girl comes towards me, a real smart one, that little Jelena, that model, who's going out with the boss of Zvezda football club...

MARA *(completely at sea, looking clueless)* Aha...

JOVAN   Well, never mind, she comes towards me and my heart's beating in a really funny way, you hear it – da-da-da, da-da-da, I stop, she looks at me, hands me the tablets and says: 'Take it easy, man'. And then you get the name of the tablets underneath. You wouldn't know it. It didn't run very often.

MARA   You don't say. I'm surprised. *(both laugh cheerfully.)*

JOVAN   And then I was in the schools programme. Chemistry for years seven and eight.

MARA   That I have seen, positive.

JOVAN   You're joking.

MARA   No, really. I always watch the schools programmes. When I practise, I mean before, when I practised, I turn the TV on, but keep the sound off and watch the pictures while I play. It's nice to see something moving. Normally I practise in the mornings, I mean, I used to. *(fills the pipe)* What about the theatre?

JOVAN *(pretends not to hear the question)* You don't practise any more?

MARA *(murmuring)* I don't have a piano. What about the theatre?

JOVAN   Don't you know anyone who's got one?

MARA   Yes.

JOVAN   Why can't they lend it to you?

MARA   Lend me the piano? You're mad. But what about the theatre?

JOVAN (*hands her the pipe*) You want it?

MARA   You're avoiding the question, aren't you?

JOVAN   What question?

MARA   You're avoiding it. Why?

JOVAN   I don't know what you're talking about.

MARA   You don't have to tell me. I mean, it's all the same to me. I told you about my boyfriend, but you don't have to tell me anything...

JOVAN (*sighs*) Nothing to tell. I had a part in a play when I was a student. Some others from my class and me – we did a Croatian commedia del arte play for the exam and then we took it out into the regions to make a bit of money. We thought people would like plays like that with sex and swearing, something a bit funny...(*he falls silent, thinking.*)

MARA (*also seriously*) And?

JOVAN   Nothing. We did four or five productions in Serbia – a mate organised it for us through the Ministry of Culture...

MARA (*serious, but patient*) And?

JOVAN   And then we got to this dump, I can't remember what it was called. We were in the school hall. The place was full of children and teachers. Well, really they weren't children, but high school kids, teenagers...

MARA   I get it. What happened?

JOVAN   We started the production – 'Father Major's Ducats'. My mate played Petronella, because we wanted to do it like it is in the original, where men play the female roles. So he starts off, and this guy stands up in the audience and shouts: 'Fuck off you shitty Croatian pooftahs!' (*he is upset, as he is every time he tells this story. Mara is also emotionally affected, however the story appears comical to her. She looks at Jovan and starts to laugh. Jovan laughs too, somewhat bitterly*) Yeh, it's funny...

MARA   I'm sorry... it's so stupid, I have to laugh.

JOVAN   I know, we thought that too. I was even sorry for the kid. I thought the teacher would grab him and take him to the head teacher.

MARA   Didn't they do that?

JOVAN   No way. The kid shouted, the whole hall laughed...
we pretended we hadn't heard anything, and carried on, then he
got up again and said: 'Didn't you hear what I said! Damned
Croatian arse-lickers!'

MARA   It's not possible.

JOVAN   Don't you believe it. We stopped, we couldn't
compete with him. He yelled: 'I'm coming up to finish you off!'
We didn't want to answer back, so we waited for somebody to do
something. There was uproar... he ran up to the stage, he wasn't
exactly small, a hefty guy, with fists like that... And we could see
that no-one was going to do anything about it. I looked round at
the Serbian teacher, the woman, who we'd arranged everything
with. But she didn't even look up. My mate shouted: 'Who're you
going to finish off?' And the guy came back with: 'You, you
Ustacha!' I could see there was going to be a fight and so I gave
the signal to let the curtain down.

MARA *(can hardly believe what she's hearing)* And what then?

JOVAN   Nothing. When it had all quietened down, we went
to this teacher to talk. We thought she'd apologise to us...

MARA   Didn't she?

JOVAN   No. She said we shouldn't have put on anything
from Croatian literature. 'The kids are sensitive, they hate Croats,
you have to understand.' This is a high school teacher talking to
me. I should understand why kids want to lynch me – nationalism
isn't forbidden in law.

MARA *(thinks)* Well, it isn't... And what did you do then?

JOVAN   Nothing. I packed my bags and came here. I was
totally disillusioned. Don't misunderstand me. I don't give a
damn about that teacher and that little twerp in that one horse
town which you can't even find on the map, but... I was fed up
with everything. *(dejected)* I was ashamed. Ashamed of my own
people... *(gloomily)*

MARA *(offers him the pipe)* You want some?

JOVAN   I can't.

MARA *(takes the pipe back)* Nor me. Have you been back to
Belgrade since then?

JOVAN   No. I had a tourist visa for six months. When it ran out I decided to stay all the same. Now I can't get out again. I mean, I could, but then they stamp your passport so you can't get back into America.

MARA   I know. But still, it's important for you to be here, – Hollywood and that...

JOVAN *(laughs bitterly)* Yeh, yeh, Hollywood.

MARA   Are you working?

JOVAN   Yes.

MARA   Where?

JOVAN   In houses.

MARA   What do you do in houses?

JOVAN   Removals. I cart furniture and that sort of thing.

MARA   Aha... and acting?

JOVAN   Acting?

MARA   So – nothing.

JOVAN   And you? Are you working? *(Mara nods)* Where?

MARA   In a café.

JOVAN   You play?

MARA   I wait tables.

JOVAN   And the piano?

MARA   What about the piano?

JOVAN   I mean, what are you going to do?

MARA   Nothing. Wait.

JOVAN   What for?

MARA   For something. Something has to happen.

JOVAN   Why did you come here in the first place?

MARA   To America? You won't believe it. I won a green card in the lottery.

JOVAN *(really delighted)* What, really?

MARA   It's a fact. The national lottery does this draw once a year. A friend put my name in, as a joke really and they picked me out.

JOVAN   What about her?

MARA　　Nothing. She's fine. She got married, works in television. She reads the news and presents the chart show. My mother says that she's even expecting a baby now... And all that in six months. (*considers sadly*) She did me a favour and now she's getting her reward.

JOVAN　　Great. Is she happy?

MARA　　No idea. We don't talk to each other. (*Jovan looks at her in astonishment*) What are you looking at me like that for? We don't talk because I don't want to. I don't want to see her ever again! Who does she think she is? What gives her the right to organise my life! What right did she have to expose me to this temptation! I've got the papers, OK, that's fine, but it wasn't my plan.

JOVAN　　You didn't have to use them.

MARA　　And have it gnawing away at me for the rest of my life because I hadn't tried it? Not sleeping at night, because I threw away the chance I'd never have had in Belgrade? Because I was too cowardly just to go and see how people live where they have it better. Where it must be better...

JOVAN　　And, is it better?

MARA　　How do I know? It could be. Isn't necessarily, though. I just have to wait.

JOVAN　　At least you can go home.

MARA　　You can too.

JOVAN　　This is my home now. (*pause.*)

MARA　　What's the time? We don't want to miss midnight.

JOVAN　　No idea. I haven't got a watch.

MARA　　Nor me. (*pause again.*)

JOVAN　　How about if we get married. I mean, first you fall in love with me and then we get married, and then as your husband I'll get all my papers and a work permit and then we can live here and we'll have a super time. What d'you reckon?

MARA　　Won't work.

JOVAN　　I knew it.

MARA　　Do you know why?

JOVAN　　Why?

MARA   We'd have to have sex first. *(continues, laughing)*
We'd have to see whether we suited each other... You can't do it
just like that!

JOVAN   Well, if it's like that, I have no objections...

*He laughs, puts his arms around Mara. They kiss lightly. It gets
serious. They look at each other for a long moment. Kiss again more
passionately. Suddenly the door opens wide. From the garden comes
loud folk music. Mara and Jovan separate. Mara, a little ashamed,
looks down at the floor.*

DACA *(in the doorway, roars, his arms out wide)* You heap of shit
... you left with the baby, because you're letting yourself be
fucked by the other guy now!

JOVAN *(jokingly)* Does he mean you?

MARA   Idiot. *(they laugh.)*

DACA   Good evening. What's so funny?
(Jovan and Mara really start to laugh. Daca's feathers ruffle up)
I asked, what's so funny?
*(We really see him for the first time. 'Medallion Man' par
excellence. Silk jacket, silk shirt, colourful pleated trousers a
good ten centimetres too long. Close cropped hair)*

DACA   Someone here want to have a go at Daca?
(Points to himself.)

MARA *(seriously)* No, really.

JOVAN   No idea. Go and ask Daca. *(laughs again.)*

DACA *(seriously)* What did you say?

JOVAN   I said...

MARA   Nothing. Jovan didn't understand the question
properly. He suggests that you ask Daca.
(Mara and Jovan laugh.)

DACA *(looks at them)* Someone here want to take the mickey out of
Daca?

JOVAN   Not at all!

DACA   D'you want to explain to me what's so funny?

MARA   Nothing, sorry. We've had a little smoke. Would
you like some? *(holds out the pipe to him.)*

DACA Drugs? Not me!
(Jovan and Mara look at him in astonishment.)

MARA Fine, if you don't want to... what's your name?

JOVAN He's told you already a couple of times.

MARA Oh yes, Daca. *(Daca nods, looks at her like a dog)* Sit down, Daca. Where are you from?

DACA *(sits, still looking suspicious)* From Tucson.

JOVAN Where from?

DACA Tucson, man, Arizona! *(Jovan and Mara look at each other, burst out laughing)* What's your problem, junkies? Someone want to cop a packet, or what...?!

MARA It's OK, Daca, calm down. We didn't mean anything.

JOVAN Oh yes we did, Daca. She's lying.

DACA I'll finish you off.

MARA *(jumps up)* Be quiet Jovan! Really we didn't, Daca. But there's this song: 'Jo-Jo left his home, from Tucson, Arizona', you know...

DACA What?

MARA Well, that's it, 'Jo-Jo left his home...'

DACA Never heard of it.

MARA Oh, you must have done. The Beatles.

DACA Who? *(looks at Jovan. He giggles secretly. Mara signs to him to be quiet.)*

MARA Do you have to provoke him? *(To Daca)* Well, I'm happy to have met you...

DACA *(looks at her)* Uh-huh, uh-huh. *(he sits down.)*

MARA *(searching for something to talk about)* You're from Arizona, then. When did you get here?

DACA Three days ago.

JOVAN Who'd have thought it. *(luckily Daca doesn't hear this remark.)*

MARA *(throws Jovan a reproachful look, does her best to make polite conversation)* And how long are you staying for?

DACA Going back tomorrow.

MARA   Only five days? Such a long journey for five days.
That's quite tiring?

DACA   How come tiring? Daca isn't a baby.

MARA   I know, but the long flight...

DACA   What flight? I came here by car.

MARA   What kind of a car?

DACA *(proudly)* My old man bought me a Cadillac for my birthday
and sent me to my Auntie in L.A. to see how it runs.
(Jovan and Mara look at him in disbelief.)

JOVAN   Hey, Mara, we must be really high.

DACA *(very suspicious. He's got an allergic reaction to Jovan)*
Something not clear here?

JOVAN *(sincerely)* Excuse me, but I really don't understand. How
could you come to America by car?

DACA   Stupid question. What do you mean come here? I
was born here.

JOVAN   Where?

DACA   In Tucson of course, idiot... Arizona, yes? My old
man emigrated twenty years ago. He knocked up my mother here,
so I was born here, logic. I'm just visiting my Auntie in L.A., like
I just said.

JOVAN   Aha!

MARA   For New Year, of course.

DACA   Stuff New Year. That's that Catholic nonsense of
those shit Ustaches. I only celebrate the Serbian one.

MARA   Oh sorry. I saw you were looking happy...

DACA   I said, my birthday...

MARA   Oh yes... which one?

DACA *(proudly)* Eighteenth.

MARA   Congratulations.

DACA   You can say that again. Eighteen, grown up, that's
something, isn't it?

JOVAN   And Daddy bought you a car?

DACA   Hmm.

MARA   Lovely. Can you drive it?

JOVAN   He told you that he came in the car.

MARA   Oh yes.

DACA   She's pretty dumb.

MARA   And can you read, too? *(she begins to laugh merrily)*

DACA *(irritated)* Say, guy, is this cunt laughing at me?

MARA   'Course not.
(She and Jovan are killing themselves laughing).

DACA *(cold, suddenly grabs Jovan by the arm)* I asked if this cunt is making fun of me!

MARA *(like Jovan, suddenly serious)* No, honestly – we were just laughing...

JOVAN   Listen, kid, this is my girlfriend so please don't call her names after sexual organs. *(Mara laughs)*

DACA *(looks at her. Laughs too. Cold. Lets Jovan's arm go)* Yeh?

JOVAN   Yes.

DACA   If you say so. Why not?

JOVAN   Because it's ugly.

DACA   Aha. *(pause, then, cold)* The cunt isn't exactly pretty.

JOVAN *(irritated)* Listen you shithead, I thought I made myself clear!

MARA   Just leave him, Jovan...

JOVAN   Wait, Mara. Let's get this straight. This pretty girl here is my girlfriend and her name is Mara... What's your surname?

MARA   Popovic

JOVAN   ...Mara Popovic... my girlfriend, OK, and also by the way a famous pianist from Belgrade. You're going to apologise to her and shove off. We want to enjoy the evening and the Californian climate alone. Is that clear?
(Daca looks at Jovan as if he has lost the power of speech. Jovan looks at Daca, not knowing what to say.)

MARA   Come on Jovan, leave him alone, you can see how he's taking it...

DACA   Shut your face, cunt. *(he's being provocative)* I'm asking myself what *getting it straight* means. I mean, if you want to give the girl one, all you have to say to me is: 'Piss off, dude, I

want a fuck…' *(Jovan and Mara are shocked. Daca becomes
more and more aggressive)* But if you don't intend to fuck her,
and it's *my* presence that bothers you, then we have a problem.

JOVAN   Oh really? What happens then?

DACA *(smiling as he pulls out a huge pistol)* Then I'll blow you
away. (*he aims at the consternated Jovan.*)
*(The music from the garden suddenly becomes loud. To the end of
the scene the actors have to shout over the bawling singer.)*

MARA *(appalled)* What are you doing, man, put the gun away!
*(Without looking at her Daca hits her with full strength in the
face. Mara screams.)*

DACA   You be quiet, cunt, or else…
*(he loads a bullet into the gun. Jovan stands up. Mara holds her
cheek)* Hey, what d'you think you're doing? Want to try it on
with Daca, eh? I'm one of the Zemun mob, you know. Know
what that is, you ape? I'm not like these American fuckers. I
know who I am and where I come from. I visit my grandparents
there every summer and meet up with the gang. So that my roots
don't wither and so I don't forget what seed I came from! *(short
pause. Then quietly, almost genuinely interested)* Where are you
from?

JOVAN   Belgrade.

DACA   What part?

JOVAN   Neimar.

DACA   Never heard of it.

JOVAN   Near the National Library.

DACA   Oh really, by the Library?… *(he suddenly hits out at
Mara again. She falls over.)*

JOVAN (*in despair. Takes a step forward, stops, shouts*) Stop
hitting her you bastard. Leave her alone, I say!

DACA   Near the Library, you said? As if Daca doesn't know
what books are, as if he never reads, you dumbo? *(kicks Mara,
laughing)* What's the matter, you pansy pig. Got a problem?

JOVAN (*shouts without moving*) I said, leave her alone! Fight like a
man!

DACA *(finds that very amusing. Imitates Jovan) Fight like a man!* Hey, you faggot dopehead, I'm going to fuck this cunt now! *(Mara flinches, appalled. Daca grabs her hair.)*

MARA   Let me go, you idiot! Let go!

JOVAN   Let her go, I said!

DACA *(laughs, pulls Mara up by her hair, grabs her breast brutally)* Now Daca's going to stick it in a bit, and you, my friend, will just watch. Is that clear? *(Jovan says nothing, tears roll down his face.)*

MARA *(almost whimpering)* Please, let go of me...

DACA *(roaring)* Do you hear what I'm asking you? Is that clear? Now you're going to watch while I screw your *beloved* and she moans. She'll be crying out: 'Oh Daca, what an enormous prick'. Is that clear? *(Jovan stays silent. Daca squeezes Mara. He shouts)* Is that clear? Say it, you educated mother-fucker. Say it, or I'll blow your brains out of your skull. *(holds the barrel to Jovan's forehead)* Say if that's clear? Come on, say it. Is that clear? *(Jovan bends his head, shuts his eyes tight, waits for the end. Sinks to his knees, urine runs down his legs. Daca takes the safety catch off. Cold)* Say it.

JOVAN   It's clear. *(he is crying silently. Mara sobs quietly.)*

DACA *(lowers the gun. Cheerfully)* That's all I wanted to hear. *(he grins)* What's the matter, kiddo? Pissed ourselves, have we? *(Jovan is still on his knees with his head bent. Beside him a pool of urine. Mara looks at Daca in horror)* Piss off, you tart. You're not my type. *(Now Jovan looks at him too. He can't believe what has happened. Mara and Jovan are silent. Daca looks cheerfully at the gun as a child looks at a toy)* A good shooter. I'm very pleased with it. *(slowly lowers the gun to the table)* I could murder a schnitzel now...

The gun touches the table top. A small bump. Then a shot. It has gone off by itself. The bullet hits Jovan's forehead. His eyes open wide, as if he hasn't understood what has happened. Then he falls over without a sound.

MARA *(struggling)* You've killed him...

DACA *(also astonished. He looks at the gun for a long time. Then he manages)* Will you look at that?... it went off by itself.

Very loud folk song.

SCENE 4, BELGRADE.
When the music from the previous scene finally fades out, the stage stays dark for a while. Then a weak light. The same flat. Ana Simovic, a highly pregnant young woman is sitting alone at the table. After a long silence a voice from off-stage.

MAN'S VOICE *(off)* Ana, where are you? Where is that woman hiding? Ana! It's nearly midnight!
(Ana doesn't react)
VOICES *(off)* Ten, nine, eight, seven, six, five, four, three, two, one... *Happy New Year!!!*

(Ana shuts her eyes and bows her head)

Blackout.
The end.

Biljana Srbljanovic

Born in 1970, graduated from the Academy of Dramatic Arts in Belgrade (1996), where she now works as a Teaching Assistant in the Dramaturgy Department.

Her first play *Belgrade Trilogy* was produced in 1997 in Belgrade's Yugoslav Drama Theater, and for that play she received the Slobodan Selenic Award (for Young Playwrights). Her second play *Family Stories* was produced in Belgrade's *Atelje 212* Theatre, and in the Deutsches Schauspielhaus, Hamburg (both in 1998). She received the biggest national award for this play: Festival Sterijino Pozorje in Novi Sad.

She lives and works in Belgrade.

OTHER TITLES BY AURORA METRO PRESS

MEDITERRANEAN PLAYS BY WOMEN   ed. Marion Baraitser
Astonishing plays from countries geographically linked but politically divided.
12 Women in a Cell, written after captivity in Egypt by dissident writer **Nawal el Saadawi**.
The End of the Dream Season, a woman doctor outwits her friends and relations to retain her inheritance, by Israeli writer **Miriam Kainy**.
Libration, a mysterious, intense and comic two-hander about two women who meet in a city park at night, by Catalan writer **Lluïsa Cunillé**.
Mephisto, from the novel by Klaus Mann, the story of a German actor who sells his soul to Nazi ideology, by the eminent French writer/director **Ariane Mnouchkine**.
Harsh Angel, a gentle Chekhovian tale of a family torn by the partition of their native land, written by Cypriot writer **Maria Avraamidou**.
Veronica Franco describes the life of a sixteenth century Venetian courtesan and poet, by Italy's foremost woman writer **Dacia Maraini**.

'...a great opportunity for those who don't see much live theatre by women to know what they've been missing.' Everywoman Magazine
Price: £9.95   **ISBN 0-951-5877-3-0**

A TOUCH OF THE DUTCH, plays by women
ed. Cheryl Robson
Introduction by Mieke Kolk.
Internationally renowned and award-winning writers.
The first ever collection in English of modern Dutch drama, demonstrating the range and sophistication of new theatre writing by women in the Netherlands.

Write me in the sand by Inez van Dullemen is a poetic portrayal of a family where layer upon layer is removed to reveal the painful secrets within. Performed to acclaim throughout Europe, available in English for the first time.
The Caracal by Judith Herzberg, Holland's leading woman writer, is a comic one-woman show about a teacher whose complicated love-life is revealed through fragmentary telephone conversations.
A thread in the dark by Hella Haasse, internationally renowned novelist, is a profound retelling of the myth of Theseus and the Minotaur, from the viewpoint of Ariadne. Widely acclaimed at home and abroad, the play won the Visser Neerlandia prize.
Eat by Matin van Veldhuizen, is a darkly humorous exploration of the lives of 3 sisters who come together to eat, drink, reminisce and celebrate the anniversary of their mother's death.
Dossier: Ronald Akkerman by Suzanne van Lohuizen, is a highly topical two-hander, detailing moments between a patient suffering from AIDS and his nurse.

Price £9.95   **ISBN 0-9515877-7-3**

313

SIX PLAYS BY BLACK AND ASIAN WOMEN WRITERS
ed. Kadija George

A landmark collection of plays for stage, screen and radio showing the range and vitality of Black and Asian writing.

My Sister-Wife by Meera Syal, a taut thriller about two women who discover they are both married to the same man.
Running Dream by Trish Cooke, tells the story of three generations of West Indian women with warmth and humour.
Song for a Sanctuary by Rukhsana Ahmad, explores the painful dilemma of an Asian woman forced to seek help from a women's refuge.
Leonora's Dance by Zindika, four women share the house of a ballet dancer, whose contact with the supernatural lays the ghosts of the past to rest.
Monsoon by Maya Chowdhry, is a poetic account of a young woman's sexual awakening.
A Hero's Welcome by Winsome Pinnock, a tale of misplaced loyalty, longing for escape and early love.
'showcases a wealth of talent amongst Black and Asian communities... often neglected by mainstream publishers.' Black Pride Magazine

Price: £7.50   **ISBN 0-9515877-2-2**

SEVEN PLAYS BY WOMEN, Female Voices, Fighting Lives   ed. Cheryl Robson

A bumper collection of award-winning plays by a new generation of women writers together with short critical essays on theatre today.

Fail/Safe by Ayshe Raif, 'a most disturbing lament for the way that some family ties become chains from which there will never be escape...' The Guardian.
The Taking of Liberty by Cheryl Robson, 'the extraordinary tale of a town in the French Revolution: when the women take offence at an improvised statue, the incident escalates into savage retribution.' What's On.
Crux by April de Angelis, follows four women who follow their own doctrine of pleasure and hedonism in opposition to the stifling dictates of the Church.
'stimulating and humorous new play.' Time Out.
Ithaka by Nina Rapi, 'theatrically inventive, often surreal, witty and funny, ...a sensitive charting of a woman's quest for love and freedom.' Bush Theatre.
Cochon Flambé by Eva Lewin, explores the sexual politics of waitressing in a comic, one-woman play.
Cut it Out by Jan Ruppe, a sharp blend of humour and pathos, tells the story of Laura, a self-lacerator.
Forced Out by Jean Abbott, a powerful drama of a lesbian teacher's confrontation with her community's prejudices, unleashed by a newspaper's gay witchhunt.
'...a testimony to the work and debate that is going on among women, artistically, theoretically and practically. It is an inspiring document.' What's On

Winner of the Raymond Williams Publishing Prize.

Price: £5.95   **ISBN: 0-9515877-1-4**

YOUNG BLOOD: plays for young performers
edited by Sally Goldsworthy

'a good value package of plays for performance for young people' Times Educ. Supplement

'....five tried and tested contemporary classics...' 95% Magazine

the girl who fell through a hole in her jumper by Naomi Wallace and Bruce McLeod. A girl falls through a hole in her jumper into a fantastical world - how will she get home?

the search for odysseus by Charles Way. An angry and awkward adolescent searches for his lost father all the way to the edge of the world.

darker the berry by J.B. Rose. A comic Caribbean Cinderella - 2 sisters struggle to break free from the poverty of island life.

geraniums by Sheila Yeger. The battle of Cable St. retold and set against the political choices of young people in the '90's.

out of their heads by Marcus Romer. The friendship and betrayal of three young people who take a trip beyond anything they ever expected.

Price: £9.95   **ISBN 0-9515877-6-5**

best of the fest ed. phil setren
new plays celebrating 10 years of London New Play Festival

'represents a rich tapestry of contemporary issues ...' Times Educ. Supplement.

'...a valuable snapshot of British playwriting at the end of the century...' NPT Mag.

WILD TURKEY by Joe Penhall. Two small businessmen struggle to keep their flagging burger bar afloat, in the face of increasingly savage and bizarre forces.

EVERLASTING ROSE by Judy Upton. Terrified of ageing, a caravan Casanova, changes wives every decade, until a woman of the 90's challenges his routine.

MAISON SPLENDIDE by Laura Bridgeman. House-sitting for gangsters, Honey and Moon enact a 'let's pretend' lesbian white wedding, parodying suburban customs.

STRINDBERG KNEW MY FATHER by Mark Jenkins. Real life descends into farce as Strindberg, on the verge of schizophrenia, loses control over his characters while writing 'Miss Julie'.

IN THE FIELDS OF ACELDAMA by Naomi Wallace. When their only child dies in an accident at seventeen, Mattie and Henry draw on her high-spirited past to find the strength to move forward.

TWO HORSEMEN by'Biyi Bandele. Banza and Langbaja, two philosophical street-sweepers, trade stories about life, sex and god in a run-down shack. Will their stories sustain them, or will they trap them in a world of make-believe forever?

Price £12.99   **ISBN 0-9515877-8-1**

ORDER FORM

- **THE WOMEN WRITERS HANDBOOK** £4.95
- **SEVEN PLAYS BY WOMEN** £5.95
- **SIX PLAYS BY BLACK AND ASIAN WOMEN** £7.50
- **HOW MAXINE LEARNED TO LOVER HER LEGS** £8.95
- **MEDITERRANEAN PLAYS BY WOMEN** £9.95
- **A TOUCH OF THE DUTCH** £9.95
- **YOUNG BLOOD** £9.95
- **BEST OF THE FEST** £12.99
- **EASTERN PROMISE** £11.99

ADD 10% UK / 20% INTERNATIONAL POST AND PACKING

NAME _____

ADDRESS _____

_____

_____

POSTCODE _____

PAYMENT BY CHEQUE OR POSTAL ORDER IN £ STERLING TO:

AURORA METRO PRESS
4 OSIER MEWS
LONDON W4 2NT. UK. TEL. +44 (0) 181 747 1953
www.netcomuk.co.uk/~ampress

TRADE DISTRIBUTION:
UK :CENTRAL BOOKS TEL: 0181 986 4854 FAX: 0181 533 5821
USA :THEATRE COMMUNICATIONS GROUP TEL: 212 697 5230
CANADA :CANADA PLAYWRIGHTS PRESS TEL: 416. 703. 0201